HUNTING with BARRACUDAS

HUNTING with BARRACUDAS

My Life in Hollywood with the Legendary Iris Burton

Chris Snyder

A Herman Graf Book
Skyhorse Publishing

Skyhorse Publishing books may be purchased in bulk at special discounts for sales promotion, corporate gifts, fund-raising, or educational purposes. Special editions can also be created to specifications. For details, contact the Special Sales Department, Skyhorse Publishing, 555 Eighth Avenue, Suite 903, New York, NY 10018 or info@skyhorsepublishing.com.

www.skyhorsepublishing.com

10 9 8 7 6 5 4 3 2 1

Library of Congress Cataloging-in-Publication Data

Snyder, Chris, (Christopher George), 1963-
Hunting with barracudas : my life in Hollywood with the legendary Iris Burton / Chris Snyder.
p. cm.
ISBN 978-1-60239-662-3
1. Snyder, Chris. 2. Burton, Iris, 1930-2008. 3. Theatrical agents--United States--Biography. I. Title.
PN2287.S6185A3 2009
659.2'9791092--dc22
[B]
2008054410

Printed in England

CHAPTER 1

'Circumstances rule men; men do not rule circumstances.'
Herodotus, Greek historian

The guard gate at the entrance to Forest Lawn made the expanse of rolling green hills seem as closed off as the lives of the movie stars who lay buried there. From high up in the hills of the cemetery you can see Warner Bros., Disney, ABC and Universal studios.

'Could you direct me to Iris Burton's funeral?' I said to the guard.

He pointed to the empty parking lot to the right of me and I saw the chapel. I pride myself on being on time and often I am very early. Now I was going to have to sit in a parking lot and wait for the funeral of a woman who I had spent half my life with. I had been asked to speak. 'You know her better than anyone,' someone had said.

I hadn't seen her in exactly seven years. We had talked on the phone occasionally, but I swore I would never see her again when I left the office on my last day of work at the Iris Burton Agency. I had quit three times in the first year I worked for her. I left for eighteen months after River died and the earthquake hit. She convinced me to come back every time, except the last. She had some strange hold over me. It was as if I had been bewitched. But you really had to know Iris Burton to understand why I went back time after time. I had

1

never met anyone like her. She was bold, brassy, funny and wouldn't take no for an answer.

Strange you never realize at the time that you're having the last phone conversation with somebody you love. Maybe she did, because for the entire week it has played back in my head over and over.

'Honey, it's Iris,' she said.

I didn't recognize her voice. 'Who?' I said.

'Iris,' she yelled.

'Oh my God, Iris, I didn't recognize your voice. It must be a bad connection. I was just going to call you,' I replied.

'Did you know it's my birthday?' Iris said.

'Yes. That was why I was going to call you,' I said.

'Do you know how old I am?' Iris enquired.

'Yes. You're seventy-six.'

'Honey, I've been doing a lot of thinking lately and I realize that I spent almost one-quarter of my life with you.'

'I guess.' I didn't really know where she was going with this.

'You were the only person that ever really cared about me. I trusted you. You watched out for me and defended me. You made me take my medicine and you used to sit with me so that I would eat my lunch.'

'Yes, Iris.' Iris was hardly the sentimental type so I kept waiting for the other shoe to drop. I looked at my watch and realized that this was going to be a long conversation.

'Do you remember the first time you met me?' she said.

'I sure do.'

'You couldn't even say "fuck". You used to say "freaken". What did I say to you?'

'You said if you can't say it, you can't do it.'
We both laughed.

The parking lot was still empty and I wondered if anyone was going to show up. I really didn't want to go into the chapel. I prayed for my phone to ring with an emergency so I'd have an excuse to leave.

I'd first met Iris Burton twenty years ago. I thought she would give me the world I had dreamed of as a child in the sleepy upstate town of New Hartford, New York.

Since grade school I'd devoured *Modern Screen* and other movie magazines. I was captivated by the ongoing affairs of Liz Taylor and Richard Burton, Robert Wagner and Natalie Wood, and Ali MacGraw and Steve McQueen. Even long-dead stars like Marilyn Monroe, James Dean and Judy Garland lived on in those fan magazines. Movie stars owned mansions, threw magnificent parties where the men dressed in tuxedos and the women wore shimmering gowns with eye-popping diamonds. They traveled to foreign cities like London, Paris, Acapulco and Rio de Janeiro. More importantly, in the photographs, everyone was always smiling. Those smiles made me want to go to Hollywood when I grew up, because everyone looked so much happier.

Iris liked to refer to herself as 'the legendary Iris Burton.' I'd been in Hollywood a year and a half so I knew the *LA Times* listed her as one of the top one hundred power people in the entertainment business. She not only handled River Phoenix, who'd been nominated for an Oscar for *Running on Empty*, but she also had the biggest roster of child stars in Hollywood. Television stars included Kirk Cameron from *Growing Pains*, his sister Candace Cameron from *Full House* as well as Fred

Savage from *The Wonder Years*. Over the years, her clients also included Kirsten Dunst, Drew Barrymore, Mary-Kate and Ashley Olsen, Hilary and Haylie Duff, Joaquin Phoenix and Josh Hartnett. And those were just the stars. Iris also handled less famous child actors who worked steadily in commercials, television and film. On her own, she had made children a viable commodity in Hollywood. According to an article about her in *Premiere* magazine she was the first agent to negotiate adult money for kids. 'Some people settle for chopped meat. I like filet mignon,' Iris said in the interview.

In my first job in Hollywood I worked for nothing: a producer at Warner Bros. hired me as an intern. Since I wasn't earning a salary, I worked in a restaurant until 1 a.m. every night, after I finished working ten- to twelve-hour days for him. It was exhilarating just to walk through the famous backlot of the Warner Bros. studio. I stepped over cables, hoses and wires; inspected the cameras, lights and wind machines. I watched as they filmed movies and TV shows on fake New York streets next door to fake Western towns. Wardrobe and make-up people followed the stars back and forth to the set and disappeared into Winnebago trailers. In the first two days of my internship, I discreetly waited by the labeled parking spaces of Goldie Hawn, Barbra Streisand and Warren Beatty. Their production companies were housed in Spanish-style bungalows on the lot. I was star-struck.

After Warner Bros., I worked as an agent for a small talent agency. I was there three months when someone recommended me to Iris. I called her over my lunch break and she told me to meet her at her house at 9 p.m. That made me suspicious. I'd never even met the woman and she wanted me to come over late at night? I'd heard enough stories to wonder if she didn't have other motives. I asked casting directors, managers and other agents about her. They said:

'She's a barracuda. She'll eat you up for breakfast and spit you out for lunch.'

'She'll cut your balls off first and ask questions later.'

'Power. She has real power.'

'She has the talent they want right now and that's all anyone cares about.'

I arrived at her large Mediterranean-style villa high in the Hollywood Hills promptly at 9 p.m. (I later learned that it once belonged to a silent film star who is now as forgotten as her movies.) I pushed the intercom and waited. She didn't answer. I peeked my head through the wrought-iron gates. From the second floor, a shadowy figure peeked out from the drapes. I pressed the intercom again.

An angry voice screamed, 'What?'

'I'm looking for Iris Burton,' I said.

'Who are you?' The deep scratchy voice sounded like a man's and I thought it might be the butler.

'My name is Chris. I'm supposed to meet Iris Burton –'

The voice cut me off. 'I don't really need anyone, honey. I've been alone for twenty years.'

'Don't we have a meeting?' I was confused.

'I changed my mind.'

'I just talked to you this morning.' There was a long silent pause. I thought she'd gone.

'Oh all right! Since you're here, you can carry my luggage down to the car.'

The door opened and I was surprised to find a woman who was only five foot two. She had on a long drapey silk shirt that hung to her knees but didn't cover her full breasts, which rested on her protruding Buddha stomach. Her short hair was dark brown and cropped close to her head. The scowl on her face contorted features that might have been beautiful in her younger days – she reminded me of Ava Gardner.

'Take this suitcase down to the garage,' she ordered.

I extended my hand. 'I'm Chris.'

She dismissed me with a nod towards her suitcase. 'I almost forgot my Jenny Craig food. I'm leaving for Palm Springs tonight. I have two homes there.'

Before I could respond she had disappeared. I headed down to the garage with the luggage as instructed.

'Hello. Hello.' I heard Iris calling from the house.

'Yes?' I called out.

'What the hell are you doing? I told you to take the bags to my car not walk them to the airport.'

I went back up to the front door of the house.

Moments later she emerged at the door with a shopping bag, which she pushed into my arms. 'I need to get in shape. My little Freddy . . .' She paused. 'You know Fred Savage. He's doing the Jerry Lewis Telethon. I have to look my best.' She dropped her cigarette squashing it like a roach. She locked up the house.

'My friend Allan Carr is having a party this weekend. The boys – they all like me. Do you know him?'

'I've heard of him.' I waited and then followed her down a patio through her extensive gardens. Bougainvillea, impatiens and roses lined the path that led to her garage. She stopped for a second, cupped her hand around the night-blooming jasmine and inhaled, before turning her face towards me and quizzically studying my face.

I looked into her eyes and for a brief second saw vulnerability. Suddenly her face became softer.

'It smells beautiful, doesn't it?' She didn't give me time to respond. 'Why do you want to work for me?'

'Because I want to learn the business.'

Iris dropped the flower and the coldness returned to her face. She faced me square on and, tilting her head

6

upwards, stared me in the eyes. I'm six foot three but at that moment I felt like her five foot two frame towered over me.

'You'll have to eat, sleep and breathe this business if you want to work for me. Are you prepared to do that?'

I froze. I couldn't speak.

'Yes or no?' Iris glared. 'Well?'

'Well . . . I –'

Iris cut me off again. 'When I ask you a question I want a response.'

Did I really want to work for this woman? 'Yeah, I guess.'

'Let me give you your first lesson on how to be a good agent. We aren't tentative. We know what we're selling and how much we can get for our clients.'

Iris walked away and headed down the path to her car. She opened the trunk. I set the bag of diet food and her suitcase inside.

She yanked open the door to her gold Mercedes convertible, slid into the front seat and lit another cigarette. 'Listen, kid, I have shoes in my closet older than you. You can't get training like this anywhere else in the city. Not even in the William Morris mailroom.' She inhaled. 'If you can hack it with me I'll show you a world you only dreamed about.' She blew smoke in my face.

Eager to have what she offered, I mustered every bit of courage I had. 'I can hack it.'

'No one else has yet.' She turned on the ignition. 'I'm tough. I hope you want this badly enough.' She started to back her Mercedes down the driveway. 'One more thing –' she motioned me over to the car and looked me straight in the eye 'I don't like liars. If you lie to me, I'll kill you. Tell the truth and we'll get along just fine. You have till Monday to let me know. And, kid, do me a favor: lose the tie and the starchy white shirt; I feel like I'm being strangled.'

Her car sped away. I watched the red tail lights wind around the curves of the Hollywood Hills as they blended into the city lights below.

Cars were slowly entering the parking lot but none looked at all familiar to me. I still didn't know whether or not to read the eulogy that I had written or do something off the cuff. I looked back up into the hills where Iris would soon be buried hoping that the answer would come and that I would lose my fear of speaking about Iris.

When I reluctantly accepted the job with Iris, I didn't realize it would be fourteen hours a day, seven days a week, with no lunch break. I brought a sandwich and ate when Iris was upstairs in the shower. There were stacks of scripts to read; appointments to get out; calls to make for Iris because she didn't like to be on hold. Since Iris worked out of her home I would have to be a witness to her disputes with the maid, the gardener, her love life and the endless parade of stage mothers clamoring to gain favor with her.

Cars were finally starting to stream into the parking lot. Nobody was leaving their cars: I watched them talking on their cell phones. I still did not recognize anyone. I guess nobody wanted to be the first person to walk into a funeral. I know I didn't.

Iris died on 5 April 2008, the same day as Charlton Heston. It was ironic because Iris had been a dancer in the movie *The Ten Commandments*, in which he had starred as Moses. She had stories about Cecil B. DeMille, who directed the movie. 'I was up on the pyramid and

Donald O'Connor had come by for lunch with his friend Sid Miller. Mr DeMille picked up the shofar horn and blew it, then called up to me, "Come down off the mountain, you have visitors." I came off the pyramid and met Sid.'

Iris later married Sid. They had a son, Barry, but the marriage didn't work. Iris became a single mom in her thirties, with no skills. She sold dishes downtown, tried her hand at being a waitress at the Playboy Club, and then landed a job in a talent agency. She started handling kids because no one else wanted to do it. She developed her clients and her reputation, then left and opened her own agency after just one year. Her first big client was Andy Lambros, who did the first big Oscar Mayer bologna commercial, singing the jingle.

People finally left their cars and headed towards the chapel. I followed the line of mourners and looked at my watch. I decided to wait outside the chapel doors in the hope of bumping into a friendly face. I had not yet recognized one person that had walked by. Part of me didn't want to accept that Iris was dead. I thought she'd live to be 100. She always seemed unstoppable. I noticed David Permut approaching. He was a big producer who had been a close friend of hers for at least twenty-five years. He glanced in my direction and walked into the chapel. He didn't seem to recognize me. David Permut had been with Iris fourteen years ago when she picked out River Phoenix's casket at Forest Lawn before his body was sent back to Florida.

Other people streamed by and nobody stopped. Had I aged that much in the seven years since I had worked for Iris Burton? I felt invisible as I opened the chapel door. A huge blown-up picture of Iris, which had been in *People* magazine, stared back at me. She sat at her desk with the headshots that she never used spread out in front of her. Behind her was a wall of pictures of her famous clients including Henry Thomas from *E.T.*

When I first started working for Iris Burton she used to say, 'Stick with me, kid, and I'll show you a world you only dreamed of.' Huge baskets of flowers, fruit, muffins and candy used to arrive daily from studio heads, producers, directors, clients and prospective clients. Joel Silver sent this huge five-foot high basket of roses. Producer David Begelman used to pick her up in his limo and take her to hockey games and dinner. Aaron Spelling had private lunches catered in for the two of them. Her lunch and dinner calendar was filled and movie premiere tickets came in daily. Iris was very sought after because she had what everyone wanted. She traveled to far-off locations to see clients while they were filming. There were blurbs about her in Army Archard's column in the *Hollywood Reporter* amongst the movie stars that he talked about. Iris Burton was a celebrity. She kept people on the phone for hours with her outlandish tales and the latest gossip. Iris had a wicked sense of humor and a throaty laugh that was infectious. She had a story for everyone and could charm the money out of the studio lawyers better than anyone. They heard it was Iris and they gave her whatever they had in the budget for the part. They figured it was easier to give her what she wanted in the beginning rather than spend weeks fighting with her. I'll never forget the time that Iris put an entire family of six into their own television series. She even made a deal for the unborn fetus that the mother was carrying. I believe that is the first and only time that has ever happened.

As I entered the chapel the casket loomed in front of me. It looked to be made of solid oak. There was another blown-up photograph of Iris on an easel in front of the casket. The picture had been taken by a client's mother at the annual Christmas party. Because the picture was blown up I noticed the sparkle in Iris' eyes. The sparkle left and never returned after River died.

I wondered if Joaquin Phoenix and his mother would show up. They had known Iris longer than anyone. They had been with her almost since the beginning of her agency. Iris had taken on the whole family and worked around them being vegans and not wearing leather. That left them out of a majority of the commercial work available to kids, but Iris didn't care. She saw something in those kids. Iris fought for her clients and she became very involved with them. She went on vacations with them, shared holidays with them and in some instances stayed as a guest in their family homes.

I found out about year after I had worked for Iris that there was a pool amongst the mothers as to how long I would last. It was ninety to one that I wouldn't last a month. People asked me all the time: 'How do you work for her? She's so tough and difficult to deal with!' Iris was a perfectionist and had her own formula. Her kids needed to look real. No make-up. No dresses. Ponytails for the girls with faded jeans and sweatshirts. The boys needed to be rough and tumble with no gel in their hair. If Iris believed in someone she went out of her way to push for them. I remember once a client fell ill while filming a television show. The client needed her appendix out and her mother couldn't take her other daughter, who was also a client, to a screen test in the morning. Iris volunteered to take the little girl to the screen test and walked her right into the studio and brought her into the room with the heads of the studio and the network. The little girl landed the job on the series but Iris was fired by two other clients because their daughters didn't get the part. They felt that she had played favorites.

Joaquin Phoenix and his mother walked into the chapel. I wondered if they would notice me. I hadn't seen Joaquin or his mother since the night before the Academy Awards in 2001. Joaquin had been nominated for *Gladiator*. I wondered how they would react to me. From across the room Joaquin's eyes connected with mine and his face lit up. He briskly walked through the mourners and before I knew it he pulled me into a great bear hug. He whispered in my ear, 'I'm glad you're here.'

'It's good to see you,' I whispered back.

Iris, Joaquin and I had shared a great deal. When I left Iris seven years ago we had placed Joaquin Phoenix on the A-list. We had fought long and hard. The chapel was filling up and Joaquin went to take a seat at the front. I looked at the picture of Iris in front of the casket and remembered all the laughs we had shared.

I remembered when Iris had told a parent that his daughter needed to prepare something uptempo for an audition. The casting director called up and told Iris that the ten-year-old girl had sung 'Like a Virgin'.

'Are you an idiot? I said an uptempo show tune not a striptease. Do you think the Disney executives want to see a little girl with a feather boa shaking her booty?' Iris said to the father.

The rabbi approached the microphone and everyone sat down. I looked around the room and saw several of Iris' rivals. I wondered why they were there, because Iris was never close to them. To my knowledge she had not seen or spoken with them in fifteen years.

A few familiar faces of mothers from twenty years ago, and some clients were interspersed amongst the strangers.

The rabbi spoke about Iris but he clearly didn't know her. He called her Irene until somebody finally called out that her name was Iris. I twitched in my seat, not the least bit happy that I would soon have to speak. I pulled the eulogy out of my pocket and clutched it in my hand.

The picture of Iris in front of the casket was the last thing that I saw before I headed for the microphone. The smirk on her face and the twinkle in her eye almost made me feel like she was there enjoying the moment. Iris had made me promise her years ago that I would speak at her funeral. 'Say something nice, kid.' We had both laughed and I had forgotten all about the promise until the phone call had come in asking me to speak and informing me that Iris had made me an honorary pall-bearer in her funeral instructions.

I paused as I looked down at the eulogy I had written and then addressed the mourners.

'When I learned five days ago that Iris had passed away, I kept trying to think of a word or a phrase that best described her. I couldn't think of anything that could sum up Iris. Then I saw this magnet with a quote on it. Jonathan Swift said, "May you live all the days of your life."Iris Burton lived her life to the fullest and because of that she always had a story.

'When I met Iris Burton twenty years ago she was one of the most successful agents in town. She had a reputation as being tough in business. Working for Iris was a grand adventure: you never knew what would happen. The phone would ring and it could be anyone from Warren Beatty, Lew Wasserman, Sid Sheinberg, David Begelman, Aaron Spelling, Joel Silver, Casey

Silver, Sherry Lansing, Leslie Moonves, Nancy Tellem, Bob Iger, John Feltheimer and David Geffen. Iris forged a path with children and young adults that hadn't existed before. I watched Iris over and over mold clients with no credits, bad teeth, eyebrows and hair and groom them into working actors and make stars. Iris negotiated adult salaries for her underage clients. Iris Burton was the last of the truly great development agents.

'Iris was a great business woman and an incredible negotiator. I watched her stand up to Harvey Weinstein and the heads of studios. She wasn't afraid to call anyone to make her case for a client. I remember when Joaquin Phoenix was up for *Gladiator* and he screen-tested several times and finally Iris said, "Chris, I want you to get the numbers of every executive, producer, writer and even the janitor at DreamWorks and Universal and we are going to call everyone of them until we find out who is holding up the deal." By the next morning Joaquin had *Gladiator*.

'Iris had an incredible sense of humor and nobody could make me laugh like she did. There were times when I would fall out of my chair because we would start laughing and couldn't stop. We had our own private jokes and Iris always had a story for me. When she traveled I felt like I traveled with her because we talked twice a day whether she was in Rome, Paris, Israel or Tahiti. I will never forget Iris calling me from Israel. "Honey, I was the only person in the whole tour bus that didn't float in the Dead Sea." She would drop her phone out of the hotel window in Paris. "Honey, did you hear that music. I am paying $400 a night to listen this bad disco music."

'Iris loved to go to spas. I remember she went to a spa on the Dead Sea. "Honey, they covered me in mud, wrapped me in gauze and threw me on a table and left me there in the dark. I felt like a mummy. I called out to the woman because I had to go to the bathroom and she didn't come. So I'm feeling claustrophobic, the mud is drying and this woman won't come. So finally she swings open the door, turns these overhead lights on and says, 'What do you want?' I tell her get this stuff off me so she yanks me off the table, throws me against this cement wall and turns a fire hose on me and blasts me against the wall. I may as well have been in a Turkish prison." I have twenty years of Iris stories.

'Iris loved pottering around in her gardens; decorating her homes; making chicken soup; putting up her Christmas tree; shopping for gifts downtown at the mart. I would like to remember her in front of her mirror, shuffling through drawers of make-up, talking to me about the day's events and putting on her make-up before heading out to a premiere with her best diamond rings on her fingers and wrapped in her full-length mink, looking every bit the legend that she was.'

I left the microphone and headed back to my seat, relieved and numb. I had to stop myself from crying twice while I was speaking. A few other people spoke and then I was asked to stay behind to accompany the casket to its finally resting place. Mrs Phoenix gave me a big hug and we watched the casket be taken out of the chapel to the waiting hearse. We parted company to head to our cars. I was stopped ten times by mourners thanking me for the eulogy and expressing their condolences for my loss before I made it to the car. All of us had gotten older and one of the mourners told me that she didn't recognize me with the short salt and pepper hair and the weight loss. At least I had an explanation as to why people hadn't recognized me until after the eulogy.

Two of the mourners were mothers who had not

talked to Iris in fifteen years. They both said the same thing: 'Iris changed my life.' I thought to myself then that no one would really know what Iris and I had shared and the influence she had had on my life.

CHAPTER 2

'There was never a genius without a tincture of madness.'

Aristotle

1992

'That son-of-a-bitch River.'

The first time I worked for Iris Burton, River Phoenix was her number-one client – a big money maker and Oscar nominee.

Dressed only in her bra and panties, she stood in front of the bathroom mirror harshly illuminated by fifteen light bulbs. Hundreds of jars of cream crowded her bathroom vanity. She was trying desperately to conceal her wrinkles. When she ranted I was her captive audience. I looked at my watch. She was going to be late to the airport.

'Don't do that to me. You're making me nervous.' She threw down her make-up brush. 'I need a cigarette.'

Since I'd known Iris she'd never been on time. She positioned the cigarette between her lips and waited for me to light it. I didn't have a lighter. I never did. She knew that. I quickly ran to the kitchen and grabbed one. Over the years I'd become quite skillful at ducking when she threw plates, cups and even phones. Her violent temper and unstable moods had forced me to walk out on her three times. Then she'd call me repeatedly, stalk me – waiting outside my apartment until I'd come out. She'd cry and make promises to never lose her temper again. And she'd hug me and kiss my hand and my cheeks. Like a fool I fell for it. Every time. Of course she never changed. By the end of the week, an ashtray would sail through the air and I'd be ducking again.

I lit her cigarette, tranquilizing her. She inhaled. 'I blame Gus Van Sant.' With each puff her face slowly released a fraction of the tension. 'Thanks, honey. What would I do without you?' She smiled at me.

The first year Iris didn't trust me. She kept me at the office until midnight going over and over and over my work, wanting to make sure I hadn't made a mistake. Hoping to catch me lying, she interrogated me on every task. And it wasn't only me Iris distrusted.

She interrogated the mothers of the children she represented. They were scared to death of her tirades. When there was a problem, the mothers sometimes made their children call the office so as to avoid her wrath.

'River was fine until he did Gus Van Sant's fucking movie. I blame him for all of this! I told you everything would get fucked up –' she shot me a look out of the corner of her eye '– but you said it would be fine.' Her cigarette ash dropped into her face powder. 'I never liked that fucking *My Own Private Idaho*. It should have stayed in the trash where it belonged.' Iris slammed the vanity drawer.

Inconspicuously, I tried looking at my watch once more.

'If you're so fucking nervous, go take my suitcase out to the car.' Her blow-dryer whined as she styled her chestnut-brown hair.

Happy to escape, I grabbed the suitcase and was almost out of the bedroom door when she started up again. I knew better than to walk away: she needed an audience for a tantrum. I stood there holding her suitcase.

'Didn't they cover up that drunk-driving incident while they were in Oregon filming Gus' fucking movie?' She looked at me expecting a response. 'Imagine, I had to find out from the movie's fucking accountant.' By then Iris' face was flushed a deep red. She slammed the blow-dryer on the counter. 'Now I have to go clean up the mess. Little old Iris. I'm the maid . . . tote that barge! Lift that bail, Burton! Well, I'm *not* a maid.' She slammed the bathroom door in my face and I knew she had to pee, because that was the only time she closed the door.

On my way to the car, I passed through the living room that doubled as a shrine Iris had created to herself. The twenty-five framed photographs of her under the age of thirty-five watched my every move. Most of the shots had been taken at a photo session during the 1950s when Iris was a contract player at Paramount Studios. She bragged about dancing in *The Ten Commandments*, *Daddy Long Legs* and the Dean Martin and Jerry Lewis comedies. She still saw herself as that beautiful contract player of forty years ago. In her bedroom, out of sight where no one could see them, she displayed the pictures of her fifty-year-old self. There weren't any photos of her at her current age, unless you counted her driver's license. For that, she'd plastered on layer upon layer of make-up. The resulting image made her look ghoulish.

Iris made her entrance into the dining room. She was dressed in a black Chanel sweater suit. The gold buttons barely contained the extra weight she'd put on. On cue, I told her how beautiful she looked.

'I never wanted River to do this fucking piece of shit movie with fucking Peter Bogdanovich either. Now I have to fly to Nashville. Not his mother! *Me*! I'm the one who has to go and babysit River!'

She pushed in her dining room chair, smashing it against the table. (That was nothing. I'd once watched her attack her desk, kicking and kicking it until it was unusable.)

'Where the fuck did I put my cigarettes? Fuck!" She stormed out of the room, the heels of her black boots furiously clicking across the wooden floors. I took her suitcases to the car in order to escape the direct line of fire.

This was the only life Iris had. Her tirades were the worst part about working for her. But I could handle them. What I couldn't handle was standing by and watching the business eat away at her like terminal cancer. In a business where the average age of studio executives was twenty-five, she was sixty-three, well aware of the cracks opening in the foundation of her empire. And in Hollywood you're only as hot as your clients. I understood her never-ending hustle for the next hot client.

Iris diffused her hot temper with an outrageous sense of humor. She said the first thing that came into her head; wisecracks or stories of her old days in Hollywood when studio executives and actors chased her around the backlot. Now it was hard to imagine anyone chasing her. She was a perfect example of how Hollywood treats you if you don't get out soon enough.

Once, a mother called the office to say she couldn't take her child on a call. Iris barked back, 'Why?'

'Because there's a horrible wind storm blowing sand across the highway and there's no visibility,' the mother replied.

Without hesitation Iris snapped back, 'Throw a white sheet around you, grab a camel and pretend like you're Lawrence of Arabia. I don't care how you do it, just get to the call.'

Our world had started to crumble on a Friday. The producer and the studio executives, as well as Peter

Bogdanovich, the director, of *The Thing Called Love* telephoned the office within minutes of each other. I juggled the calls because Iris was at Geisha Nails, having a manicure by Thang. She did this every other Friday. Her nude lacquered nails were her pride and joy. To me they were claws to strum tables or the sides of the phone when agitated.

'Tell her it's an emergency,' I said to the receptionist.

I never called her at the nail salon. 'What's wrong?' Iris's voice sounded panicked.

I imagined Thang holding the phone to her ear, trying not to ruin her manicure.

'John Davis, Karen Rosenfelt, John Goldwyn, George Folsey and Peter Bogdanovich are all looking for you,' I said.

Iris loudly repeated the names as if to impress the other customers in the salon. She always wanted everyone to know she was a top Hollywood agent. Then she lowered her voice. 'Shit . . . this isn't good. Not good at all. What do you think they want?'

'What do *you* think they want, Iris? River's fucking up,' I answered. 'The rumors have been flying for the past two weeks. We've both heard them.'

'What should I do?'

I didn't have an answer. There'd been problems with River before but this time the studio was involved. Iris knew the scene better than me. Producers, studio executives and directors only called an agent for two reasons: either they wanted to sell their client on a project, or they were having trouble on the set. It wasn't the former so it had to be the latter.

'Why didn't you deal with it? You're my associate,' she snapped.

Why was it whenever there was a problem I was her associate? I was only her assistant.

'It will have to wait until my nails dry. Tell everyone I'm unreachable. And find River!' She slammed the phone in my ear. It was going to be a long Friday afternoon.

River wasn't easy to locate. Like all movie stars, he knew how to disappear from fans, producers, agents, lawyers, publicists, business managers and anyone else who wanted a piece of him. He had become a star through his work in the movie *Stand By Me*. Millions of people identified with the character he portrayed: an outsider, the adolescent who never really fitted in. After *Stand By Me* he made a string of movies that revolved around the same theme: the teenager's struggle to become an adult. In *The Mosquito Coast*, *Little Nikita*, *A Night in the Life of Jimmy Reardon*, *Running on Empty*, *Dogfight*, *Sneakers* and *My Own Private Idaho* the characters he portrayed struggled with lost innocence and secrets that made acceptance into normal society difficult. River had become a household name. He had also become the new grist for the Hollywood rumor mill. Iris and I had heard them all:

River was difficult on the set.

River was gay.

River drank too much.

River did drugs.

Rumors sold newspapers and magazines. Their covers made actors into stars. There's an old saying, 'It doesn't matter what they say as long as they spell your name right. If nobody hears about you, then you must be dead.' Besides we knew River. We'd never seen any of his bad behavior. He had a girlfriend. He'd always had a girlfriend. Just because he chose to play a gay hustler with narcolepsy in a film, didn't make him gay. And if he drank, well, everyone his age got blasted on weekends. Only nobody followed them into bars and snapped photographs. As for drugs, we'd never seen any evidence of them.

A half-hour later, cigarette in hand, Iris burst into the office. She dropped her purse to the floor and threw her keys on the phone table next to the white wicker chair. Her nails were freshly coated their signature nude. 'Oh God,' she said. She was exasperated. Iris didn't like being rushed by anyone, especially on a Friday afternoon. The furrowed lines around her eyes and lips seemed deeper. The smell of Fendi for Men overpowered the room. (Iris preferred the heavy scents of men's colognes to the flowery ones that women usually wore.)

'Lets go. Start dialing.' She waved her brown Sherman cigarette like a conductor's baton. 'John Davis first! Snap to it!'

When I was there, she never dialed her own phone. She wouldn't even know where to find the numbers to call anyone.

'What the hell is going on in Nashville? Christ almighty!' She smashed out her cigarette in the baccarat ashtray. Only seconds passed before she lit another. 'For all of them to call . . .' She took another drag. 'Haven't you gotten him yet? For Christ's sake!'

I didn't bother to tell her I was waiting for his assistant to answer the phone. John Davis and Iris had known each other for years and had recently been working together on a television deal with one of our other clients.

'Go ahead,' the secretary said.

I couldn't believe she'd found him. In Hollywood a casual game of phone tag could go on for days. John Davis had made it clear from the beginning he wasn't that interested in River. Iris had called in every favor she had to secure River the lead in *The Thing Called Love*. We hadn't heard from John Davis in months because he was currently in production on the new Tom Cruise movie *The Firm*. For him to be found this quickly, I knew there was trouble.

'Iris. Have you talked to River since we started the picture?' John asked.

'No.' Iris fidgeted causing the white wicker chair to creak. She grabbed her letter opener and poked at the ashes in the ashtray.

'Well, I think you should. I'm going to send you the dailies. I want you to see River's performance,' he said.

'What's wrong?' she asked.

'I'm not going to say anything until you look at the dailies. You'll have them in an hour.' He clicked off.

Iris hung up and growled, 'If the studio calls, I'm not here.' She stormed out of the office and slammed the door behind her. 'Fuck!' She yelled so loudly it caused the gardener to drop his rake.

One hour later, I was summoned into the house. The living room was filled with smoke. Iris only chain-smoked when she was feeling insecure. She closed all the shutters in the living room making it pitch-dark. I struggled to find the slot on the VCR and pushed play on the remote. The first take was River opening the door to a truck. Instead of walking to his mark, he stumbled and almost fell. His face was ghostly white and his blond hair, freshly dyed black, was slicked back. He looked awful.

'Cut!' the director yelled.

Iris and I watched as River did his scenes over and over. His eyes were unfocused. He mumbled his lines into the ground not looking at the other actors or at the camera. In an hour of dailies, there wasn't one good scene. Even after twenty takes he never managed to get it right. Usually, River absorbed every nuance of his character like a sponge. He took months to shake off a role and his vulnerability oozed out of him onto the screen. For the first time, I watched the camera become River's enemy. It exposed his flaws.

'Enough,' Iris said signaling with her arm to pause the tape. River stumbling, almost falling but not quite hitting the ground, froze on the screen.

'Get me John.' Iris choked on her cigarette smoke. 'Jesus Christ, River, what the hell are you doing?' she muttered, shaking her head.

After a day of arguing with Paramount Studios, the producers and River's mother, Heart Phoenix, Iris had no choice but to fly to Nashville where they were shooting *The Thing Called Love*. No one wanted to confront him – not even his own mother. Iris had decided to forgo the limousine the studio had offered to send. Despite the fact it was Sunday she had volunteered me to drive her to the airport so she could drill into me the tasks she wanted completed in her absence.

I looked at my watch. Iris was stalling. I'd left her twenty minutes ago. Her make-up was finished and she was dressed and packed. She was going to miss the plane and, knowing Iris, that's exactly what she wanted. Iris did not like face-to-face confrontations. She was great at screaming and cursing over the phone but in person she could be shy. I rang the doorbell.

'All right . . . I'm coming. Leave me the fuck alone!' she yelled from inside.

If I wanted Iris to be on time, I had to trick her and give her a fake time.

'I can't find my charms.' The door swung open. Panic registered on her face. 'Fuck! You have to help me find them.'

'Which ones?' I replied.

Iris had Catholic medals, a Jewish star and the evil eye all pinned to the inside of her bra with a rusted safety pin and faded red ribbon that had belonged to her mother. She also had a small pouch with an ivory elephant, a pyramid and a stone from Egypt.

'The pouch,' she barked.

I had to haul Iris's tote bag back in the house. It weighed thirty-five pounds and was filled to the brim with the contents of her bathroom. I was always searching for things she'd lost. Remembering that she'd used another travel bag on her last trip, I located the charm pouch and coaxed her into the car.

'Shit! Where's my ticket?' She rifled through her purse and found it. Five minutes from the house, as I barreled down La Cienega Boulevard, Iris yelled out, 'Fuck! I hope I didn't leave the gas on again.'

Iris had a habit of leaving the gas on after she lit her cigarettes off the stove. 'I'll check it on the way back. I promise.'

'Thanks, honey.' She patted my knee and held it for a minute. 'How many times did I throw that fucking script in the garbage pail?' Her fists smashed my dashboard. 'It all started on the set of *My Own Private Idaho*. The drinking started there. Nobody is going to tell me differently.' Iris batted her lit cigarette around in my car.

'I resent having my Thanksgiving ruined and being forced to go to Nashville and save the day again, little old Iris. Why the fuck doesn't Peter say something to him? No, they make me disrupt my week. What about his mother? What am I supposed to do? Give him a spanking?' Iris looked at me.

'I really don't know, Iris. They just don't like him,' I said, rolling down my window to let out some smoke.

'I know they wanted the other guy. What's his name

. . . the one who sings "Achy Breaky Heart"?' Iris waved her cigarette almost in my face.

'Billy Ray Cyrus,' I said.

'Whatever! They should have gotten him and my achy breaky heart wouldn't be achy breaky right now,' Iris said.

I laughed and so did she.

CHAPTER 3

'A man's character is his fate.'

Heraclitus, Greek philosopher

Iris pulled River out of the limo. They had just returned from Nashville where location work on *The Thing Called Love* had finally been completed. River was wearing a ski mask and looked like a terrorist rather than a Hollywood heart-throb.

Iris had remained in Nashville to ensure there were no more incidents. River had avoided Iris the first full day she was there. She had confronted Peter and he assured her River's acting was fine. He blamed everything on the studio not understanding River's interpretation of the role. He couldn't understand why they'd made Iris fly to Nashville. In his defense, River shot his scenes all day long and recorded his musical numbers at the end of the day's filming.

Iris was finally able to lock River down for breakfast before he left for the set. She told me later that she had confronted him about the rumors of his drug use. 'He cried on my shoulder, Chris. He swore that he didn't do drugs. That he would never do anything to hurt me. Then he sobbed in my arms telling me it was the grueling production schedule.'

Iris had called me from the limousine and asked that I meet them in the office in five minutes. Iris was the first to step out of the stretch limousine. She hurried over to me. 'He's been wearing that since Nashville,' Iris whispered glancing towards the ski mask. 'You don't know how embarrassed I've been.'

River stared at the ground and shuffled his feet. He wouldn't look me in the eye.

'Honey, are you hungry?' Iris patted his arm. 'I could take you to lunch.'

'No . . . I gotta go,' he mumbled. He stepped back into the limousine without another word.

'Bye, baby.' She blew him a kiss.

I stared at Iris in disbelief. River was in a ski mask and she was pretending everything was fine.

I made a call to River's mother. 'You need to come to town,' I said. 'We can't have any more problems, he's still acting strange.' Mrs Phoenix agreed. She came and watched over him during the remainder of the LA shoot.

A few weeks later, Iris and I visited River on the set at Paramount. They were still shooting the interior scenes of the movie. We were in River's trailer. He was in great spirits. Iris told war stories of her days on the Paramount lot. River and everybody else laughed. The film wrapped without any further incidents. I felt relieved. It seemed he'd gone back to his old self. But fewer scripts were being sent and they weren't A-list films. The phones had stopped ringing.

In April, I celebrated my thirtieth birthday. Iris went on vacation. I didn't have to see her for almost ten days. When I arrived at the office I heard the phone ringing. I struggled to unlock the door and punch in the alarm code. I noticed it was the third button, Iris's private line. When she was out of town it was my signal to drop everything. I was sure it was her doing her routine check-up. She didn't want me taking advantage of her absence. I wondered why she bothered to go on vacation. She spent the entire trip checking up on me. I ran across my office and picked up the phone.

Her voice sounded like she was in an echo chamber. 'Do you know how much they charge for a ship-to-shore call from Tahiti?'

I dropped into my chair. 'No, I don't, but I'm sure you're about to tell me,' I replied.

'I'm not spending all this money to argue. This ship's a nightmare,' Iris complained. 'This fucking boat is loaded with a bunch of old married couples from Orange County renewing their wedding vows. And the fucking toilet paper . . . I may as well wipe my ass with sandpaper.'

'I'm *so* sorry Iris,' I said. 'I thought cruising the islands would be relaxing.'

The last thing I felt like was dealing with Iris. Regardless of the cost, I knew Iris could stay on the phone for hours, especially when she was unhappy. I grabbed the other phone and dialed our office number several times. Every phone line in the office rang.

'Hang on.' I pushed the hold button.

'Don't put me on hold,' I heard Iris say as I clicked the button down. I flipped through some papers and watched the flashing red light. I knew I was pissing her off but I didn't care.

A few minutes passed before I picked up Iris' line again. 'Got to go, Iris. Last minute casting session for Nestlé's cookies,' I said. Then I clicked the receiver knowing Iris was already calculating how much money she'd make if we booked a Nestlé's commercial.

With Iris away I could do anything I wanted. I put my feet up on the desk and tried to decide if I felt like drinking a cup of coffee. Iris never made coffee and she didn't like me to bring it into the office. She thought I might spill it and stain the rugs.

I left my office in the guest house and went into the

main house. It was a small English cottage. Despite the charming outside appearance, inside the house was sparsely furnished. The living room didn't have any end tables or coffee tables. There wasn't anywhere to put down a drink or a magazine. Not that it mattered, she didn't like people to sit on her furniture, not even herself. While I brewed coffee, I plunked down on the sofa.

A knock on the back door startled me. I jumped up. The door creaked open. River poked his head in. 'Hello. Hello?' he called tentatively.

'I'm in the living room,' I called out.

I'd forgotten he was in town. He'd flown in for a meeting with the director of *Dark Blood*. We wanted him to do the movie. He couldn't have cared less.

He hugged me. My God, this wasn't the same River who'd come back from Nashville in a terrorist mask. He actually looked healthy. His skin glowed. When River hugged me he had a hard time letting go. I disengaged from him. 'Iris is in Tahiti.'

'I know. That means we can go to lunch. We never spend any time alone.' He looked me squarely in the eyes and smiled.

'Cup of coffee?'

'No thanks.' He put his arm around my shoulder and walked me towards Iris' refrigerator. He rummaged inside, pushing around bottles of soda and water searching for something to eat. Whenever River came to the office he raided Iris' refrigerator. Iris bitched about it but always smiled as she turned on the microwave to bake him a potato or pop popcorn.

'There's nothing in here.' He shut the refrigerator door.

'I told you. Iris is away.'

The phone rang. I grabbed my coffee and headed out to the office. River followed me, plopped down in the wicker chair and pulled out a cigarette. I couldn't help but notice that he looked just like the publicity still from the movie *The Mosquito Coast* that sat directly across from him on the bookcase. His blond hair blowing – young and innocent River was the poster child for vulnerability.

'Shit . . . I left my cigarette lighter at the hotel.' He glanced in my direction and instantly I dropped what I was doing to help him. I opened my desk drawer and tossed him the spare Bic lighter Iris used.

River lit up and took a long drag. A smile broke out on his face. 'Tahiti. What the hell is she doing there?'

'Vacation.'

We both laughed.

River tossed the lighter back to me and went into the garden. I watched him through the window. He smoked and paced the ten by ten foot backyard. When he came back in, he tossed the cigarette butt over his shoulder into Iris' perfectly manicured English garden. He sat back down in the wicker chair. 'Am I bothering you?'

I looked up from the ledgers where I was logging the clients' checks. 'No. Not at all. How was your meeting this morning?'

'I told the director I loved the movies he'd made.' He lit another cigarette. 'Blah, blah, blah. I've never seen one of his fucking movies. I told him I *loved* the script and that I *really really* wanted to do his movie. The usual.'

We shared another laugh.

River flicked his ashes into Iris's flowerbed. He had a troubled look on his face. 'From now on I need to be careful which films I chose. I want to leave a legacy that I'm proud of. I want my children and my children's children to be proud.'

His legacy? Too bad he hadn't thought about that before his last two films. The only place they belonged was in a bonfire. 'River you have a long time to start thinking about those things.'

'No I don't.' He tossed another cigarette into the garden. 'I don't even like this business any more. I don't know if I ever liked it. I wasn't exactly given a choice.' To make money to support his family he and his brothers and sisters sang and danced on the street corners in Westwood. River started acting when he was nine years old and now his income supported his entire family, including their properties in Florida and Costa Rica.

'Maybe I'd like to take a break from acting . . . go to college.' His eyes locked onto mine. 'Can you still go to college at twenty-two?'

'Sure you can, River. You can go to college at seventy.'

'You went to college, Chris. Tell me about it.'

'There were a lot of reading assignments, papers and deadlines. But there were parties and friends. I hated it while I was going but now after working for five years, I wish I was back in school.'

'Do you think I'm missing anything by not going to college? You know I didn't even go to high school.' He paused and lit another cigarette. 'I played the part of a high school student but never actually experienced it except on the set.'

'River, how can I tell you that you're missing something? I don't know what you want. If you want to be a doctor, lawyer or engineer, then you're missing something. But if you want to be an actor, then you're not missing a thing.'

'I don't know what to do,' he said. 'A lot of people depend on me.'

'River, you have to do what's best for you.' I wanted to hug him and tell him it was all right to quit the business, but I couldn't. If he took a break from the business now, he'd be yesterday's news. Someone else would get the roles he turned down.

'I'm tired. Really tired,' he said 'Please come to lunch with me, Chris.'

As we left he spotted the publicity still from *The Mosquito Coast*. 'Iris still keeps this picture of me?' With a forlorn look he picked up the photo and gazed at it.

I put my arm over his shoulder. I didn't know what to say.

The phone jarred me awake at 3 a.m. It was probably Iris. What time was it in Tahiti?

'Hello,' I barked into the phone. This time I wasn't going to be nice to Iris.

'Chris, it's Marcy, from Iris's answering service.'

The service had never called me at home before.

'River's on the phone. He's demanding we find you.'

'It's three in the morning,' I said, annoyed.

'Shall I put him through?'

What could he want? 'Yeah.'

'Chris?' River barked.

'Yeah.' I sat up in bed.

'What the fuck's . . . going . . . on?' He could barely get the words out.

'What do you mean?' I was perplexed by the change in his attitude. He'd been so nice at lunch. It was obvious from his voice he'd been drinking.

'The fucking scripts, man. You haven't sent all of them, have you? You're hiding things from me.'

'Everything that comes into the office I mail directly to you, River.' Maybe if you read them you wouldn't be calling me at three o'clock in the *morning*!

I heard the sound of street traffic on the phone. Where the hell was he? I wondered.

'What's it called, Sam?' he asked his current girlfriend,

Samantha Mathis. She'd been his co-star in *The Thing Called Love*.

'*Reality Bites*,' she whispered.

'*Reality Bites*,' River slurred into the phone.

'Reality *does* bite, River! You've had that script for a month. I've asked you to read it *five* times. You told me to pass on it for you.'

'I want to do it! I want to do it!' he whined.

'How can you want to do something you haven't even read? You don't even know what it's about.'

'Samantha said it's great. I trust her. I don't trust you!' He was yelling into the car phone. Police sirens blared in the background. God, I prayed the police were going in the opposite direction. He sounded drunk to me.

'Who's driving the car, River?' I demanded.

'Why? What the *fuck* does that matter?'

'Because you're *fucking* drunk, River . . . and if you're drunk you'd better not be driving a car.'

'Samantha's *driving*,' he said mockingly.

'Has she been drinking too?' I asked.

'What are you, the fucking FBI? I just want to do the fucking movie!' He banged the phone on something.

'No. I think Samantha wants to do the *fucking* movie. Is she your new agent? I'm sure Iris will be glad to hear that . . .You're fucking drunk!'

'I'll have you fucking fired, you cocksucker!'

'Good. Call Iris in Tahiti right now. Wake her ass up and we'll see who's fired at sunrise.' I paced back and forth across my studio apartment, 'You want the script . . . you'll have it tomorrow . . . but tell Samantha . . .Winona Ryder already has the part she wants.' I slammed down the phone and then went back to bed.

My head was throbbing. I reached for my trusty bottle of Motrin. In bed I tossed and turned. Unable to sleep, I popped a movie into the VCR: *Shirley Valentine*, a film about a middle-aged English woman. Feeling trapped in her suburban life she goes on a two-week vacation to Greece. There she realizes that she's lived her life for everyone else and somehow lost herself in the process. When the film ended, I finally drifted off dreaming about Greece. What a perfect escape that would be.

The next day, when I told Iris what had happened, even the phone lines couldn't filter out her screaming.

'Why the hell didn't you just say yes to whatever he wanted?'

'Hmm . . . The next time you go away I'll sleep with your phone number under my pillow. Then I can have him call you so you can listen to him in a drunken rage.'

'How do you know he was drunk?' she snapped.

'Because. I *heard* him Iris, you didn't.'

'Have you talked to him today?'

'Considering it's only eleven in the morning, he's probably still sleeping,' I said. 'Why don't you wake him up?' I dared her knowing she wouldn't do it. 'I'll give you the number.'

She cut me off snarling, 'Just get him the script.'

'He's already got one,' I said.

'I don't care if he has five and he uses them for toilet paper. Get him another one, make him happy.'

'He should read Samantha's, she riled him up.'

'Get him the script!' Iris yelled. 'And when you've found him and gotten him the script, you find me! Understand?' She hung up without a goodbye.

The St James' Club on Sunset Boulevard is a landmark art deco hotel that resembles a miniature version of the Empire State Building. There was always a traffic jam as cars, taxis and limos backed up on the Boulevard. I waited in the line of cars and eventually pulled up to the curb in front of the valet and tried to attract his attention. If he could deliver the script to the front desk, I wouldn't have to see or talk to River.

The valet's eyes glanced at my Mazda 323 and figured there wasn't a hefty tip in it, so he refused. 'You need to valet the car and take the script to the concierge desk,' he said.

Great! Iris didn't reimburse me for expenses. I yanked the keys out of the ignition and slapped them into the valet's hands. I intended to pay the three-dollar fee in nickels, dimes and quarters.

'I can't drive your car because it's a stick shift,' the valet said. 'You'll have to drive it down to the garage yourself.' That was fine with me. Then I wouldn't have to worry about tipping him.

By the time I reached the front desk I was angry. The concierge refused to take the script. That made me even angrier. Instead, he called River's room. Now I would have to face him.

I became more anxious as I watched each number on the elevator panel light up. I would drop the script at the door and leave. From the end of the corridor I saw a huge stack of room service trays. I knew that was his room. I hurled the script down the hallway. It hit the door and smashed into the dishes.

I ran back towards the elevator. Frantically, I pushed the down button. I wanted out. Just as the elevator door dinged to close, River's head tentatively stuck out of his room. I was caught. As I walked towards him I berated myself for not using one of those room service carts to hold the elevator open.

'Chris,' he called out and walked up the hallway wrapped only in a towel.

'I didn't want to bother you.' I said, making something up so it didn't look like I was sneaking away. I was in enough trouble after last night. As he came towards me I realized his hair was wet and dripping down his neck and chest. He smiled and pulled me into him as if nothing had happened. How could he have forgotten what he'd said? I certainly hadn't. The water from his hair soaked my shirt. We pulled apart. I looked down.

'Sorry,' River said. 'Come back to my room and we'll dry your shirt. Maybe we can have dinner? Come.' He pulled me by the hand down the corridor into his room.

I was stuck now. 'I have to go, River. I have another script to drop off.'

His smile was charming. 'Who's more important than me?'

The bathroom door was open. The light was on. 'Is Samantha here?'

'No,' he said as he pushed some clothes off a chair onto the floor. He invited me to sit down and carelessly tossed the script onto the bed. It lay along with the sheets, his jeans and six other scripts that I didn't recognize. Obviously other agents and producers had found out he was at the hotel and had been sneaking their projects to him without going through Iris.

'I read it again. It's not bad,' I said.

'I read Samantha's copy. You're right, this project isn't for me.'

River pulled a pair of jeans from a pile on the floor then casually dropped his towel. I didn't want to see him naked. I closed my eyes, embarrassed.

'Have you read *Interview with the Vampire* or *Dark Blood*?' I glanced around the floor seeing if I could spot them amidst the mess. He shook out his long wet hair, spraying water all over. 'I really don't want to do any of these scripts,' he announced.

'*Interview with the Vampire* is the most highly anticipated movie adaptation since *Gone with the*

Wind.' I located the script on the floor and handed it to him.

He yanked it from my hand. 'I don't care about any of these.' He hurled the script across the room. When it hit the window the force of the impact broke the binder and the pages fluttered down to the floor.

'Do you have any idea how hard Iris and I have worked to get you considered for these parts?' I said, frustrated.

River lit a cigarette.

'The studios aren't exactly bombarding us with projects for you.'

He glared at me from across the room as the last pages of the script settled to the floor.

'I don't want to work any more. You can tell Iris and my mother! My passion is my music.' He walked away from me and moved towards the window and the lights on Sunset Boulevard. He stared at the billboards that advertised everything from liquor to Calvin Klein underwear. I walked over to him. Maybe I'd said more than I should.

'If you don't want to work then don't, but I'm not going to be the one to tell Iris.'

River's face broke into a smile. 'I have to work. After all these years in the business I still don't have enough money to just say "Fuck you" to this town. The band is expensive. So is Costa Rica.'

'Maybe you can cut back some expenses and take some time off,' I reassured him.

His eyes were sad. 'Do you think there's a way that Iris can have a bank account with only my name on it. I want to take more control of my money.'

'I don't know, River.' I didn't want to get in the middle of this. 'You should ask Iris. I'm sure you have more money than you think.'

'Not enough to never have to fucking bleed in front of the camera again.' He looked away from me. 'Maybe I should just disappear for a while.'

'This town forgets about people quickly,' I replied.

'What does it matter, when my next two films are released I'm only going to be doing B movies.'

'That's why it's important that you really look at these two projects seriously. They could put you back on top.' River was right about the B-list, he'd be on it soon even with his Academy Award nomination. Iris always said, 'An Academy Award and a nickel might get you a cup of coffee in a diner.'

'Time for me to leave.' I gently patted River on the back and he gave me a hug then turned his attention to the lights of the Sunset Strip.

I walked out and closed the door behind me.

CHAPTER 4

'I count him braver who overcomes his desires than him
who conquers his enemies; for the hardest victory is the
victory over self.'

Aristotle

The studio called. River was on the press junket for *The
Thing Called Love*. He'd thrown a cell phone off his
hotel balcony and one out of his limousine.

'What about the people you could have injured? Or
the accident you could have caused,' I scolded him.

'Did anyone get hurt, cocksucker?' River mocked me.
'The fucking phones didn't fucking work, Chris. If they'd
given me fucking phones that worked instead of cheap
pieces of shit, maybe I wouldn't have thrown them.'

'Don't act like a two-year-old,' I said.

'Fuck off.'

I hung up. River wasn't pissed about the phones.
He'd seen *The Thing Called Love* and knew that both
the movie and his acting sucked. Luckily, his other
unreleased film, *Silent Tongue*, was so strange it hadn't
even found a distributor. We'd never wanted him to
make it. The film was a twisted story about a grieving
widower (River) who guarded the decaying corpse of his
Indian wife as it rested on the funeral pyre. He refused
to ignite the fire that would set her spirit free.

For the first time, the studios weren't coming to us
with offers. It took Iris and I six months to secure him

41

his next role in *Dark Blood*. More importantly, we'd been able to secure him a part in *Interview with the Vampire*. With Tom Cruise and Brad Pitt already signed on, a huge box office was guaranteed.

River was unappreciative and felt he should have been cast in one of the lead roles instead Brad or Tom. The studio hadn't wanted River and he knew it. The truth was he really didn't want to work. As far as *Dark Blood*, he would film that prior to *Interview with the Vampire*. He hated the script and only agreed to do it after we convinced him it would bolster his standing with the independent market. River needed *Dark Blood* more than he knew. We couldn't allow him to screw up. *Dark Blood* was produced by Neil Jordan, the director of *Interview with the Vampire*. If he screwed up on *Dark Blood* he'd be replaced in the other film.

River was five weeks into production on *Dark Blood* and there hadn't been a single incident. The studios said the dailies looked great. I wanted to believe that River had exorcised his demons. The sun was shining when I arrived at the office.

Alan, Iris' neighbor, was watering his garden. 'Why can't Iris watch TV in her bedroom instead of the office? I can't get any sleep. You'd think she'd have a little more consideration.'

The word 'consideration' wasn't in Iris' dictionary. He was talking about the woman who screamed, 'Shut the fuck up, you little brats,' terrorizing the young children that played in the neighborhood. 'I don't know, Alan,' I said and quickly opened the office to escape his complaints. I couldn't explain anything she did. Why she sat in my office watching TV all night was a mystery to me. Often she went through all my papers and files. Entering the office, I patted the television monitor directly across from my desk. The screen was still warm. That meant Iris had recently gone to bed. At least I could get some work done.

The phone rang. I leaped to answer it.

'Iris Burton Agency.'

'Chris? JoAnne Sellar here.' JoAnne was the producer of *Dark Blood*, River's current film. 'I need Iris right away.'

'She's at a breakfast meeting.' I gave JoAnne my pat response, the one I gave to anyone who called while Iris was still sleeping. Even when she had a good night's sleep she was far from pleasant.

'When she calls in please have her call me,' JoAnne said. 'Immediately.'

'What's wrong?'

'River's acting bizarre. Please find Iris.' She hung up the phone.

JoAnne called back at 11.30. 'Is Iris back yet?'

Two calls in two hours. I didn't want to wake Iris but my instincts told me to.

'Hold on, Joanne,' I said. I grabbed the keys to the house from the trophy cup Iris had won for being the Most Beautiful Child in New York at the age of nine.

Outside her bedroom door, I hesitated. She didn't sleep with any clothes on. I'd been with her for five years and was still uncomfortable seeing her naked. The sheets were twisted around her still shapely dancer's legs. Iris had put on a great deal of weight during the past year so her stomach protruded out as if she were eight months pregnant. Her firm round breasts were also exposed. One thing I could say for her, you'd never have known she was sixty-three by looking at her breasts. They were the breasts of a thirty-year-old woman.

I whispered, 'Iris . . . Iris.' I took two more steps into the bedroom. 'Iris.' I waited. 'Honey . . . Dear.'

'Huh,' Iris mumbled.

Finally some movement! 'Wake up,' I said.

She lifted her head off the pillow and reached towards the nightstand for her Sherman cigarettes. I grabbed the lighter on the dresser and lit the cigarette that dangled from her mouth.

'What time is it?' She pulled herself up against the headboard. She hadn't removed her make-up from the night before and it was smeared across her face. 'Why are you here?'

'JoAnne Sellar is on the phone. She says it's urgent.'

Iris sat up in bed and pulled the sheet over her exposed breasts. 'God almighty! Why do I need to wake to this crap?' She waved her cigarette at the red flashing hold button. She grunted and picked up the receiver, 'What's up, JoAnne?'

'We have a problem here. River has stopped production,' JoAnne said.

Iris coughed into the phone. 'Jesus fucking Christ.'

'We need you here, Iris . . . River wants you,' JoAnne said.

Iris pushed the phone towards me so we could both listen.

'There's a dead snake in the scene we're shooting . . .'

'Yeah.' Iris looked at me.

'River doesn't believe that the snake died of natural causes,' JoAnne said.

'What?' Iris pounded her cigarette out in the ashtray. I lit her another one.

'River wants us to provide him with the death certificate for the snake.'

I looked over at Iris' closet filled with at least fourteen leather and fur coats. She never wore them around River. He was an animal rights activist. But a death certificate for a snake?

'I'm not a pet coroner for Christ's sake!' Iris bounced out of bed, wrapping the sheet around her naked body.

'Hold on. I'll put River on the phone,' JoAnne said.

Iris put on the speakerphone. A few minutes passed. We could hear JoAnne pounding on River's dressing-room door and calling his name.

'River?' we heard her call. 'Iris is on the phone. Open your trailer, please.'

River's voice came through the speaker. 'Iris, is that you?' he said.

'Yeah, baby. What's going on up there?'

'Iris, they're killing snakes ... They want me to work with murdered snakes. They poisoned them. Or strangled them. I don't know. They're liars. . . They say that the snake died of old age. I don't believe it.' River sounded near tears.

'River, honey,' Iris said, 'JoAnne assured me that the snake died of natural causes.'

'They're liars ... fucking liars ... all of them ... They killed the snake. THEY'RE MURDERERS! MURDERERS!' River just kept shouting.

Iris turned to me her face drained of color. 'Jesus Christ,' she mumbled. 'Jesus Christ.'

Then the phone connection went dead.

My legs felt weak. 'What are we going to do, Iris?' I sat down next to her on the bed.

The phone rang. 'Hello,' Iris said.

'It's JoAnne. He threw the phone out of his trailer.'

River was good at throwing phones.

'Let's get a lab to fax a death certificate or maybe a pet shop,' I suggested.

'Did you hear that JoAnne?' Iris said.

'We tried it already. Iris, you have to come. We're already behind schedule. Judy Davis and the director are having problems too.'

Iris cut JoAnne off. 'Does the studio know?'

'Not yet, but we need you here today. I've booked you on a flight this afternoon. Someone will pick you up at the airport in Salt Lake City.'

Iris did not want to go to Salt Lake City any more than she'd wanted to go to Nashville last year. She was afraid of what she'd find. Besides, she kept saying she had a business to run. 'Where the hell's his mother? Why do I have to go?' she moaned.

'I tried the house in Florida. They said she was away. Iris, you have to come. He seems to straighten up when you're around. He's afraid of you.'

'Well, isn't that just fucking great?' She slammed the bathroom door.

Several more attempts to find Mrs Phoenix failed. I reminded Iris that River was a significant portion of her business.

While Iris pulled on a sweatsuit, I helped her pack.

'What are we going to do, Chris?' For the first time since I'd known her, she looked defeated.

'I don't know, Iris . . . Pray? Pray he makes it through these next two films.'

CHAPTER 5

'He can always find another agent to represent him.' Iris looked at her watch. She was late for lunch with River. He'd just arrived back in LA where they were filming the interiors for *Dark Blood*. 'You should come to lunch with us. It won't look good if you don't.'

'I'm not going. He doesn't mouth off to you. And he's never called you a cocksucker, Iris. So you deal with him.'

She pulled out a cigarette and glared at me. 'I insist you come.'

'I'm not going,' I said emphatically.

'If you don't come –'

I cut her off. 'You'll fire me? Go right ahead, Iris. I'm sick of him and I'm sick of you pretending he's fine. He hugs me one minute and curses me out the next. It's not normal.'

She left, slamming the door. Damn! The script to *Safe Passage* was still on the chair. That was her whole reason for meeting with him.

Three hours later, I heard her heels clicking down the driveway. Iris must be back from lunch. And there was another set of footsteps dragging up the driveway with her. Shit! It must be River. No wonder she left the script behind. She wanted an excuse to bring him back to the office.

'Chris . . . Chris . . . honey,' Iris chirped. 'I have River with me. He wants to see you.' Iris trying to be sweet was scary. She slipped into the office ahead of River. 'I can't have the two of you not getting along,' she whispered.

I shrugged. 'Iris, it's not my fault we're not getting along.'

'Be nice. He wants to make up with you.'

River appeared in the doorway. Iris stopped talking and plastered a fake smile on her face. He didn't enter the office. She lit a cigarette. Jesus, he looked like a corpse. His skin was pasty and white, almost as if he'd been ravaged by illness. His jet-black hair looked as if he'd cut it himself without looking in a mirror. And he was so thin. I glanced over at the enlarged publicity still from *The Mosquito Coast*. River's blond hair hung over his blue catlike eyes and begged to be pushed back. Chills went down my spine. His eyes were cast down as he studied the carpet in front of his feet. He shuffled in the office doorway but wouldn't enter.

'River and I had lunch, didn't we, honey?' He didn't look up. Iris' attempt to engage him in conversation failed. She waved her hand and pointed at him, mouthing to me, 'Say something.'

'That's nice,' I said.

River kicked the stones in the pathway. Five-year-old boys who auditioned for the agency did the same thing. They wouldn't come into the office without their mothers.

'River?' Iris held out her pack of Shermans. 'Baby, do you want a cigarette?'

He took one and dangled it from his mouth.

Iris handed River her lighter. 'Chris wants to talk to you about a script. It's really good, isn't it, Chris?'

'Yeah, it's great,' I said. 'Susan Sarandon has signed on to play the mother.'

'I'll leave you two boys alone.' Iris left a trail of cigarette smoke lingering behind.

River still hadn't made eye contact with me as he moved to sit down in the wicker chair across from my desk. He used to have such soulful eyes. Now he was afraid of what I'd see.

I handed him the script. 'It's called *Safe Passage*. There might even be roles for your brother and one of your sisters. It's about the dynamics of a family. About a mother trying to give her children safe passage into adulthood. Oh, and Sam Shepard plays the dad.' Sam had directed him in *Silent Tongue* and River liked him.

River reached for the script. 'Sounds good,' he said unenthusiastically.

His arm was as thin as the stems of the calla lilies in Iris' garden. 'The studio can push the start date. That way you can do the movie a few weeks after you finish *Interview with the Vampire*.'

River flicked his ash, narrowly missing the ashtray. 'Great . . .When can I meet the director?'

'He's directing a play in London, but he can fly in on Friday for one day. I checked with the producer of *Dark Blood* and you're off work that day. Should I set up the meeting?'

'Yeah fine . . . If you like it, I'm sure it's good.' River stood up, headed towards the door leaving the script on the chair.

'River?'

He turned.

'You left the script.'

Awkwardly, he approached my desk. He put his hand on my shoulder. At last our eyes connected. For a moment he was the old River with his captivating wounded-deer eyes. 'I'm sorry . . . I yelled at you and woke you up in the middle of the night.' He looked about to cry. 'I'm sorry I swore at you.'

I felt uncomfortable, 'That's OK, I'm sorry I called you a fuckin' drunk.' Unable to look in his eyes any more, I picked the script up.

'No, it wasn't OK.' He hugged me tight and for a moment rested his head on my shoulder. I didn't know what to do, so I put my arms around him. He was so thin I felt his skeleton. His body shook as he sobbed. If something wasn't done soon, he wasn't going to make it.

'River,' Iris called from the porch. 'River?'

Reluctantly he broke away.

'Don't forgot this again.' I handed him the script.

He patted my shoulder half smiling. Obediently, he joined Iris on the porch. I followed.

Iris politely smiled at River and then at me. 'Isn't it better now that you two have made up?' I couldn't look at her.

River hugged me again. 'I gotta go.'

Unable to hold back, I finally blurted out, 'You're so thin, River.'

'He lost weight for the part,' Iris said, dismissing my concern.

I watched as he shuffled down the driveway, dragging his feet all the way. The script to *Safe Passage* dangled from his hand. He barely held on to it and it seemed to take every bit of his energy just to keep moving.

'Chris . . . I can't . . . the . . . meeting.' The voice on the other end of the phone was incoherent, almost a whisper. I wondered if he was drunk.

It was 4.30 p.m. I'd been trying to reach River all day. The director for *Safe Passage* was on his way from the airport to the Hotel Nikko, where River was staying. They had a meeting.

'You have to . . . cancel,' River mumbled.

'I can't cancel. The director flew all the way from London just to meet you. Don't hang up. I'm going to call the hotel on the other line and have coffee sent to your room.'

I dialed the concierge at the Hotel Nikko. 'Hello . . . Could you please send the biggest pot of coffee you have to Earl Grey [Earl Grey was his alias. He'd gotten it from a tea bag] in room 5408.' I switched back to River's line.

'River . . . River . . . River.' I yelled his name into the phone. No response, 'RIVER!' I screamed louder praying he'd only dozed off.

Iris swung open the back door of the house. 'Why the hell are you screaming?' She was wearing the white cotton kimono she always wore. She never belted it, so it was always falling open.

'It's River on the phone, Iris. He's either stoned or drunk, and he wants to cancel the meeting with the director,' I yelled.

She looked at me confused. 'Why is he in bed at 5 p.m.? He didn't *work* yesterday. The director is on his way to the hotel?'

'River! River!' I yelled again.

'Stop fucking yelling his name! Do you want the whole fucking neighborhood to hear?' Iris went back into the house slamming the door. I picked up the phone again and, finally, I heard River's labored breathing. I was relieved.

In the house, Iris picked up the phone extension, 'River, it's Iris . . . River . . . honey.' She was very calm.

'Huh?' River said.

'River, what's wrong?'

I interrupted, 'What's wrong is that I'm calling his mother, Iris.'

'Don't you dare call her! River?' Iris said again.

I pushed my hold button and dialed Mrs Phoenix in Florida. Even if she was home I still needed to figure out a way to cancel the meeting with the director. If word leaked out that River hadn't made a meeting because he was drunk, he would be finished. I could stall the director by saying he was called into work or was running late. What really mattered was that we had to do something about River's problem. It couldn't be swept under the rug any more. I dialed Mrs Phoenix again.

'Hello?' she answered the phone.

'Heart, it's Chris. River needs to talk to you. Hold on.' I patched her into the line with Iris and River.

'I'm ... so ... tired ... just want to sleep...' It sounded like he was drugged. I hoped they finally heard what I'd been hearing for some time.

'River, what's wrong?' Heart asked.

'Tired ... just tired,' River said.

I looked through my Rolodex to find the casting director's phone number. 'I'm calling Pam Dixon. She'll stop the director.'

'River, why are you so tired?' Heart asked.

I interrupted, 'Pam isn't picking up. River, get in the shower. Drink the coffee that's coming up to the room. It should be there any minute.'

'Get in the shower, honey,' Heart said.

'Drink the coffee,' Iris said sweetly.

'Maybe Iris should go to the hotel,' Heart said.

'I don't want ... anyone ... here,' River said. 'No!'

'I can't get ready that fast,' Iris said.

'I don't want to work ... I need to be alone,' he said.

'River, a shower will make you feel better,' Iris said.

River hung up the phone. None of us knew whether or not he'd show up for the meeting with the director.

'So you both still think he's fine after this, huh? Something has to be done. This can't go on. We have to find out what the hell is wrong with him once and for all.'

Dead air. No one spoke.

It was decided that Iris would go to the set with River the next day. Heart would fly out to LA on Sunday. After the conference call ended, Iris came into my office with cigarette in hand.

'What the hell are we going to do? I can't protect him if he keeps pulling this shit. He'll be finished.' She paced back and forth in front of my desk.

I stood up. 'Iris, we have to confront him.'

She inhaled. The tip of her cigarette glowed orange. 'With what, Chris? Rumors?'

'With the facts, Iris. It's not just the drinking.' It suddenly dawned on me. He was on heroin. It was currently the most popular drug in town. 'My guess is hard drugs . . . maybe heroin.'

Iris's eyes bulged like a bull ready to charge. 'Don't you *ever*, *ever* say that again. It's a fucking lie!'

'How can you stand here and tell me nothing's wrong?'

'I told you. He got thin for the part.' She waved her cigarette around.

'There have been rumors for a long time, Iris. You choose to ignore them. You saw him yesterday. We both saw him, Iris!'

'You know him, he likes to change his look for every film.'

'Bullshit, Iris! Bullshit! He's emaciated.' I pointed to *The Mosquito Coast* publicity photo on the shelf. Then I moved so close to Iris I could feel her breath. 'He doesn't look like River any more.'

'River's fine! He doesn't do drugs! He swore to me!'

'Then he's lying!'

Iris spun around and marched from the room. When she slammed the door, the publicity still fell to the floor, toppling another glass frame with it. It smashed. I looked down at River's young and innocent face covered in shattered glass.

CHAPTER 6

'Miserable mortals who, like leaves, at one moment flame
with life, eating the produce of the land, and at another
moment weakly perish.'

Homer, *The Iliad*

It was the night before Halloween. Only fifteen more
hours until Heart Phoenix arrived, then River would be
her responsibility. Until then, Iris was supposed to watch
over River. I called to see how they were doing. But Iris
didn't call me back. Iris *always* called me back. I left
several more messages with the service and never heard
back from her. That meant she was avoiding me, that
she hadn't honored her promise to watch over River on
the set of *Dark Blood*. I couldn't shake the feeling that
something bad was going to happen.

By dusk, I had a horrible headache. I decided to walk
it off. I simply couldn't sit around my apartment and
worry about River any more. The eerie orange light of
the gigantic harvest moon guided me towards Santa
Monica Boulevard. In West Hollywood, Halloween
was the biggest holiday of the year. The streets were
mobbed. It was the time when the world of the living
met the world of the dead. I pushed my way through
crowds of men dressed as ghosts, skeletons and witches.
Others dressed in drag. It was nothing I cared to do.

I was gay but had never even ventured into a gay bar.
My two closest friends knew I was gay but no one else

did. Not even Iris. None of the clients knew, certainly not River. In the past, I'd walked down Santa Monica Boulevard thousands of times and I'd always been too afraid to enter the strobe-flashing, music-thumping clubs. I knew I couldn't measure up even when it wasn't Halloween. I didn't fit in with the thin, muscled men wearing skin-tight jeans or tight shorts. They walked around shirtless. Some even pierced their nipples or wore dog collars around their necks. I wasn't thin. I didn't work out at a gym. I didn't even know how to dance. I certainly couldn't imagine dressing the way they did.

But this was Halloween and the masks of the men passing me on the street gave me courage. Besides, I was uptight about River. The first gay bar I approached was Motherload. It seemed to be less threatening than Rage and Revolver across the street, where the chiseled men posed like marble statues.

I would've walked away if there'd been a line in front of Motherload. Inside, men were packed six deep. The maze of bodies created an obstacle course. I forced my way through to the back of the bar. Anonymous hands groped my ass. I stood by the pool table while my eyes adjusted to the dim lights. I smelled the potent mix of beer and sweat. Nervous and unsteady, I wanted to find somebody who would help me forget my problems.

I leaned against the paneled wall. I wanted to order a drink but remembered the five Motrin I'd taken earlier. Was it safe to mix the two? All around me I watched men rub their own crotches. Their tongues seductively licked their lips. Asses gyrated to the rhythm of the endless techno music. Eyes darted about the room searching for sex. Next to me, two men cruised each other. It reminded me of two dogs sniffing. I didn't know how to respond to the unfamiliar body language and was feeling out of place when a total stranger walked up and kissed me on the lips. Then he simply smiled and walked away. I was grateful for the wall's support. I didn't know how to respond. I'd only had three sexual experiences: the first was with a church deacon, the second with a theatre director and the third a UPS man. All of them had left me feeling empty and alone. I wanted a Danielle Steele romance. I thought two people should meet, fall in love and stay together for ever. It wasn't just about sex.

Out of the darkness, a man seemed to be looking in my direction. Or was he staring at the guys on either side of me? I looked for an exit sign and tried to move away. He moved quicker than I did. His face was partially covered by a thick black beard and moustache. He was dressed head to toe in black – boots, tight jeans, body-hugging T-shirt and a leather biker jacket. I looked down at the floor and counted peanut shells until his black polished boots crushed them. My stomach churned. Maybe he wanted me. His rough calloused fingers lifted my chin until I met his gaze. His blue eyes locked on mine and reminded me of my favorite marbles from childhood, the ones I wouldn't trade. I didn't know what to say. Without a word the stranger began to rub my neck. I felt his warm breath on my ear. His whiskers brushed my cheek. His stomach muscles were as hard as granite and he held me captive, pinned against the wall. His lips came down on mine and he slipped his long tongue into my mouth. I put my arms around him and pulled his body closer. When I hugged him tightly I noticed the sleeve of his leather jacket was empty. We kissed harder and our hands began to grope each other's stomach and waist. Running my hand up along his chest to his shoulder I discovered a small stump where his arm should have been. I tried to move away but he held me tighter.

'Let's go,' he whispered in my ear.

'Where?' I said. I didn't know what was supposed to happen next. But I did know that tonight I didn't want to be alone.

'My place,' he said. 'I live alone a few blocks from here.' He guided me through the crowded bar. Out on the street he maneuvered me through skeletons, gay goblins and drag queens drunkenly yelling, hollering and shrieking. His grip was so tight that my hand hurt. The crowds lessened as we walked away from Santa Monica Boulevard towards Sunset Boulevard. When we reached his street, he pulled me close and we walked side by side. I smelled his new leather jacket mixed with the scent of the crisp autumn air.

'My name's Michael,' he said.

'Chris,' I replied. Suddenly, I realized I knew nothing about this man, except that he was a good kisser and had one arm.

'My apartment is at the top of the stairs.' He pointed up. When he opened the apartment door a pair of agate eyes beamed out of the darkness. Startled, I jumped back.

'That's Serena,' Michael said as he flipped on the lights. The black cat scampered across the wood floors, jumped on the couch and then leaped on top of the bookcase. She hissed at me.

'Serena. Stop that.' Michael threw a small stuffed mouse at the cat. She jumped down and headed into the kitchen. Before she disappeared she arched her back and hissed again.

'Sorry about her. She doesn't like strangers.' He lit some candles and I noticed oil paintings filled every inch of wall space in his loft apartment. In the corner, a sheet covered an easel and canvas. Curious, I wanted to lift the sheet.

'I'm a painter,' he said as he dimmed the lights and turned on the radio to soft classical violin music.

His paintings were beautiful: clean and fresh, full of bright blues and crisp whites. In them, boats glided on blue tranquil waters, Ancient Greeks dressed in classic white robes strolled by marble columns. Gods looked down from the clouds upon the mortals. The paintings reminded me of *Shirley Valentine*.

I admired a painting of two lovers under an apple tree. They were entwined in each other's arms.

Michael came up from behind and kissed my neck. 'Adam and Eve,' he whispered in my ear before turning me to face him.

He was naked and I was embarrassed. His smooth muscled body with the right arm sheared off looked like a classical sculpture discovered in an archaeological dig, toppled by an earthquake thousands of years ago. Michael embraced me before he slowly peeled off my clothes. His tongue, as skillful as one of his paintbrushes, stroked my whole body. He lingered on my neck and chest. Relaxed by the music, his warm touch and the soft lighting, I let him gently guide me to his bed. By then, I not only felt safe, I also wanted to be with him.

A cold draft from the window caused the candle to flicker and woke me up. Where was I? I felt a warm leg draped over mine. Then I saw Michael's beautiful coal-black hair framing his face. The bedside clock read 3 a.m. It was officially Halloween. Perched on the shelf above us was Serena. Her agate eyes bored down on me. I hated cats. When I was a child, my grandmother crossed to the other side of the street and made the sign of the cross whenever she saw one. She said cats brought bad luck. I shivered, then got up and shut the window. Something was still wrong. I felt it in my bones.

Whereas earlier by candlelight, the paintings had

seemed beautiful, in the darkness they became ominous. I saw the blood that ran down the sides of the white marble altar where the lamb was being sacrificed. I noticed the indifference of the gods, the fear of the mortals who stared towards Heaven with beseeching looks.

I had to leave. The paintings were giving me the creeps. While I gathered my clothes the cat's eyes trailed me, as if to protect her master. I didn't want to wake Michael. If I did, we'd have to exchange phone numbers. I looked at his stump and felt ashamed that I was sneaking out. Serena happily replaced me in his bed, nestling up to Michael's leg. I decided not to kiss him goodbye. Besides, the cat hadn't stopped glaring at me. I grabbed my shoes and socks and quietly left, closing the door behind me.

At the bottom of the steps I stopped and laced my shoes. The streets were hauntingly still. The moon darted in and out of the fog. Shivering, I buttoned my shirt. I walked back across Santa Monica Boulevard. All the costumed gay men were gone. The night air hung still. It was so still I could hear the leaves rustle. All I heard were my own footsteps and the occasional wail of an ambulance siren heading towards Cedars-Sinai Hospital.

Once safe in my apartment, I double-locked the door. I was relieved to be home. I checked the answering machine. No messages. Iris still hadn't returned my phone calls. I looked at my watch. Only nine more hours and Mrs Phoenix would arrive. I tore off my clothes, dropped them haphazardly in a trail as I walked towards my bed. My Motrin bottle was on the nightstand. I shook out three and swallowed them. I jumped into bed and pulled my down comforter over my naked body.

At first I thought I was dreaming. Make the ringing stop. Blinded by darkness I groped for my glasses on the bedside table. My head pounded. Where was my Motrin? I was cold. I'd left the patio door open to let in some fresh air. I pulled the covers over my shoulders. Glasses finally in hand, I negotiated them to my face. The bedside clock read 4 a.m. Even Iris wouldn't call this late and it was too early to hear from my family in New York.

The phone finally stopped but the respite was only temporary and it soon started its incessant ringing again. I took two more Motrin and headed for the bathroom – I may as well pee. With the blinds shut my apartment felt like a tomb. I didn't want to turn the lights on but the light from outside slipped under the front door. The entire time I was peeing the phone continued to ring. The last time I'd picked up a phone in the middle of the night, my grandfather had died. Mercifully, the phone stopped. My headache was back in full force. I needed to lie down.

The minute I returned to my bed the phone rang again. Shit! Had I taken my wallet when I left Michael's apartment? Jesus. I hope I didn't leave it at his place. Then he'd have my phone number. I'd have to explain why I had left after sex without even saying goodbye. The phone rang and rang.

My wallet wasn't on the kitchen counter where I usually left it. It wasn't in my coat pocket or my pants pocket. The phone rang. I knelt and swept my hand across the carpet. Finally I found it. I hadn't left it at Michael's. Then I crawled over to the phone and picked it up.

Out of the receiver came screams, followed by uncontrollable sobs. No voice. Just screams. 'Hello. Hello?' I said into the phone. Suddenly, someone shrieked like a wounded animal. I hung up, figuring it must be some sick Halloween crank call. At sleepovers, when we were younger, my brother, sister and I randomly dialed phone numbers from the telephone book. When someone answered, we screamed and then hung up.

I crawled across the floor. I couldn't stand upright. My head hurt too much. I opened the vertical blinds and the moonlight beamed in. I pulled the sliding glass door closed, but that didn't stop the chill that ran from my spine to my skin. The phone rang again. I started to shake. Where was my robe? I grabbed my blanket and pulled it around my body.

When I answered the phone again, there were more loud continuous sobs. If whoever it was hadn't screamed, 'R . . . I . . . V . . . E . . . R!' I would have hung up. I heard only static on the other end of the phone; whoever it was had dropped it.

'Hello. Who is this? If you don't tell me who you are I'll hang up.'

I heard a scuffle on the other end of the phone. 'Chris . . . it's Samantha.' Her voice was cold, almost calm – this obviously wasn't the person who'd been sobbing.

'Samantha?' I said.

'Yes, it's Samantha Mathis. I'm with Iris.' In the background the sobs grew louder. I finally recognized the sobbing – it was Iris.

'Why are you with her?' I asked, but I knew why. I felt it in my gut.

'River's dead.'

I leaned back against the wall, slowly sliding down to the floor

'RIVER!' Iris screeched his name. Then she wailed like an old Greek woman; the ones who dressed in black, pulled at their hair and pounded their breasts when someone dies.

'RIVER!' I heard once more before the phone went dead.

*   *   *

On the morning after his death, it took forever for the sunrise to appear. Ever since I had received the call, I remained on the floor wrapped in a blanket, staring out of the sliding glass doors. I waited for the Halloween moon to vanish. Every ten minutes I checked my watch. Even though it was Sunday I would have to go into the office. The phones were probably already ringing and Iris was at Samantha's house. I turned on the morning newscast and waited for the press to confirm what I already knew: River was dead. I poured a cup of coffee and like a zombie watched the TV screen. Finally, the first CNN news report aired.

'River Phoenix, one of Hollywood's up and coming stars, dead at twenty-three. He died outside the Viper Room, a nightclub owned by actor Johnny Depp. The exact cause of death is still unknown, but drugs seem the leading cause.'

I turned off the television. This wasn't a bad dream. Coffee in hand, I grabbed a fresh bottle of Motrin and pulled on my sweats: it was time to head to the office.

When I arrived at the office, Iris called and, for a moment, she managed not to cry.

'They made me identify his body . . . He looked so helpless lying on that steel tray. I kissed his forehead . . . He was cold,' Iris sobbed again. 'Jesus Christ, Chris . . . River is dead . . . My baby . . .' She broke into sobs and hung up the phone.

Mrs Phoenix's plane still hadn't landed. She was unaware that her firstborn child was in a cold steel drawer at the coroner's office.

I headed into the office, friends of Iris and of the Phoenix family called wanting to know if it was true that River was dead. There wouldn't be any meeting with River that day, no confrontation about his problems.

When Heart Phoenix arrived, Iris finally came home. Her nose wouldn't stop bleeding. She'd cried so much, a blood vessel in her nose popped. I put her to bed and then unplugged the phones, so she wouldn't be disturbed. In my office the phone never stopped ringing. The press called from all over the world. I talked to Sky, River's assistant, and he asked me to find a plane to fly the Phoenix family home to Florida. The producer of *Dark Blood* found a private jet, but ultimately they decided to go back home on a commercial airline.

The only time I left the office was for twenty minutes to get some food. Iris wouldn't come out of the bedroom to see those who had come by to pay their respects. Sunset brought the children in their Halloween costumes. I put the candy on the porch steps. They rang the doorbell anyway. Since they might be Iris' friends, I had to answer.

The phone continued to ring. Not only did I have to answer all of the lines, I had to make an appointment for Iris with the doctor to have her nose cauterized. I popped Motrin by the handful, but they didn't stop my headaches.

At lunchtime, I found out that Mrs Phoenix had left LA without River's body. His dog had also been left behind and wouldn't stop barking. Nobody planned on the mounds of paperwork: death certificates, coroner's reports, police reports and hospital reports all had to be filled out and signed in triplicate before the body could be released. The coroner was still running tests. River was dead. No tests were going to bring him back. The funeral director who handled celebrity deaths at Forest Lawn told me he wouldn't release River's body without the death certificates signed by the coroner. It had become my job to get the dog, Iris and River's body all on a plane. Someone had to go to Forest Lawn and pick out the casket for him. With the phones ringing I couldn't leave the office. I couldn't find Sky either.

I located Iris at her doctor's, where I'd sent her to get her nose cauterized.

'Iris, you have to go pick out a casket for River. I can't find Sky and Heart has left LA,' I said.

'I can't.' Iris started to cry again. 'I can't do it. He's my baby ... my baby,' she sobbed.

'Put David on the phone,' I said.

To avoid the crazy fans and the phones that wouldn't stop ringing, Iris had temporarily moved in with David Permut, a producer and close friend. 'You have to take her to Forest Lawn, David ... help her pick the casket out. I'll take care of the rest.'

'I don't think she can do it,' David replied.

I heard her muffled sobs in the background. God, now she started crying again.

'She has to David. I can't leave the office and she's the only one that can – just go with her and she'll be fine.'

CHAPTER 7

'Look now how mortals are blaming the gods, for they say
that evils come from us, but in fact they themselves have
woes beyond their share because of their own follies.'

Homer, *The Odyssey*

River's memorial service became the hottest ticket in
Hollywood. People who didn't even know him begged
Sue Patricola, River's publicist, and I to be put on
the guest list. We were coordinating the full-blown
Hollywood memorial service to be held at Paramount
Studios. Ironically it was in the same theatre where Iris
and I had screened and watched River fumble through
his last completed film, *The Thing Called Love*. Family
services had already been held in Florida. This service
was for friends and associates on the West Coast.

For two weeks prior, I fielded phone calls from
grieving fans and the news reporters. Then there were
the crazies, like the young female fan who wanted a
piece of memorabilia. She threw herself at my feet and
grabbed my ankles. 'Please, mister, just a picture of him.'

I struggled to unclasp her fingers from my ankles.
There were tears in her eyes. When I finally escaped, she
chased me all the way to my car. I slammed the car door
shut. She banged on the window, crying hysterically.

Another male fan paced back and forth in front of the
agency insisting that he be allowed to talk to Iris. 'River
has been reborn in my body and I want Iris to represent

him through me,' he claimed. He screamed obscenities when I walked away. I didn't respond and he pounded on the hood of my car. I had to threaten to call the police before he finally left.

Johnny Depp called. He owned the Viper Room. Fans had scribbled messages and poems on the Viper Room door. He wanted to send the door to us. 'What are we going to do with it?' I said, 'I'd rather you send it to his family if you have to send it somewhere. I'll give you the address.'

Garbage bags of fan mail filled the garage. Funeral wreaths and flowers appeared at the office door every day. The phones never stopped ringing. I emptied three bottles of Motrin a week. The fans and the press wouldn't let River die. On top of that, it was business as usual for the many other clients that our agency represented. Iris wasn't any help. The pressure of the workload took its toll. Nothing stopped my headaches.

The day of the memorial service, I was stuck at the entrance checking the list to make sure unwanted fans didn't crash. Approximately 100 people milled around outside the Paramount theatre smoking and talking about film projects, like it was a fucking movie premiere. I had no choice but to listen to their trite conversations.

'I think we can get Uma Thurman,' a producer said.

'What about Julia Roberts?' a director asked.

'Nah. She can be difficult.'

'What about that Sandra Bullock girl?'

'Did you hear Christian Slater has stepped into River's role in the vampire movie,' a woman dressed in a black Chanel suit chirped.

'Yeah. Leonardo DiCaprio almost got the part. I hear they were neck and neck,' her Armani-clad friend gossiped.

Who were these people? I wanted to evict them all.

Shit! Was that Bill Richert? I looked over at Sue. She'd seen him too. Bill Richert, the director of *A Night in the Life Of Jimmy Reardon*, wanted to play a tape-recorded phone message that River left on his answering machine a year ago. Two days ago, Sue and I had listened to the tape. It was an incoherent rant that went on for twenty minutes. Why would anyone save a message like that? We'd asked him not to bring the tape. Offended, he slammed the phone down.

'If you have a tape recorder Mr Richert, you'll have to leave,' I intercepted him.

'Does it look like I'm carrying a tape recorder?' He flashed open his long black coat and flapped his arms like a bird. 'Where do you think I'm hiding it?' He looked weird and I didn't want to search him. Sue let him pass. She didn't want a scene either.

'Go in. But we'll be watching you. You're not to play that tape. Understand?'

Richert stared me down on his way to the lobby.

Finally the last of the mourners took their seats. I slipped into the back of the theatre. In the middle of the stage there was a speakers' podium and two big baskets of flowers. On the easel was the publicity still from *The Mosquito Coast* (yes, the same one that had fallen to the floor two days before he died). It was illuminated by a klieg light.

Iris had come out of seclusion for the big event. She was with her best friend David and they were seated three rows in front of me. I had made sure not to sit next to her. Let her dig her nails into his arm instead of mine.

As the service dragged on, I paid more attention to my watch than to the famous speakers: Sidney Poitier, Rob Reiner, Jerry O'Connell, John Boorman, Christine Lahti, Peter Bogdanovich and Helen Mirren. Rob Reiner told a story about River losing his virginity in a tent decorated with flowers at the age of fourteen during the filming of *Stand By Me*. What a strange topic for a memorial service. There was so much I never knew about River. Someone else read letters from Tom Cruise and Brad Pitt who were in London filming *Interview with the Vampire* (River was to have started filming that picture after Christmas). Christine Lahti spoke about how hard it had been to visualize River as her son when they filmed *Running on Empty*. He was too sexy. She didn't know whether to mother him or date him.

God almighty, my head throbbed. I popped more Motrin. No matter how many I took, the headache wouldn't go away. I was glad the service was almost over. I couldn't wait to leave. The chairs were uncomfortable and my constant squirming made mine squeak.

I glanced at the program and noticed that Iris and Heart were scheduled to speak next. I wanted to leave. I envied the small clusters of smokers who escaped outside, slamming the metal door as they went in and out. It was the same metal door Iris had kicked open after the first screening of *The Thing Called Love* so many months ago. I remember how vacant River's eyes had been in that film.

In the last three weeks, so much had been printed in the newspapers and magazines. So-called friends sold every last piece of dirt to the press. The headlines unmasked the very illusion that they'd originally created. The press had built River up. And now that he was dead, they were just as quick to tear him down.

River's contemporaries – Christian Slater, Ethan Hawke, Brendan Fraser and Jerry O'Connell – sat directly in front of me. Had they known River's secrets? Had anyone really tried to help or had they, like Iris and I, turned the other way? I had suspected he had a problem for a couple of years. Why hadn't I done more?

When I glanced up at the podium, Iris was speaking. I hadn't even realized she'd taken the stage. She was almost through with her speech.

'This innocent little bird got his wings clipped in the most evil city in the world,' she said.

Then Heart walked to the stage. 'We believed we could use the mass media to help change the world and that River would be our missionary. I sensed from the beginning, as my labor extended to three and a half days, that River didn't want to be in this world. I woke up two days after his death, understanding for the first time why dawn is called morning and suddenly had a vision of how God had tried to convince River to be born one more time. River told God, I'd rather stay up here with you. So they bargained, God was persuasive, and River offered to go for five years, and then ten and finally agreed to visit Earth, but only for twenty-three years. River is still with me. Whenever the wind blows, I see River, when the sun shines I see River, when I look in someone's eyes and make a connection, I see River. To have death transformed into another way to look at life is his huge gift.'

Whereas Iris had been overwhelmed with grief, Heart read her speech without much emotion. I didn't understand how she kept from crying. Certainly I wanted to cry, but not in front of all these people.

'Please, let's join hands,' Heart said, 'and think of River and then if anyone has any thoughts about him please share with us.'

Please not that. I always hated it in church when they asked us to hold some stranger's hand. Thank God no one was sitting near me. I closed my eyes.

When the moment of silence ended, Jane Campion, the director of *The Piano* stood up. 'I didn't know River but I just lost my ten-day-old son. I had to come so that I could try to understand why these things happen.' Heart left the stage and walked towards Jane. They hugged. It was as if I was watching this from above the room. It seemed like a dream. This couldn't be happening. The theatre was so quiet that the muffled sobs of Jane were a welcome relief. Nobody knew what to say or do or how to end this awkwardness.

Obviously inspired, Louise Stratten, the wife of Peter Bogdanovich, stood up. 'Peter and I adopted this stray cat that came around the house every day. We know my sister Dorothy is reincarnated in that cat.'

Samantha Mathis spoke from her seat. 'River was a sensitive . . . He had so much compassion for everyone and everything that he had a weight on his heart . . . He was obsessive. When he wanted to eat artichokes he would eat ten at a time. He did everything to that degree.'

John Boorman blurted out, 'Is there anybody here who can tell us why River took all those drugs?'

I looked over at Heart. She looked shocked that anyone would dare bring up how River had really died. The cause of death was still speculation as far as she was concerned. River's sisters, Summer and Liberty, stoically left the theatre in protest.

I didn't want to be in the theatre. I had to get out. I ran up the aisle and charged into the restroom outside the theatre. I turned on the cold water, wet a paper towel and put it on the back of my neck. Nothing would stop my head from throbbing. I sat on the toilet seat hoping that I'd wake up and this would all be a nightmare. I wanted to get off the Paramount lot before I had to talk to anyone else. By the time I left the bathroom, people were exiting the theatre.

'Chris!' I heard Iris's voice behind me. I kept walking. 'Honey?' she called again.

'Shit,' I muttered under my breath. I didn't want Iris throwing herself at me in front of all these people. I felt David's hand on the back of my shoulders. Iris joined us. She was out of breath but she waited for her cigarette to be lit.

'David and I are going to Kate Mantilini for dinner. Come with us,' she pleaded.

Thank God she didn't hug me or start to cry. I looked over her shoulder. Outside the theatre mourners surrounded River's mother. If I was going to talk to anyone I felt I should talk to Heart. I just didn't want to. I felt awkward. Perhaps even a bit guilty. Should I have gone behind Iris' back and let Heart know more of what was happening with her son.

'I have a headache, Iris,' I said. She put her arm around my waist and pulled me so close her cigarette smoke drifted up my nostril.

'Come on ... Come to dinner with us,' David encouraged. He rubbed my back. 'You're just hungry.'

I pulled away.' No, I have to go.'

'Chris,' Iris yelled after me 'Chris.'

I ignored her and quickly walked away. I was halfway to my car when Mrs Phoenix called out to me. I turned around and walked towards the theatre. She motioned me to her side and quietly whispered, 'Chris, I just heard that Christian Slater is donating his salary from *Interview* to River's favorite charity. Please go over and tell Christian that he should send the check to me in Florida, care of the Foundation.'

Mrs Phoenix was going to start a foundation. But as the charities listed in the obituary had been approved prior to being published, I wasn't going to approach Christian Slater. I just walked away.

On the passenger seat I saw the bottle of Motrin. I pulled off the top and poured four of them into my hand. Then I washed them down with a warm can of Coke. Now that I'd escaped from all those Hollywood people maybe I could cry at last, then maybe my head would stop throbbing. I leaned back against the headrest for a moment before I pulled out of Paramount's main gate. The same gate that River had gone through on his first audition, when he and his family had first arrived in LA fourteen years ago.

On my way home, I drove by the Hollywood Memorial Cemetery where Rudolph Valentino, Tyrone Power, Douglas Fairbanks and Marion Davies were buried. I bet nobody visited those monuments any more. They were forgotten idols.

I stopped my car, leaned my head against the headrest and rolled down the window to let in the crisp autumn air. The cemetery was uncared for. Vines, trees and bushes grew wild and crept over the top of the wrought-iron fences. Cement crumbled onto the sidewalk and weeds choked everything.

Like them, River Phoenix had been a star. His vulnerability emanated from the movie screen. Fans wanted to touch him because he made them feel. To do that, he gave up a part of himself. Other parts of himself he gave up to lawyers, agents, business managers, producers, directors, his family and friends. In the end there weren't any parts left to give.

He couldn't trust anyone. Their motives were never really clear. A quintessential child of Hollywood, he'd been raised under klieg lights. Movie sets had served as temporary homes. The other actors in whatever movie he was filming became his temporary family. He worked adult hours. The ten-hour days included seven hours devoted to acting, two hours for schooling, one hour to eat and play. The stages were his playground. Even when River went home to his real family, he couldn't go to a regular school and was taught privately.

At eighteen, he received an Oscar nomination for the movie *Running on Empty*. Overnight he was elevated to the status of an idol. His face appeared on national magazine covers. Fans camped outside his hotel and tried to sneak onto his movie sets. People invited him to the A-list parties in Hollywood and New York. Designers gave him clothes to wear. Other people paid his travel, food and drugs. Everyone wanted him because he was a star, one of the chosen, an immortal.

I don't know when he discovered that people only wanted him to sell their magazines and movies. Towards the end, his films quit pulling in the audiences. The same people who had worshipped him, talked about him behind his back. Maybe that's why he wouldn't let the camera see his eyes. He didn't want to give any more. Nobody wanted to see that he was in trouble. If they had, they would have had to admit their part in it.

What bothered me most was what happened outside the Viper Room. As River lay on the sidewalk, the paparazzi and the fans crowded in around his convulsing dying body, trying to snap one last picture.

'No paparazzi, I want anonymity,' were River's last words.

CHAPTER 8

'Even Time, the father of all, cannot undo what has been
done, whether right or wrong.'

Pindar, Greek poet

For the past week the phones had finally quieted down.
Now, the day before my Thanksgiving holiday was to
begin, Heart had published an article in the *Los Angeles
Times*. It stirred up the incessant ringing of the phones.
Iris was gone.

'Iris Burton Agency. Please hold.' I placed line one on
hold.

'Iris Burton Agency. Please hold.' I placed line two on
hold.

I let the third line ring. I didn't care any more.

Let all the phones ring. I reached for the Motrin bottle.
Empty. Shit! I slam-dunked it into the wastebasket.
The third line continued to ring. If only I could dispose
of the phones as easily as I had the Motrin bottle. I
pulled another bottle from my briefcase, unwrapped
the cellophane and popped the childproof cap. The two
lines I'd put on hold earlier, blinked silently.

'Shut the fuck up!' I screamed at the third line.

Suddenly I felt nauseous and a cold sweat broke out
on my forehead and my chest. Then I must have blacked
out. When I came to, I was petrified. If I had blacked out
here, I could black out anywhere. I was out of control.

Two hours later I sat in the doctor's office. I had gone

to see him during my lunch break. 'Your blood pressure is 190 over 100.' He shook his head. 'I'm not surprised. It's probably all stress related.' He unfastened the blood pressure cuff.

'Is that what's causing the nausea?' I asked.

'No. I believe you're having panic attacks,' the doctor responded.

'Panic attacks? How do I get rid of them?'

'I can prescribe Prozac or Valium.' He looked at his watch and quickly scribbled out a prescription. 'You can fill this at the pharmacy downstairs.'

Panic attacks? I reached over and picked up the prescription. Prozac? Mental patients took Prozac. I crumpled up the prescription and tossed it in the wastebasket. I wasn't going to start taking drugs. That's what River had done. Now that I knew the warning signs for the panic attacks, I could pull off the road or head to the nearest bathroom.

I went back to the office. I didn't have any other choice. 'Iris Burton Agency. Please hold.'

But before I could push the hold button again: 'Don't you dare put me on hold!' Iris yelled. 'I'm using the phone in the hotel manager's office.'

David had taken Iris to the Canyon Ranch, a celebrity spa, for a week. Since River's death, she'd gained an enormous amount of weight. She was gigantic. Her 5 foot 3 frame was now carrying well over 180 pounds, the largest I'd seen her since we'd been working together. She needed to shed some weight.

'I have two lines holding Iris,' I replied tersely.

'I don't care if Steven Spielberg is holding on the other line,' she snapped.

I was silent.

'Let them hold until I'm finished! Don't you dare pick up another line.'

'Yes, Iris,' I said sarcastically.

'Did you find out who sold the pictures to the *National Enquirer* yet?' Iris said.

'Does it even matter at this point?' I shook four Motrin into the palm of my hand.

'It matters to me! That's all you need to know.'

The *National Enquirer* had published a disgusting photo of River in his coffin. His black hair was in sharp contrast to the pasty white pallor of his skin. It was dehumanizing. Some sleazy photographer must have bribed someone to get into the funeral home.

'I have better things to do, Iris,' I snapped.

'It must have been someone close to the Phoenix family. That's what really makes me sick,' Iris yelled into the phone. 'Whoever the sick son of a bitch is, should be strung up!'

For once I agreed with her. 'Look, Iris, I'm not a detective and I have *your* business to run. River's publicist says that we'll never find out who did it. Should I make that priority or do you want me to handle the lawsuit that Warner Bros. and New Line are planning to file the minute the coroner's report is released?'

I reopened the Calendar section of the *Times*. Should I even bother to tell Iris that Mrs Phoenix had sent a letter to them explaining River's death? There wasn't anything she could do about it anyway.

'I want answers, Chris. I want this taken care of,' she said.

'Yeah? Well, there are other problems, Iris,' I said. My day had been ruined. I might as well ruin hers and let her know why the phones hadn't stopped ringing. 'Heart published a letter in the *Los Angeles Times* today.'

'What? Why would she do that? What does it say?' I heard the click of Iris' lighter through the phone. That meant she was ready to listen.

A MOTHER'S NOTE ON HER SON'S LIFE AND DEATH

River Phoenix, one of Hollywood's rising young stars, died of a drug overdose on Oct. 31. He was 23. His death was particularly shocking because he had been dedicated to causes that espoused healthful living and cleaning up the environment. He was one of five children of parents who had been wanderers in the 60s, who were strict vegetarians and who were, at one time, missionaries in South America for Children of God, a controversial Christian sect that now calls itself the Family. The late actor's mother, Arlyn, of Gainesville, Fla. – who prefers to be called Heart – sent this article to the *Times* to explain her feelings about her son's death.*

'Iris, did you know about the cult?' I'd never heard that story before.

Iris cut me off. 'Who knows what the hell they were into? Keep reading,' she commanded.

I continued. Heart Phoenix's letter was heartfelt, if somewhat overwritten. She wrote of how River, the strongest influence on her life, was from early on 'a soul filled with passion and a sense of service to others'. He was responsible and liked to share the talents that had been given to him. His acting – a mix of 'openness' and 'vulnerability'–had reawakened audiences the world over. Although the coroner's report had stated that the cause of death was due to drugs, Heart believed that he was not

* Copyright, 1993, *Los Angeles Times*. Reprinted with permission.

a habitual drug user and had just returned to LA from 'the pristine beauty' of Utah, where he had been filming.

'Tell me she didn't say that! I went up to Utah when River freaked out about the snake. Not her! Pristine beauty my ass . . . keep reading,' Iris huffed.

I read the rest of the letter – an apologia for her dead son. How many kids had died through recreational drug use? The world was a 'confusing place' for the young and drugs were a symptom of this fact. More importantly, River's death had allowed her to make sense of the chaos of the world and see how divorced from nature mankind had become.

'It's Sue –' River's publicist '– Heart didn't write this by herself,' Iris revealed. 'I never liked Sue since the day you told me River had hired her.'

Heart finished her letter with the words, 'thanks dear, beloved son, for yet another gift to all of us'.

'Jesus Christ! Is that it? Tell me that's the end of the article.' Iris exhaled her cigarette. 'Why the hell did she do this? Didn't she realize that we are going to have to deal with the nutcases?'

'We already have, Iris,' I sighed.

'You'll be glad to know you've ruined my day!' She slammed the phone down.

Sure Iris could slam the phone down and go get a massage. The 'us' she'd referred to was only me. I was the one stuck answering *her* phones in *her* office. I only hoped I didn't have another panic attack. I retrieved the messages from the answering service. Several more calls had come in while I was on the phone with her. More reporters had called. I looked at the clock. Two more hours until I could take more Motrin, not that it mattered – I had already exceeded the amount allowed for one day. I yanked the phone on my desk out of the

jack. The hell with everything! I flung it into the garden.
I stormed into the house and pulled every phone (there
were six of them) out of their jacks. I tossed them all
into a heap in the middle of Iris' English garden. If
gasoline had been handy, I would have built a bonfire.
Instead, I sat down on the same steps where River used
to sit

Silence at last.

The Thanksgiving holiday gave me a rest from the
phones. I checked with the service a couple of times and
the calls from the press and fans had not diminished. I
only wish we could have forwarded the calls directly to
Mrs Phoenix.

The publicist faxed me two editorials that responded
to Heart's article, they reflected the sentiments of a
large majority of the calls I had received. Although they
sympathized with Heart as a mother, they both blamed
River rather than society's ills. They seemed to have
some validity.

I carried the fax into the house and left it with Iris'
papers, a significant pile had amassed since she'd been
out of town. Then I went back into the office and ordered
a pizza. I couldn't remember the last time I'd gone out
to lunch.

CHAPTER 9

'Know the right moment.'

The Seven Sages

During December I was still having regular panic attacks. Iris spent every day crying to anyone who would listen. I tried answering the phones as much as possible. I didn't care who was calling but I wanted to spare any unsuspecting soul from Iris' rambling rants. It didn't matter if it was the pool man or the head of studio, I was forced to listen to the same calls and they all ended the same, with Iris sobbing uncontrollably.

'I had to identify his body at the morgue,' she said during each of the twelve phone calls. 'I picked out the casket and paid for his funeral,' she said the sob beginning to sneak back into her story.

Iris wasn't exactly paying for the whole funeral, no matter what she told everybody. She had paid for the casket at Forest Lawn but not the Milam Funeral Home in Gainesville, Florida. They kept mailing, faxing and calling the office regarding the $1,745.25 bill for the funeral services they insisted she owed. She chose to ignore them. So I had to deal with the irate funeral director on top of my daily responsibilities.

Iris finally hung up the phone. I handed her a tissue and decided to make her deal with the funeral bill.

'What is this?' Iris didn't even look.

'It's the bill from the funeral parlor in Gainesville.'

I shoved it in her hand, 'River's funeral service in Florida.'

'Why are they sending it to me? I never said I would pay for that,' she spat.

What the hell was she talking about? That's all she'd told anyone since she had returned from the memorial service in Florida.

'I heard you tell everyone, including Mrs Phoenix, that you were taking care of all the bills for the funeral.'

She stood up and slammed the paperwork down on my desk. 'You call them up and tell them to send the bill to Heart. You give them her address. Do you understand?'

'I think you should pay it,' I said admonishingly.

'You work for me and when I tell you to do something you do it,' she snapped.

'Iris it's only $1,700 dollars.'

'Do you know how much money I lost? I did not receive the rest of the money from *Dark Blood* and we lost the commission on *Interview with the Vampire.* I'm not paying!' She stormed out of my office and slammed the door.

'I'm not calling!' I yelled back.

Eventually, I called the Phoenix's personal assistant and he handled the bill without telling Heart. Now the funeral director was off my back.

I was never so happy to go on vacation. The way things were going I couldn't stand another minute around Iris. As usual, I'd spend my Christmas holidays in Delray Beach, Florida at the winter home of Sitto (grandmother in Lebanese). Most of all, I looked forward to Sitto's home-cooked meals. She always encouraged me to eat all my favorite childhood foods. At the same time, she nagged me to lose weight. Normally, she hated parking in the airport parking structure but this time she was so eager to see me she actually greeted me at the gate.

Christmas Eve, I had to accompany Sitto to Saint Thomas Moore Catholic Church. The choir sang 'Silent Night'. The priest and the altar boys made their procession to the altar. One minute I stood up in the pew, the next thing I knew I was perspiring profusely. I thought it was the change in climate. But when the sweat soaked my hair and dripped down my brow, I realized something was wrong. Out of the corner of my eye I saw Sitto give me one of her concerned looks. I smiled reassuringly then slipped out of the pew and headed for the bathroom. I was probably having a panic attack. Except this must be a new symptom. No sooner had I entered the restroom than I passed out on the hard tile floor.

I regained consciousness while the choir was singing 'O Come All Ye Faithful'. Every muscle in my body ached and I was still sweating. Whatever was wrong with me, it wasn't good. I peeked out of the bathroom door. The Communion line had already formed. I must have missed quite a bit of the service. I scanned the church for Sitto knowing she always left at Communion. She liked to be the first person out of the parking lot. Outside I found her standing by her brand-new white Cadillac, her arms crossed.

'Where did you go?' she questioned.

As I drew closer she could see I was still sweating, she uncrossed her arms. She put her hand on my forehead. 'You're all sweaty. Are you OK?'

I wasn't about to tell her I'd just passed out on the church's bathroom floor, any more than I'd tell her I was gay. 'I don't feel well. Could we skip dinner?'

'I was going to take you to the Firehouse. It's your favorite restaurant.'

'Another night,' I apologized.

She drove me back to the house. I went right to bed. When I woke up at 2 a.m. my sheets and pillowcases were soaked with sweat. I was so cold I grabbed two blankets from the linen closet and wrapped both of them around myself. My teeth chattered as I staggered out into the hallway. The light from Sitto's TV lit up her room the same way it had when I was a child and had fallen asleep at the foot of her bed.

'Sitto . . . Sitto,' I whispered.

'Huh,' she said sleepily. Then she saw me. 'Christopher, what's wrong?'

'I need to go to the hospital. I'm really sick.'

She knew I hated doctors. If I was asking to go to the hospital then I must be seriously ill. Without even a word she threw on her jogging suit.

The hospital emergency room nurse took my temperature. It was 105 degrees. I must have passed out again because the next thing I knew a strange voice was discussing me with my grandmother. I thought I felt an IV in my arm but couldn't be sure because I kept my eyes closed. I hoped the voices would just go away.

'Is your grandson an air traffic controller, Mrs Spinella?' the doctor asked my grandmother.

'No, he's a talent agent,' she replied.

'Well, he's showing signs of stress-related exhaustion and he has pneumonia. I'm still waiting for the X-rays but his sinuses are badly infected. His liver panel is also very strange . . . I hate to ask you this, but does he have a drinking problem?'

'As far as I know he doesn't drink,' my grandmother said. 'He lives in that Hollywood place though and they're strange there.'

'Whatever he's doing, it's not good for him. His teeth

84

are completely ground down in the back of his mouth,' the doctor said.

'Will he be able to come home today? I have Christmas dinner in the oven.' My grandmother had been preparing her famous lasagne dinner for weeks.

'I suggest you cancel your plans. The pneumonia is contagious, besides I doubt he'll be hungry.'

I waited until they both left my bedside before I opened my eyes. If my teeth were ground down, it was because I had as many secrets as River. I was gay, I owed $20,000 dollars in debt and it was probably safe to say I was addicted to Motrin. That must have been the reason for the strange liver panel. I feared the idea of another bill so I pleaded with the doctor to let me go home. Thankfully, he let me go later that day.

Sitto picked me up at the curb outside the hospital. 'That *Iris* woman called,' she said spitting out her name. 'I told her you were in the hospital. She didn't even ask what was wrong with you.'

'It's because she's leaving for London and she wants to make sure someone's running the office while she's away,' I said dismissingly.

'She ordered me to tell you that you'd better get back to work on 2 January. She didn't even say Merry Christmas.'

'She's going to visit Kirsten Dunst who's filming *Interview with the Vampire*,' I explained.

'I don't care who's filming what. I said you were in the hospital! What kind of a woman is she? I don't like her and I've never even met her,' my grandmother persisted. She shook her head as we drove away from the hospital.

For the next two weeks I lived the life of my seventy-three-year-old grandmother, the perfect pace whilst recovering from an illness. We watched endless old movies, game shows and sitcoms. She fed me chicken soup. We played Yahtzee, her favorite game. She could play it day and night. She always won. She was the luckiest person I'd ever known. She could sink forty-foot putts on the golf course, bet 50–1 shots at the horse track and win, and she could throw the dice at the craps tables for hours and come out ahead.

The only thing we didn't do was discuss my problems. I was too ashamed to let her or anyone else know how badly I'd failed in Los Angeles. I put up a front because I'd wanted everyone to be proud of me.

It was all I could do to get myself to go back to work. Neither the doctor nor my grandmother wanted me to leave Florida. He recommended bed rest for at least another month but I didn't have one. Iris left for London and I flew back to Los Angeles on 2 January. Thank God she wasn't there the first two weeks. I didn't have the energy to deal with her.

Her first night back she called me six times. I ignored the calls. I did not want to talk to her. It was bad enough that I was going to have to see her the next morning. All I wanted to do was sleep but I was struggling with insomnia. Instead of watching the clock, I chose to watch *Shirley Valentine*. This was probably the fifteenth time in three weeks I had watched it. But even the movie couldn't stop the pounding in my head. Something bad was going to happen, I could sense it. Maybe there was going to be an earthquake. I turned the lights out and prayed I would fall asleep.

I must have dozed. When I woke the clock showed 4.18 a.m. Wearily I reached for my Motrin bottle, when suddenly the room began to shake violently. Quicker than a baseball player heading for home base, I ran the length of my studio apartment to crouch under the dining room table. It was totally dark, I couldn't ever remember being in such darkness. All around me dishes, plates, pottery, wine bottles and lamps crashed to the floor. Then the bookcase fell causing the items to ricochet off my legs.

When the shaking stopped, the darkness became even more terrifying. Alone under the table, coughing and trembling, I swore to leave LA. The only sound I heard was a symphony of car alarms and the creaking of my apartment as it settled back onto the foundation. The few remaining bottles of wine rolled from the rack and crashed to the floor. Even the hallway light was out. Complete darkness.

More shaking. Was it another earthquake or an aftershock? And what was coming next? For years the experts had predicted the great earthquake, the one that would plunge the entire state of California into the bottom of the ocean. The dark silence was so deafening, for a minute I wondered if I'd been buried alive. I looked for my flashlight. I crawled out from under the table and blindly stumbled across the room. My foot caught on something and I tripped and fell to the floor.

I hurt my right arm so badly that I blacked out from the pain. When I came to, my arm was throbbing. I tried to stand up but I couldn't support myself with my right arm. I pulled myself erect with my left arm. In my bed I found the flashlight. I clicked it on and scanned my apartment. It looked like I'd been vandalized. Everything had been tossed about. Candles, books and magazines had spilled off tables and shelves. My mattress had moved off its frame and knocked over the nightstand, TV and VCR. Hundreds of videocassettes were strewn across the floor. There was a huge red stain on the floor from broken wine bottles. In the kitchen the refrigerator had toppled over; broken jars of mayonnaise, mustard, ketchup and pasta sauce had all converged into a puddle in the middle of the floor. I shoved my cut and bloody feet into my work boots. I didn't even bother to tie them. The quickest and safest route out of the building was down the back stairs.

Outside my apartment, the dark hallway was like a catacomb. My neighbors seemed to have the same idea and we all converged on the back stairs. Another aftershock. Behind me two children cried. I raced down two flights of stairs. My injured arm and feet ached. I needed to take care of my wounds. Next door in a twenty-story apartment building people were screaming from their balconies. Large waves splashed the sides of the swimming pool. I didn't know where to go. In shock, I wandered up Doheny Drive. The streets were empty; I felt like the last person on earth.

I wanted someone to tell me everything would be all right. The next thing I knew I was heading towards Iris' house three blocks away. Her lights were on. Even an earthquake didn't dare inconvenience her. Through the window I saw her straightening the pictures. Why was she bothering? Earthquakes generate thousands of aftershocks. I banged on the door.

Startled, Iris jumped. 'Who's there?' She grabbed the poker from the fireplace.

'Chris,' I called out. I stood in front of the window so she could see me. 'It's me,' I said more gently.

She unlocked the door.

I followed her into the living room. 'I can't believe you have electricity, mine is out.'

'The head is missing from my Lladro porcelain milk maiden,' she bitched.

No hug. No kisses. She was preoccupied. She knelt down and groped under the couch. My knees were bleeding. My arm was in a sling, hastily assembled from a scarf that had been a gift from Kirsten Dunst. I felt the dizziness of a panic attack. I sat on the couch and heard a crack. Something hard and sharp needled my buttock. 'Shit!' I jumped up. I'd sat on the glass from a broken picture frame.

'Jesus Christ, Chris,' Iris said.

I tried to sit back down.

'No!' Iris screamed. 'You'll get blood on my couch.'

I jumped and almost lost my balance, 'I need some Band Aids, Iris.'

'I have to find that head. Maybe I can glue it and put in a claim to my insurance company. You don't have to give them the broken stuff do you?' Iris questioned.

I really couldn't have cared less. I wiped my brow. I had started to sweat and knew a panic attack was on its way. 'I'm going out to check the office. Have you been in there?' I called out as I walked towards the back door.

Another aftershock hit but didn't deter her search for the missing Lladro head. 'Where the fuck did it roll?' she screamed.

I ran to my office. It was better to be alone. The walls of the office were shaking. I went into the bathroom and pulled the door closed behind me. The toilet seat vibrated with another aftershock. I started to cry. My stomach clenched up. Cold sweat mixed with hot tears. There was a wall phone installed in the bathroom so I would never miss a call. Now I was glad for it. I dialed my grandmother's phone number in Florida. My mother was visiting her.

'Hello,' I heard Sitto's voice.

'Sitto.' I held back tears, 'It's Chris.'

'Christopher . . . Why are you up so early? Annie, it's your son,' my grandmother called out.

'We just had a terrible earthquake . . . I'm alive . . . I just wanted you to know I'm alive.' I started to sob.

'Christopher it'll be OK . . . Annie, he's crying. You'd better get on the phone.'

'Chris, what's wrong?' My mother's voice soothed me.

'I could've died ... I still might ...' I said between sobs.

When I walked back into the kitchen sometime later, Iris was packing her Waterford crystal into boxes. 'Help me pack my crystal. There might be a bigger quake.'

I stared at her in disbelief.

'Hurry up!' she barked.

'Can I please have some fucking Band Aids! Can't you see I'm fucking bleeding!'

Iris almost dropped the bowl that was in her hand. The dogs started to bark, which meant another aftershock was on its way. I gripped the sink with my left arm.

'Don't raise your voice at me.' She put the bowl down, looking me straight in the eye. 'What do you need a Band Aid for anyway?'

'My knees and my feet, Iris.' She followed me into the bathroom.

'I think we should go and check my other house. I'm worried about those crystal goblets I bought in Paris. They cost $150 each,' she said.

I sat on her toilet. I felt the vibration from another shock. I took off my boot. My feet were bloody.

'Jesus Christ! Let me get you one of my old towels. . .You'll get blood all over my white tiles,' as she tossed it to me.

I attended to my feet. 'Maybe to you this is just an earthquake but to me it's a catastrophe, one in a long line. The first was my walking through your door five years ago.'

'What the hell do you mean by that?' Iris shrieked.

'I mean, I fucking quit, Iris! I can't fucking stand one more day with you in this office.' I wrapped a piece of gauze around my foot and grabbed the tape from her hand.

'Now you listen here. I'm willing to let these comments slide because you're upset.' She glared at me.

I cut her off. 'Upset . . .? I can't go through a day without a fucking migraine. I'm having panic attacks and I can't even breathe without wheezing . . . or maybe you haven't noticed? Like you didn't notice that my body is bleeding. Or that River was taking drugs. Fuck your precious crystal! And fuck you!' I shoved my bandaged bloody foot back in my boot and pushed past her.

She ran after me. 'I could fire you for what you said.'

I ran onto the porch. 'I *quit*, Iris. I quit! I quit! I fucking quit!'

'Would you keep it down,' Iris hissed, 'the neighbors will hear you and how do you think that will look?'

'I don't care, Iris,' I hissed back mimicking her. 'There's nothing left between us. There hasn't been since River died. You didn't notice River had a problem and you can't see I'm having one. It's all about you! I don't want to live this way any more! If I die today I don't want the last person I see on this earth to be *you*!' I spun around and walked down the street.

Iris ran after me and screamed at the top of her lungs, 'YOU'RE FUCKING FIRED!'

CHAPTER 10

'Life is short, the art long, opportunity fleeting, experiment
treacherous, judgment difficult.'

Hippocrates (460–377 BC), *Aphorisms*, sec.1,1

Two days after the earthquake I was answering the
phones. Iris had convinced me to come back to work,
full of promises that things would be better. She said I
was just uptight and in a few weeks I'd forget all about
the earthquakes. I thought maybe our relationship was
as shattered as her Lladro porcelain.

When a huge aftershock hit, almost as big as the
original earthquake, I thought it was the end of the
world. I ran out of the office, jumped in my car and
drove towards my apartment. But I didn't know if I'd be
safe there, so I pulled off the road and parked. Where
would I be safe? I needed someone to comfort me and
hold me. Safety didn't exist in Los Angeles, the mythical
place of my childhood dreams. River's death had shown
me how empty those dreams were. Now I sat in my car
trembling uncontrollably with the realization that there
was no stability in life.

It was odd, but Iris was the person I was closest to in
LA. She never had anything good to say but she could
enumerate all your flaws. The ground beneath me would
never stop shaking if I stayed with her.

When I returned to my apartment I sat in the middle
of the floor and held the phone. Another aftershock hit.

I had always resisted asking my family for help. Now I wanted to savor my last breaths of freedom. I had to accept defeat and be handed the sentence for ignoring them for the past ten years to chase after my dreams. I'd have to admit they were right about Hollywood and accept the life they wanted me to live. They told me I would fail and the stacks of credit card bills and my empty checking account proved they were right.

Since I was sixteen I'd worked full-time and supported myself while I attended high school, college and finally graduate school. I'd always worked hard and saved my money so that I wouldn't have to answer to my family. Up till now I'd done everything on my terms because I never had to ask them for anything. While I punched each digit of my grandmother's phone number I felt the noose tighten around my neck. I choked and prepared for my ultimate humiliation.

My grandmother didn't answer the phone, my mother did. I cried for what seemed like hours, which spared me any lectures. I sobbed that I couldn't live like this any more. Within two hours my mother had located a moving van; the only catch was that it was leaving LA in the morning. I had one day to pack up what was left of my belongings.

Talking to my mother helped me to feel better. I was going home. Soon I would be with people who cared about me, instead of Iris whose only concern was the missing head of her Lladro milk maiden.

As soon as the clients found out I was leaving, my phone never stopped ringing. My answering machine screened every call. Most of them were from Iris and I didn't want to talk to her. I scanned the contents of my apartment. I had a tremendous amount of packing to do before the movers arrived in the morning.

The next day at 8 a.m. I left for the supermarket in search of boxes and heavy-duty green garbage bags; I'd used every container I had for packing. When I returned Patricia Bryant had left a message that she had a job for me. I was suspicious because I'd represented her daughter Clara and was sure she wanted me to start work at her friend's new agency. I balanced the phone receiver on my shoulder, while I continued to shove sweaters into garbage bags.

'Hello,' Patricia said.

I looked at the clock. The moving van would be here in an hour.

'Is it true . . . are you quitting?' I heard the panic in her voice.

'I can't do this any more.' I yanked a winter coat off a hanger and threw it to the pile on the floor.

'Jesus, what are we going to do? I don't know if we'll be able to handle Iris with you gone,' Patricia said.

'Give her a chance, Patricia. I'm sure it will be fine.'

'Chris, if you really are leaving . . .' She hesitated. 'I have a job for you.'

'I'm not staying here. Patricia. I told you –'

'Just listen to me for one minute,' she cut me off. 'Joannie and Thomas my friends – I think you know them – own Le Petit Greek restaurant. I've taken you there before.'

'I don't want to be a waiter, Patricia,'

'Would you just let me finish . . . They own a bed and breakfast and they need someone to run it from April to November.'

'What?'

'The bed and breakfast is in Greece,' she continued.

I found another empty suitcase and packed in a few more sweaters. 'Greece?'

'Santorini, Greece – it's one of the southern most

94

islands, closest to Crete. Chris, I've seen pictures of it and it's just spectacular. According to Joannie, it's one of the most beautiful islands in the Aegean.'

'I don't think I can move to Greece right now. I'm buried up to my ears in credit card bills. How am I supposed to pay those?' I stuffed more clothes into a dresser drawer. 'Let me ask you a question: do you think I have to empty the dresser drawers for the movers, or can I just tape them shut?'

'Chris, stop packing! Just listen to me for one second. I've talked to Joannie and Thomas. They remembered you and they're willing to meet.'

'I don't speak Greek.' I grabbed the tape for the dresser drawers.

The downstairs buzzer rang. 'Hold on, Patricia.'

'Moving company, sir,' the voice said.

'Shit. You're early.' I buzzed them up. ' Hold on, Patricia. The moving company's here.'

'Chris, what do you have to lose?' Patricia said.

Damn it. I looked around. How was I going to get all this packed on time?

'I'll pick you up in an hour. Be ready.' She hung up.

The movers banged on my apartment door. I couldn't run a bed and breakfast in Greece. Could I?

'You should've shaved.' Patricia glanced at me on the drive over to meet Joannie. 'You're starting to look like a bum with that beard. When's the last time you shaved?'

'I don't have time to shave. I *should* be home packing. I'll never get this job, Patricia.'

'Now there's a healthy attitude. Some of us can't pick up and leave. I have a home and a daughter.'

We pulled into a strip mall next to a gas station. It had a laundromat, a video and liquor store, and a Thai restaurant that I followed her into.

'Gee, real classy place, Patricia. And you were worried about how I looked?' I scrunched up my nose at the smell of cooking oil. That was why I didn't eat in Thai restaurants.

'Knock it off,' she said pinching my arm.

Patricia hurried across the room, hugged a woman with shoulder-length blonde hair. Joannie was voluptuous with bosoms almost as big as Dolly Parton's. Her full hips were encased in black spandex pants that hugged her legs all the way to her high heels. She waved and her diamond-loaded fingers and her wrists glittered. In the car, Patricia had told me Joannie had been a successful opera singer. She now coached aspiring artists.

'Tell him about the island and show him the pictures, Joannie,' Patricia said.

'I *will*, Patricia,' Joannie said.

'Show him the hotel and tell him.'

Joannie cut Patricia off. 'I think you should sit over at that table for a minute, so Chris and I can talk.' Joannie sat down. She motioned for me to sit across from her. 'I apologize that my husband couldn't be here.' She pulled out some photographs from a folder. 'Our two restaurants were damaged in the earthquake – a lot of broken bottles and glass.' Joannie pointed to a picture of two tables with huge white umbrellas on a white tiled patio. 'That's the view from the rooftop terrace.' It showed a huge island that looked like a crater surrounded by blue seas and blue cloudless skies. It was a peaceful scene.

'Can I see?' I heard Patricia from the next table.

'Later,' Joannie said.

The next photograph in the album was a little, elfin-like man. He was missing his top row of teeth.

'That's Gregory, Thomas' father,' Joannie said.

Gregory's eyes sparkled like a child who knows that

he's getting away with something. He was holding out a red bougainvillea to the camera, proud of the gardens and the flower box behind him. He looked relaxed, serene and without a care in the world. I envied him.

I flipped through the photographs of the hotel lobby, kitchen and bedrooms. There were altars behind the beds. According to Joannie it had been a monastery back in the sixteenth century. There were winding staircases and vaulted ceilings. The rooms were Spartan; everything was uncluttered and to the bare minimum, with whitewashed walls and shutters that opened to the sea. It looked charming.

'This would be your room.'

From the photograph it appeared as if my room burrowed into the cliffs. It resembled a cave. A long altar ran along the backside of the tiny room.

'It's built into the volcanic rock. But you have a patio.'

'It must have been where the monks went to flagellate themselves for having impure thoughts,' I responded.

Joannie laughed. ' I never thought of that, but you might be right.'

I flipped back and forth through the photos a few times. 'How'd you find the place?' I asked politely.

'Gregory works on the island. When it came up for sale, he told us about it. Twenty years ago an Englishman tried to turn it into a bed and breakfast but he ran out of money and abandoned the project. It sat empty and rotting. Gregory said it was a steal. We flew to Greece on holiday. We fell in love with the island.' She laughed. 'We've spent a fortune renovating the place.'

I looked at the brochure. It showed the hotel fully restored to its simple style. 'What's that?' I pointed to a small chapel on the other side of the sidewalk in the brochure.

'The old chapel where the monks prayed; we don't

own that. Here's another picture of it.' She flipped through the book.

The chapel literally hung on the cliffs with a 2,000-foot drop to the sea. Those monks must have been isolated up on the cliffs with nothing to do except pray. Isolation from mankind, blue waters and blue skies – it all sounded good to me.

'We pay coach airfare, room and board and $250 a week. The guests leave tips too. Cindy, the girl who ran it last year, made a fortune. Gregory, by the way, is a great cook. He'll make all your meals.'

'Why isn't Cindy going back then?' There must be something she's not telling me. It seemed to good to be true.

'Gregory didn't get along with her,' she said.

'How long do I have to stay?' I countered.

'You'd stay six months, until November. We won't need you after that, but you'll have to learn Greek. Gregory doesn't speak English . . . or he pretends he doesn't.' She smiled. 'I have these great Pimsleur tapes. The foreign diplomats use them. You have two months to learn Greek.'

'Is there a phone?' I asked.

'No phone. It takes three years to put one in. We're on the wait list,' Joannie said as she grabbed her purse.

I would be cut off from the world. Neither the credit card companies nor Iris could find me.

I could just vanish.

CHAPTER 11

'As to the gods, I have no means of knowing either that they exist or that they do not exist. For many are the obstacles that impede knowledge, both obscurity of the question and the shortness of human life.'

Protagoras, Diogenes Laertius, *Life of Protagoras*

The moving company packed me up and I loaded my Mazda 323 with the clothes, valuables and books that I didn't trust with them. By sunset, I was ready to begin my journey. Endless highways unspooled in front of me, leading me across the scorched and mostly barren landscape of California, Nevada, Arizona, New Mexico and Texas on my way to Florida. Occasionally a small town popped up but I was lost in thought. My life had become as unlivable and dry as the deserts I crossed. Exhausted, my arrival in New Orleans finally made me realize it was time to stop. Had I driven far enough from Los Angeles that neither Iris nor the ghost of River could haunt me?

I rented a hotel room in the heart of the French Quarter for two days. According to the literature in the lobby it had been a bordello 150 years ago. Georgian columns held up the ceilings, plush red velvet curtains covered the windows, green potted palm trees filled the courtyard and red wool carpets covered the stairs. It was straight out of *Gone with the Wind*.

After checking in I decided to wander the streets and

explore. I could sense the ghosts as I walked past the old cemeteries in the Vieux Carre. The damp fog had a life of its own as it slithered down the cobblestone streets and around tipped gravestones which were half-sunken in the ground. Wrought-iron gates and fences guarded the stately mansions. What were they trying to keep out?

I decided to stay an extra day and explore Anne Rice country before I had to face my family in Florida. Three months ago I'd been scheduled to visit Kirsten Dunst and her mother here on location while they filmed *Interview with the Vampire*.

The next morning while sipping coffee I came across an old copy of the *Chicago Sun-Times*. As fate would have it, Roger Ebert reviewed River's last completed movie, *The Thing Called Love*:

THE THING CALLED LOVE
By Roger Ebert

Of course you go to River Phoenix's last finished film in a certain state of mind. You remember his clarity and power in films like *Running on Empty* and *Dogfight*, and against those images you hold shots of his dead body on the sidewalk outside the Viper Club. His death still seems all wrong. How could he have been so careless of his responsibility to his own future?

These thoughts are there as Peter Bogdanovich's *The Thing Called Love* begins, but there are more pragmatic thoughts, too: Will his performance reveal signs of the drug use that ended his life? Or will his farewell performance show him at the top of his form?*

---

* © Roger Ebert/*Chicago Sun-Times*.

I guess I knew the answer to Ebert's questions. I'd sat through the film at least seven times. Every time they re-edited the film, they held another screening to gauge the audience reaction. It was never good. The editor could only cut away from the star of the picture so many times in a scene. Iris couldn't even bear to sit through the film after the first screening. I finished reading the review:

In Phoenix's first scene, it is obvious he's in trouble. The rest of the movie only confirms it, making *The Thing Called Love* a painful experience for anyone who remembers him in good health. He looks ill – thin, sallow, listless. His eyes are directed mostly at the ground. He cannot meet the camera, or the eyes of the other actors. It is sometimes difficult to understand his dialogue. Even worse, there is no energy in the dialogue, no conviction that he cares about what he is saying.

Some small part of this performance may possibly have been inspired by Phoenix's desire to emulate James Dean or the young Brando in their slouchy, mumbly acting styles. And maybe that's how Bogdanovich and his associates reassured themselves as they saw this performance taking shape. After all, Phoenix came to this project as one of the most promising actors of his generation, and perhaps somehow an inner magic would transmit itself to the film.

It does not. The world was shocked when Phoenix overdosed, but the people working on this film should not have been. It is notoriously difficult to get addicts to stop their behavior before they have found their personal bottoms, and so perhaps no one could have saved Phoenix, who was not lucky enough to find a higher bottom than death. But his performance in this movie should have been seen by someone as a cry for help.

Bogdanovich does what he can. Samantha Mathis is plucky and spirited in the lead role, and the milieu is entertaining (everyone in the movie, even cops and taxi drivers, seem to be aspiring songwriters). But at the center of the film is an actor whose mind and heart are far, far away, and he is like a black hole, consuming light and energy.

He's running on empty. Sometimes there are even scenes where you can sense the other actors scrutinizing Phoenix in a certain way, or urging him, with their tones of voice, to an energy level he cannot match. It is all very sad.

I tossed the newspaper back on the table and headed out into the murky streets of New Orleans, the city that would have been the setting of River's next movie, *Interview with the Vampire*. He'd been cast as the interviewer who chronicles the vampire's story. Even after River's character hears the vampire's sad tale of the loneliness and the difficulty of a life lived in the shadows, he still asks the vampire for immortality. The last year of his life, River repeatedly spoke about his film legacy. Perhaps it was his desire to be immortal.

The fog drifted across the narrow cobblestone streets. A chill went through me and I pulled my coat collar up around my neck. I looked up, in front of me was a church guarded by menacing gargoyles.

I entered the dimly lit church and walked down the center aisle towards the main altar and approached the huge crucifix. The blood that dripped from stigmata wounds on Jesus' hands seemed real. Didn't people in ancient times run to temples to escape the wrath of the gods, spirits and ghosts?

Roger Ebert had seen River was in trouble and he'd only watched the film once. I had watched it seven times.

Why hadn't I recognized River's call for help, when a total stranger had? It looked to me like an attempt at James Dean or Montgomery Cliff sensitivity, when he was screaming for someone to stop him. But instead we'd ignored his cries for help and signed him up for more movies. I felt blood stained my hands too. If I had shouted louder rather than ignoring the rumors, would Heart Phoenix have come to Los Angeles sooner?

Candles flickered on the prayer altars all the way down the aisles. I searched the faces of the saints, seeking one that would grant me absolution. My heels clicked on the marble floors and echoed in the stone chamber. I knelt at one of the prayer altars and pulled four dollars from my wallet to pay for offertory candles to acknowledge loved ones recently lost. I lit a candle for each of my dead grandfathers, my grandmother and also one for River. He had been in trouble for a long time. I should have been able to do something. I gazed over at the huge crucifix and realized River's blood was on more hands than mine.

As I continued my exodus to Greece, my family had created a detour to Florida with hopes that I would stay and live the life they had already mapped out for me. All the debts I'd incurred in Los Angles loomed over my head. The only chance I had to avoid bankruptcy was to cash in my pension plan from the Iris Burton Agency, but that would require Iris's cooperation. It was highly unlikely that she'd sign the necessary papers, considering I had mailed her the key to the office from a hotel in Texas and never said goodbye.

Once in Florida my family left me alone. I guess the defeat that registered on my face was enough. I isolated myself from everyone and spent my days walking miles up and down the beach learning Greek, passing the very same lifeguard stations from my childhood. I was thirteen and gazing at the lifeguards, when I realized I was attracted to men. I was always scared that my glances would reveal my secrets to my father.

This was the same beach where I had made my first awkward attempt at kissing a girl when I was twenty-one, and discovered it did nothing for me. Shortly after that I admitted to myself that I was gay. I knew that the prying eyes of my grandmother would stop me from experimenting. It was then that I decided to pursue my childhood dreams of movie-making. I saved my money for two years and I applied for graduate school in Los Angeles.

Nothing had changed. After nearly seven years in LA my family still didn't know I was gay and I still had not accepted myself. Here I was wandering aimlessly up and down these same beaches.

As I boarded the plane at JFK bound for Greece, I hoped the answers and a sense of inner peace would be found in the ancient mysteries of Santorini.

CHAPTER 12

'No man can be an exile if he remembers that all the world
is one city.'

C.S. Lewis, *Till We Have Faces*

The scraper clanked as it hit the white marble terrace.
I began to loathe the Santa Fe orange paint that had
been splattered on every window, mirror and most
of the marble tiles of the former monastery that was
now my home. I looked down at my hands; blisters
had formed on top of blisters. Since my arrival one
month ago I scraped and cleaned from morning until
night. I was now certain that a blind man or someone
who had swallowed too many bottles of ouzo had
been hired to repaint the Le Petit Greek Bed and
Breakfast. On top of the scraping, every single one of
the nine rooms had a layer of dust, dirt and cobwebs
that looked as authentic as any haunted house set I
had seen in Hollywood.

Santorini was the most picturesque and romantic
island in Greece according to all the travel guides that I
had read. The guidebook I found in the reception area
of the hotel described Santorini as the Devil's Island.
Jagged and scorched cliffs dropped thousands of feet
to the sea. Centuries of volcanic eruptions, earthquakes
and devastating winds had created a particular kind of
beauty – one wrought from tragedies. As I stared off
into the landscape I definitely understood why. There

105

was something almost electromagnetic in the air, an energy that set a person on edge, with an undercurrent of something violent that I couldn't quite put a finger on. I noticed this energy increased more with the full moon.

The cool breeze revived me enough that I reached for the bottle of water. Sweat poured down my body but I didn't even bother to wipe it away any more. I had simply grown accustomed to being sweaty. I glanced out at the blue Aegean Sea with its patches of shimmering gold. I found it hard to believe that a month had gone by. I hadn't done this much manual labor since I was a boy. I climbed up and down four long flights of stairs all day long as I completed my routine tasks. I had dropped three waist sizes in a month. Iris had never been to a spa like this.

As I stared off into the harbor I wondered what had ever possessed me to leave Iris Burton and my job as an agent. River's death had been awful and Iris and I had a lot of problems but *what had I been thinking*?

What kind of career trajectory was there for a toilet bowl cleaner and paint scraper? I had nothing to think about except the shame of my impending bankruptcy. Iris had made it perfectly clear through her lawyers that she was not going to release my pension money. It was at her election and she elected not to. She had been very hurt by my quick departure but there was no other way to leave. Iris did not let go. The look on her face as I walked down her driveway still haunted me. She looked like a child that was lost in the mall.

There was supposed to be a maid and a cook. The maid never materialized and Gregory, the owner's father, was never where he was supposed to be. It was a good thing I knew how to cook. Gregory was like Zorba the Greek on happy pills – he smiled all day. He also drank all night. He looked like a 5'3" lawn gnome. Even when he did something wrong his toothless smile quickly evaporated the anger. I spent hours trying to communicate with him because he spoke only a few words in English. I was so isolated that I found myself talking to the bathroom mirror.

Day after day as I scraped the orange paint, I thought of River Phoenix's death. Leaving Los Angeles had not removed Hollywood. If anything, I felt like I had abandoned something inevitable. I wasn't finished with Hollywood and it wasn't finished with me. Hollywood is like an addiction to alcohol, drugs or gambling. Any degree of success in Hollywood is a million to one shot and there is no high quite like beating the odds. That's what makes the game so intriguing. Iris made everything all the more interesting because she was the rogue swimmer, the one who swam against the current. God help me, I even missed Iris. It was impossible to call anyone because there was no phone in the hotel. I was desperate for news of the clients and Iris. If I wanted to make a phone call I had to go to the American Express office in town, which was a twenty-minute walk. I felt like I had banished myself to the ends of the earth.

A stampede of donkeys raced by the hotel on their way to the port. There were no roads on the cliffs so supplies had to be carried in by donkey. The road ended ten minutes from the hotel. No cars or buses except in town. It was as if I had been transported back in time. I resumed my work determined that I would make the best of this exile and try to make some sense out of what had happened so I would never have to go through such a horrible experience again.

It was during my second month in Santorini that Gregory's girlfriend Stella arrived. Stella was 5' tall and weighed at least 300 pounds. It took her a half an hour to get from the bottom of the hotel to the kitchen. Once she arrived in the kitchen there was no getting her out. She was an incredible cook.

About a week after Stella arrived I was hanging the laundry out on makeshift clothes lines when I noticed a mysterious woman dressed from head to toe in black. A black lace mantilla even covered her face. Gregory waved frantically and smiled.

'Stella. Stella,' Gregory called down into the kitchen and then turned to me. 'Athena.' He pointed to her as if I should know who she was.

'*Kalimera*,' I said smiling and extending my hand.

'*Kalimera*,' she said in return clasping my outstretched hand and not letting go. Blue veins popped from her knobby fingers, one of which wore a simple gold band. I would later learn that Athena was Stella's best friend from Athens and summered in her family's ancient homestead on the island. Her family went back 500 years on Santorini. They had originally fled Spain due to religious persecution. I was a bit unnerved that she had still not let go of my hand after a few minutes. I caught glimpses of her leathery skin and wisps of gray hair poked out from behind the veil.

Athena had buried three husbands and vowed she would never marry again. Supposedly she also possessed psychic abilities. Not more than three minutes after her arrival in the hotel, Stella hurried onto the roof terrace with a serving tray. She set a coffee pot and two ancient looking demitasse cups on the table. After she served Athena the dark milky liquid, she poured a cup for herself but she didn't serve Gregory or me. Stella quickly sipped her coffee and when she was finished flipped the cup over and spun it on the plate several times and then pushed the cup towards Athena.

Athena flipped up her mantilla. Her intense blue eyes fell into a trance and as she rocked back and forth her bones creaked. She passed her hands back and forth over the upturned coffee cup and then she carefully turned the cup and flipped it over leaving the coffee ground residual on the plate.

'The only thing I see is that Stella will be washing a dirty plate with coffee grinds on it,' I said.

Athena raised her hand authoritatively to halt the chattering. She began a monotone, melodic hum that sounded similar to the Greek Orthodox priest's prayer from the Easter service that Gregory and taken me to in my first week on the island. Stella wrang her hands and her head hovered close to the cup. Almost on cue the wind began to blow. Scraps of paper skittered across the terrace. Gregory pulled his hat down so it wouldn't blow away. Stella scrunched her face so hard that she was almost in tears. Athena suddenly spoke but I didn't understand a word of what she said.

'A storm comes, so great that the end of the world will seem near. In one month the ground will shake . . .'

Athena screamed, ' Catastrophe!' Then louder – 'Catastrophe!' And finally and shrill – 'Catastrophe!' I felt like I was watching the climax of an opera. Athena's arms stretched to the sky for a final dramatic touch and then she pushed the cup away and slumped on the table. Her body trembled like electric currents were moving through it. What an actress! I looked up in the sky. It could not have been a clearer day.

I should have listened to Athena because an hour later, as I was halfway over the mountains headed towards the beach, the winds picked up. When I say winds I mean the car was having a hard time staying on the road. The skies were still clear but the winds were harbingers of something awful.

Back at the hotel, Gregory was on the roof waging a battle of his own with the tables, chairs and umbrellas. I reached the rooftop terrace in enough time to help him save a table from being dragged off the roof. He had locked his feet against the wall to keep himself and the umbrella on the roof. I ran over, grabbed his belt from behind and pulled him and the table back onto the roof. We managed to secure the table by lashing it to the refrigerator with rope. We stored the remaining chairs behind the refrigerator, along with the two umbrellas that had been saved. Stella and Athena stood in the doorway of the kitchen fingering their worry beads.

Then it began to hail. Hard rocks of ice the size of ping-pong balls stung my face and hit the back of my head. Gregory signaled that we needed to go in. I could see the lightning in the distance against the black skies. We managed to secure the kitchen doors and then headed down into the safety of the hotel. The four of us huddled in the kitchen. The noise of the wind, hail and thunder was deafening. Minutes seemed like hours. Intermittently the hail stopped, only to be followed by a new assault. Then the power went out. Without lights and with all the shutters securely fastened, the hotel resembled a tomb. Gregory reached for a kerosene lamp. Athena decided to chant. I lit another lamp and decided to head down into my room. I had the best room in the bed and breakfast as far as safety was concerned because I was in a windowless cave that was carved out of the hillside.

I placed the kerosene lamp on the night table and picked up the book that I had been given by one of the guests some time before. There was a shortage of

English language books on the island. The only way to obtain them was to hope that the tourists wanted to lighten their loads of books that they'd read. I'd finished all the books that I had brought with me already. The book was called *The Killing of the Unicorn: Dorothy Stratten (1960–1980)* by Peter Bogdanovich. I had resisted reading the book because Peter had directed the last film that River Phoenix had completed. I looked at my watch, it was only 1 p.m. From the sounds of the wind howling and the pounding rain on the patio door I wasn't going anywhere for the rest of the day and night. I reluctantly picked up the book.

At 6 p.m. Gregory called me to up to dinner. Apparently Athena was spending the night in one of the unoccupied rooms. We didn't have any guests in the hotel, as the tourist season had not yet started and we had intermittent business. The rain was still pounding down and the wind continued to rattle every shutter in the place. Gregory had kerosene lanterns lighting up the kitchen and the staircase. We ate dinner in silence, which made me even more aware of the storm outside. I had almost finished the Peter Bogdanovich book and I wondered if he would write a book on River Phoenix. I found it amazing how tragedy just seemed to follow some people. He was one of the most acclaimed directors of the 70s and his life took a downward spiral after the brutal murder of his girlfriend Dorothy Stratten.

It was strange that Peter Bogdanovich was associated with so much tragedy. My mind kept wandering back to *The Thing Called Love*. Everything had pointed to River having a serious drug problem. I kept rerunning that last year in my mind. There were plenty of opportunities to do something. Looking back I think Iris was just as afraid of the truth as I was. We both just wanted to pretend that the problem didn't exist. River was the crown jewel of the agency. Iris' power and respect in the industry was associated with River.

I remembered one of the last times I was with River alone – he had stopped by the office and Iris wasn't there. It was before he did the movie *Sneakers*. River was talking about his legacy. He was very worried about how he would be viewed by future generations. I found it odd that some one who was in his early twenties was worried about his legacy. It seemed like River knew that he was destined for a short life. What could I have done any differently? I am sure that Peter Bogdanovich blamed himself for Dorothy Stratten's death. But could he have stopped Dorothy's husband from killing her?

It was 10 p.m. and the storm still raged. I had to shove towels under the crack in the patio door because the sheets of rain that were coming down were flooding into the room. I put *The Killing of the Unicorn* down on the nightstand and turned out the kerosene lamp.

I woke up. My room was warm – almost balmy. I couldn't move my legs or my arms. The thunder still clashed and the wind pummeled my door. The lightning illuminated the figure of a man. I wanted to scream but nothing would come out of my mouth. My stomach clenched. I felt short of breath. The man approached my bed. I was hyperventilating. He came to the side of my bed and then I saw his face. It was River. He seemed so calm and serene. He kept saying, 'Let go,' over and over. Then he was gone. I woke up and threw myself out of the bed. I dripped sweat. I had to escape. There was an inch of water on the floor. I slid across it and banged into the balcony door, I opened the door and was assaulted by a cold wind and driving rain that reassured me there were no such things as ghosts.

The Greek postal service was so slow that I was halfway through my stay on Santorini before the onslaught of mail from former Iris Burton Agency clients found its way to me. The mothers' grapevine was unbelievable as I was only corresponding with one person in Hollywood. The tales of the mass exodus that was taking place from the agency were sad. Iris was having a hard time keeping anybody in my position. Any client that didn't have a contract with the agency scattered. Iris had also managed to filter messages through my close friends that she missed me and she understood why I left. I was glad that she understood. I wasn't sure I did.

Santorini could have been used as the backdrop to a movie about heaven. Everyday the warm waters of the Aegean were my giant bathtub. I had a great tan and once Gregory and I came to an understanding, life was good. I swam every day for an hour after my chores and then ate a feta and tomato sandwich before I took a nap on the beach. I would ponder what I was going to do when I left Santorini. I had always wanted to be in Hollywood, since as far back as I could remember. What was I going to do when I returned to the States? I was homeless and jobless.

I walked up on the beach kicking at pebbles and watching the fishing boats. I really kind of admired the fishermen and the simplicity of their lives. I knew damn well that my life would never be that simple. I wondered what made me hesitate from saying what I should have said to River, Iris and Heart Phoenix. I wondered what had instilled in me such a deep fear of the truth. I was gay and had known I was gay since I was a child, but I also knew what happened to people who showed any signs of not conforming. They were ridiculed and taunted as they walked down the hallways of school.

They were spat at and laughed at on the streets. I had allowed myself to wear the mask of the conformist. I even tried to hide being gay from Iris. I was too afraid that she wouldn't accept me. I didn't even accept me so how could I expect anyone else to accept me?

CHAPTER 13

'Seek not, my soul, the life of the immortals; but enjoy to
the full the resources that are within thy reach.'

Pindar, Greek poet, *Pythian Odes*,III 1.109

My daily visit to the American Express office to pick up
my mail did not net me the results that I had hoped. My
mother had retained a lawyer in an effort to release my
pension money from Iris Burton. Her business manager
responded that it was at Iris' election to release the
money and that she chose not to. So much for a chance
to start over without any debts. There was no way that
I could pay off the charge card bills that I had amassed
in Los Angeles. My mother suggested bankruptcy. I
considered that the ultimate failure. The money that I
would make over the summer wasn't significant enough
to even put a dent in the debts I owed. Iris sealed my fate
with the denial of the pension money.

I walked back to the hotel without even a stop to visit
my friend Susannah at the jewelry store. I only had a
couple of months left in Greece and then it was back
to reality. For the first time since my arrival, no winds
stirred. It was 100 degrees in the shade and an oppressive
humidity cloaked the island. It had been days since I had
been able to get a good night's sleep. We were all on
edge. I was soaked with sweat by the time I arrived back
at the hotel. I went straight to the shower and didn't
even bother to turn on the water heater. I took an icy

cold shower with water straight from the well. I heard the dinging of the bell in the reception area. 'Shit,' I muttered. I waited to see if Gregory would take care of it but when the bell rang again I turned off the shower, grabbed a towel and headed up to the reception area. It was probably just somebody who wanted to know the price of a room. I crouched behind the banister.

'Hello,' I called out. 'Hello.'

I could see the customer but he couldn't see me. He was bald headed with big round glasses too big for his face. Around 5'8' and skeletal, he reminded me of E.T. On his arms, face and neck were the black tumors of AIDS. I'd seen enough of them when I had done volunteer work with Tom, an AIDS patient in LA. The man that stood in the reception area was clearly in the advanced stages. I stuck my head around the banister and kept my body hidden behind the wall. 'I'm up here,' I yelled.

His name was Stephen and he was an American expatriate living in the French countryside. He'd purchased his home with the money his dead lover had left him. They'd been together seventeen years. Stephen used the restroom twice in the first ten minutes and he kept looking at his watch while he clutched the satchel that contained his medicine. He asked me for a glass of water and I watched him take his pills.

A flood of memories returned and I remembered Tom. Tom had died about a month before River had begun his final decline. It took Tom eight long months to die. He was in and out of the hospital so many times. No one came to visit him except for me and his mother. In the last few months his mother moved to Los Angeles and she leaned on me for support. The apartment had pictures scattered about of Tom before he became sick. He was a beautiful, popular, active man who had been reduced to a skeletal shell of his former self. I thought I had left AIDS behind me. I thought I could escape AIDS by not having relationships or sex. I glanced up at Stephen as he swallowed the last pill and hoped that he wouldn't stay at the hotel. I showed him a room and he was very non-committal about whether he would be back. I wasn't the least bit concerned. As I waved goodbye I realized that I was still wrapped in a towel. I returned to my room and slipped into some shorts and picked up my book. The bell rang again and I reluctantly walked up the steps to the reception area again.

'Coming,' I called out as the bell rang once more. When I rounded the corner to the reception area a man that could have fallen out of a Marlboro billboard was standing in front of the reception desk. He looked like Steve McQueen with wheat-colored hair that fell across his forehead. His eyes were an incredible blue and he had a moustache.

'You must be Chris,' he said as he extended his hand.

I had no choice but to take his hand. An electric current shot through me when our hands connected. 'Who are you?' I said.

'I'm Stephen's friend, Richard. I thought I'd bring the luggage ahead while Stephen settled up with the hotel.'

I opened the door to the room, which was right off of reception.

'Wow! This is quite the room. Stephen was right.'

He made me nervous – as nervous as when I first realized I was attracted to men sixteen years ago.

Richard cleared his throat. 'I left the luggage on the landing.' He smiled as he walked by me.

'Let me help.' I followed him down the stairs. Stephen had arrived and the two of them were deep in conversation. Their eyes darted in my direction, or maybe I was just being paranoid. When I approached them Richard looked at Stephen. 'You were right.' He smiled at me and I noticed that he had blushed.

I helped Richard carry the bags to the room and then I took a walk into town to buy supplies for breakfast.

When I returned Richard was sprawled out on a patio chair dressed only in a pair of white shorts. He had well-muscled legs. When I walked by he popped up and gave me a huge grin.

'If you don't have any plans tonight Stephen and I would love to take you to dinner.'

'That would be nice,' I said as I walked by.

'How's eight o'clock?' he called after me.

'Great.' I walked up the steps to the kitchen. I'd never been asked on a date before. What a wonderful feeling.

Santorini's majestic sunsets were revered – by the islanders as well as by the tourists. The 'sunset ceremony' as I called it wasn't a formal mandatory directive like Sunday church services, but a simple way to give thanks for the day. In the five minutes that it took for the sun to swoop down from the heavens and splash into the sea, a meditative calm transported me inwards to a sense of peace I'd never known in Los Angeles. Of course there were sunsets in LA but I never left the office until it was dark and I never really took the time to watch. Iris was not really a nature girl. She was more of a 'go shoot the mink and I'll wear it' girl. I had lost touch with the outdoors while I lived in LA and I had spent most of my time hiking, camping and being outside before I worked for Iris Burton.

I looked out at the sunset with great anticipation of my dinner with Richard and Stephen. I asked Susannah to join us. We went to our favorite restaurant in the next town which had a beautiful view of the bay.

During dinner Stephen told us the story of his French lover. For three years Stephen had saved his money for a trip to Paris where he felt destined to meet his future lover. The very first day in Paris, in the exact spot he'd always imagined (a bridge facing the Cathedral of Notre Dame), he met his lover. He was a high-ranking officer of a bank. By the end of the three-week vacation Stephen agreed to stay because he was in love. Unfortunately, Stephen's lover's family were not enthusiastic. They'd always hoped their son would outgrow his homosexuality. Stephen found a job washing dishes in a restaurant (the only job obtainable in France without the proper work papers). Despite the family's meddling, they were able to live happily for ten years until they were both diagnosed with AIDS. Stephen's lover died first and left Stephen his estate. Unfortunately the family was well connected and Stephen was forced to settle out of court or face losing everything.

Richard sat right next to me at dinner and I felt his knee brush against mine under the table. He smiled at me when this happened. We knocked knees all through dinner, unbeknownst to Susannah and Stephen. We talked about movies and music and Richard mentioned that his favorite piece of music was the love theme from the film *Somewhere in Time*, coincidentally, my favorite movie. It was a movie about the quest for the perfect soulmate. I'd brought the CD with me to Greece. On more than one evening I had played it while the sun was setting and dreamed of one day finding my soul mate. Stephen tired quickly and we retuned to the hotel. He walked directly into the room.

'Let me put him to bed and I will be right out,' Richard said and closed the door.

Susannah smiled at me. 'I think someone is smitten.' She winked.

'I don't think so,' I said.

119

'Well, I'm leaving. You two don't need a chaperone.'

'Susannah!' I called after her as she ran up the stairs.

Richard and I sat on the roof for hours talking about his ex-lover and how lonely he was in the farmhouse that they had restored together. They'd been together for sixteen years. He hadn't dated anyone since the break-up two years ago. Stephen had taken Richard on this trip to get him out of the funk that he had been in. Richard was thirteen years older than me. He was strong, stable and safe. I told Richard my story and he listened attentively. The night flew by and before long it was three in the morning. Richard walked me to my room. I opened the door and he leaned in and kissed me. It was a long lingering kiss. We said goodnight and I drifted down the steps to my room happier than I had been in my whole life. The next day Richard and Stephen asked me to dinner again. Stephen wanted to go early at around 6 p.m. I invited Susannah. Halfway through dinner Stephen excused himself because he wasn't feeling well and Susannah graciously offered to escort him back to the hotel amidst the protests of Richard.

'I'll be fine,' Stephen said.

Susannah winked at me as she left the table. I wanted to crawl into a cave because I was sure that Richard had seen the wink. There was still a bottle of wine on the table. Richard rubbed his knee against mine and reached for my hand under the table. I half wondered if Stephen hadn't left on purpose.

I leaned in to whisper in Richard's ear. 'Listen, Richard, nobody knows that I'm gay here.'

'Come on! I'm sure Susannah knows.'

'Well, if she does we don't really talk about it. I don't really care if she knows it's the men that I care about. People get funny.'

'I think it's only you that gets funny.'

'Let's go. There's someplace I want to take you and something I've dreamed of doing the whole time that I've been here.'

Richard was right, it was me that had the problem. I grabbed his hand and pulled him further up the trail that led to the castle ruins. The castle had once been inhabited by the Venetians and they could see their enemies approaching for hundreds of miles from the promontory that it was built on. The view was spectacular, particularly at sunset, and from a distance the castle appeared suspended over the sapphire sea in the darker blue horizon.

Richard stopped and leaned against the wall to catch his breath. 'You didn't say we'd be hiking.'

'It's just up ahead around the next bend,' I reassured him. 'Hurry, we don't want to miss the sunset.'

'We have plenty of time.' He lifted his hand and placed it under my chin. Then he stared at me intently with his brilliant blue eyes. He kissed me on the lips right on the main walkway. My eyes darted from side to side. Richard drew me closer. His chin brushed mine. Behind me I heard the clanging of bells. The donkeys were stampeding our way. This was not the place to kiss. I felt his hard body pressed against mine. I wanted more. We jumped off the trail into an alley just as the donkeys flew by. As soon as the donkeys had passed I pulled Richard quickly along the trail until we were standing in front of the land bridge to the castle, which jutted out 2,000 feet above sea level. The only entrance was over the volcanic rock bridge. I'd never thought it was safe and I practically ran across it. After all, this was an earthquake zone. There were no railings to hold on to and Richard grabbed my hand and led me across the bridge. I tried not to look down at the sea but the waves crashed up against the cliffs. I froze for a minute.

'You brought me here. Don't stop now.' Richard's blue eyes were hypnotic. I would have followed him anywhere. Before we knew it we were standing in the ruins of the castle. He pressed me against the ancient wall and brushed my hair back from my brow. He moved in to kiss me again.

I put my hand up. 'No, Richard. Not now. For five months I've dreamed of coming to this castle and being kissed at sunset.'

Richard massaged my neck and brushed my hair back again. 'If that's what you want, I'll wait.'

The wind grew colder but he held me tighter. I lost myself in a comfort that I hadn't known existed. As Richard held me tighter, I leaned my head on his shoulder and glanced towards the horizon. The sun slowly slipped into the Aegean. Gold light shimmered across the sea. His warm hands caressed my back and I felt his breath on my ear. Finally he kissed me. My body tingled. I closed my eyes and when I opened them I saw the first star of the night.

Richard pulled me towards a fallen column. I closed my eyes as he unbuttoned my shirt and slowly pulled it off. I shivered as he drew me against his chest. Then he took his shirt off and he laid me down on the stone floor. Seconds later he rested on top of me. While he kissed me on the neck, shoulders and lips, not even the wind could find a space between the two of us. I enjoyed the warmth of his stomach against mine but when he started to unbuckle my pants I pushed him away. 'Not here, Richard.'

He kissed me on the neck then I pulled away. 'We'd better get back to the hotel. I'm sure they're wondering what we're up to.'

'Yeah,' he said reluctantly.

Richard went to stand up but I didn't want him to leave. I reached for his hand. He lay back down and I rested my head on his chest and waited. Then I heard it, his heartbeat. I listened to the rhythm and felt safe for the first time in my whole life. He was for real. The missing link. Beat. Beat. Beat. It was almost as soothing as the waves lapping onto the cliffs below. We had six more days to fall in love.

Richard and I spent every night together and he would sneak back to his room before Stephen woke up. We didn't want him to feel bad that he was in the most romantic place on the earth without a lover. Stephen napped a good deal of the day so Richard and I had plenty of time together.

Stephen was obsessed with the idea of hiking to the top of the mountain above Perissa Beach. According to the tourists that came through the hotel, there was an ancient Roman town at the top. The locals didn't really talk about it that much so I hadn't bothered to hike up there. But the locals tripped over ruins in every direction so I guess I wasn't surprised at Stephen's persistence. Richard asked me if I would take Stephen because he had a very fair complexion and tried to avoid the sun as much as possible.

The bus to Perissa Beach was crowded but we were able to find a seat. Stephen and I talked and he seemed eager to divulge information about Richard's past. Richard's last lover, a decade older, had grown weary of the extensive renovations on the farmhouse they'd purchased near Cooperstown, New York. The commute between the farmhouse and New York City proved too taxing on him so he ended the relationship. Richard was so devastated at the break-up that he hadn't dated in two years and channeled all his energy into the renovations. The location of his home seemed too good to be true. He lived an hour away from my parents, where I'd decided to live once I returned from Greece. I need to stabilize my finances and figure out what I wanted to do before I moved anywhere.

It wasn't until the bus stopped in Perissa Beach that I realized what a daunting task it would be to reach the ruins of Ancient Thira. We would have to hike 2,500 feet to the top of Mesa Vouna Mountain. As we passed the base a group of archaeological students were working at the excavation site of a 2,000-year-old slave village. Ten minutes into the hike my backpack, filled with water bottles, guidebook and sandwiches, was already a burden. I couldn't help but imagine the miserable existence of the slaves who once carried food, water, wine and supplies up to the residents of Ancient Thira. Even though I'd been walking everywhere for five months I found it difficult to breathe as the incline gradually increased. We hadn't been gone twenty minutes when Stephen had a wheezing fit. I sat him down on a boulder and made him drink water until it had passed. It was the same wheeze I remembered from Tom; he was thirty-six years old when he was battling the final stages of the disease. In all the training classes I took no one could teach me how to numb myself to the never-ending empty beds in the AIDS ward. I never knew and was afraid to ask if a patient had gone home or died, all I needed to do was look into Tom's eyes.

What distressed me the most was watching Tom's mother cope with his untimely death. I'd never really mourned Tom's death because I needed to be strong for her as she sifted through her son's secret life. By the time I put her on the plane back to Florida, I was sure that there was nothing more I could have done. Richard was the first person I had allowed myself to be vulnerable with. I figured that if I didn't have sex or open up to anybody then I wouldn't have to worry about AIDS.

The climb grew steeper and I kept glancing back over my shoulder to make sure that Stephen was OK. I was beginning to understand why people did long pilgrimages because there was certainly nothing to do when you were hiking up a mountain but look ahead and reflect on the past.

In the year prior to River's death there were warning signs and whispers of his secret life. Whenever I called attention to an article in a magazine or a photo layout and made a comment that he didn't look healthy, Iris lashed out at me. I was in River's company just as much as she was and it amazed me that she didn't see the mood shifts and the weight loss. It became such a source of contention between us that I stopped bringing up anything about River with her.

I looked back over my shoulders again and saw that Stephen had stopped twenty feet back. I turned around.

'Chris, I can't make it. It was stupid for me to try,' he whispered.

'It's OK.' I was actually relieved that I didn't have to hike any further as the shade of the mountainside was disappearing as the sun moved higher in the sky. I helped Stephen up and he leaned into my ear and whispered, 'Please, take my camera – be my eyes. It's the only way I can see Ancient Thira.' So much for a pleasant day at the beach. I really didn't understand what was so important about a bunch of ruins.

'There is a temple to Apollo up there and I would like it if you could put this letter there. It's really important to me.'

'OK, but let me help you back down the mountain.' I said.

'Going down is easy. You'll waste too much time.

I'll wait for you down on the beach. I'll grab lunch. I'll watch your progress up the mountain.'

I was about three-quarters of the way up the mountain when the shade of the mountain disappeared and my already overheated body began to boil. My t-shirt was soaked. A trail of donkey shit guided me through the treeless volcanic rocks. I may as well have been hiking on the moon. Nothing lived on this mountain. I was glad I had Stephen's extra bottles of water. I enviously glanced down at the cool Aegean below and the people that frolicked in the water. The temperature climbed past ninety degrees. There was no wind. Why had I said yes? Because of Tom? Because I promised Richard? Or was it simply because I knew that Stephen was going to die.

I noticed the symbol of a lion carved into the rock. I dropped my backpack and consulted my guidebook. This was the symbol of Apollo. I had been told by my Greek friends that Apollo was worshipped for his ability to heal the sick as well as his ability to see the future. I continued to follow the wall until I saw the carved image of an eagle, which I knew was the symbol of Zeus who had the final judgment on all matters mortal or pertaining to the gods. Next up was a carved dolphin, the symbol of Poseidon. I guess living on an island you wouldn't want to forget the god of the sea. Since no one guarded these ancient carvings I traced my fingers along their smooth edges and hoped to somehow absorb their ancient energy. I realized I was searching for answers just like the ancient people that had carved these symbols. This was the closest to heaven I'd ever been outside of a plane.

After I traced the lion, the eagle and the dolphin, I closed my eyes and waited for a sign. A breeze stirred but there were no voices, no burning bushes. Nothing. I squeezed my eyes closed. An image of Iris popped into my head. Good Lord, of all the images that was one I really didn't need up here. Was I supposed to pull out a chisel and carve an image of Iris into the mountain? It would look strangely like Medusa. Legend has it that Athena had Medusa slayed for having sex with Poseidon in one of her temples. She gave two vials of Medusa's blood to Asclepius the healer. One vial could heal; the other could kill instantly. Iris could be the nicest, funniest and most helpful person if she liked you but she could turn on somebody like a poisonous snake. It was difficult for me to understand how duplicitous she could be. Maybe it had to do with the way I left. I hadn't exactly clearly thought things out. Was Iris really the problem or was it my inability to deal with life in Los Angeles? Then the clicking of cameras and the echo of foreign voices made me open my eyes. Did I somehow think that I would unlock the gates of heaven and bask in the radiance of golden light or that an angel would explain why Stephen had to die, why River overdosed, why Tom died, and why I had exiled myself to a Greek island?

I knew that I was close to the top of the mountain. The sun hit mid-heaven. I shook a pebble from my sandal and walked another ten minutes before I reached the gates to Ancient Thira. A guard sat under an umbrella with a gun at his side. He motioned me through the crumbled columns. I hesitated before I approached the ancient steps once traversed by the footsteps of men far greater than I. Conquerors such as Alexander the Great, Julius Caesar and Hadrian of Rome could have placed their feet in these well-worn grooves on the steps. I couldn't believe they allowed people to even walk on 2,000-year-old steps. Philosophers and maybe even Aristotle himself could have taught here. The blue sky and sea merged into an endless horizon too beautiful for words, magical as Mount Olympus, the fabled home of the Greek gods.

I walked up into Ancient Thira and stared at the remains of a large village. It was so spectacular. I closed my eyes and pictured myself in Ancient Thira 2,000 years ago surrounded by Plato and his pupils in white flowing robes as they debated the meaning of life. Naked young men bathed after an athletic competition. Their skin glistened with scented oils. I gasped as I encountered the semicircle of an ancient Greek theatre in an olive grove with only the sea for a backdrop. I could picture the stone benches filled with people as they watched a performance of Aeschylus's lost play *Myrmidons*. In the play the Greek soldiers dragged the naked body of Achilles' male lover Patroclus onto the stage. Achilles did not want to believe he was dead and threw himself on the corpse and sobbed, 'Why did you take Patroclus? I was supposed to have died on the battlefield, not him.'

I imagined maidservants and other soldiers as they joined Achilles, lament and pounded their breasts and chanted to heaven: 'Patroclus is dead! Patroclus is dead! Felled by Hector who now wears your armor.'

Achilles' mother, Thetis, heard her son's plea and rose from the depths of the sea. 'Achilles, why these tears? The gods granted your wish.' Achilles answers, 'Not at the cost of Patroclus' life.' At the end of the play the ghost of Patroclus appears and asks Achilles for their ashes 'to be as one forever'. Perhaps that was what Stephen had written in his letter to Apollo.

I'd wanted to be part of Hollywood and the movie business since childhood and those dreams had led me to encounters with some of the unhappiest people I'd ever met. River had lived the dream that I had fantasized about: fame, wealth, adoration and the freedom of expression. But why had he tried to escape it through drugs and alcohol? Perhaps the message of Patroclus and Achilles still holds true. Be careful what

128

you wish for because the consequences aren't always apparent.

I walked the ancient cobblestone streets of Thira and searched the endless horizon and realized that the lives of River, Stephen, Tom and myself weren't even a grain of sand against the infinite horizon of the past. All that mattered was what lay ahead. I had the strangest feeling that I would soon be back in Los Angeles with Iris Burton. The mantra of 'It isn't finished between you and Iris,' kept repeating in my head. My gut told me it wasn't over as well.

The cawing of a black bird brought me back to my mission, which was to find the temple of Apollo. As if trying to get my attention the hawk circled around my head five times. When it flew east I didn't follow. But when the bird came back and circled around my head a second time I took it as a sign and walked directly underneath him until he guided me past the monument markers, through the fallen columns and into the remains of a temple. I flipped through my guidebook and realized that there are two temples of Apollo in Ancient Thira. Stephen hadn't told me where to leave the envelope. Scattered rocks and broken columns revealed no clues as I searched the temple's skeletal remains. The black bird rested on a column split in two (perhaps by a thunderbolt) and his eyes followed me in my search. I read the guidebook and learned that the Temple of the Pythian Apollo had been an oracle presided over by the Pythia, a woman appointed by Apollo to be the voice of his oracle. She sat on a three-legged stool at the back of this temple illuminated by oil-filled sconces. While bay leaves smoldered, she went into a trance and sought the guidance of spirits. If the Pythia's ghost were to appear what would my questions be? Is Richard HIV positive? Is he the man I have longed for my whole life? What price would I have to pay if I was granted his love? Despite the heat of the day I felt a chill in my spine. Her response had been given so often it was carved at the entrance to Delphi: 'Know thyself' followed by 'Nothing in excess'.

The bird cawed again. I backed out of the temple and bumped into the guard who had been at the entrance. I was startled. He chewed as he spoke. 'You lost, mister?'

'Yeah. I'm looking for the Temple of Apollo, not the one where the Pythia resided.' I decided whatever Stephen had to say to Apollo should go straight to the source.

'Over there.' He pointed north-east, 'The tall building with the columns in front, that's the remains of the Temple of Apollo.' They all had columns. He probably meant the standing columns.

'Thanks,' I said and headed in the direction of the columns. I looked up in the sky and noticed my bird friend followed. When I entered the ruins of the Temple of Apollo I remembered that Apollo had needlessly lost his male lover Hyacinth. According to the myth, the jealous wind killed Hyacinth with his own disc during an athletic competition. Apollo was unable to bring the youth back to life. The blood that seeped from Hyacinth stained the grass and became a white flower with deep purple markings of the Greek letters AI-AI (signifying Apollo's last tribute to his great love).

I pulled my backpack open, took out Stephen's letter and, as tempted as I was, didn't read it. Instead I placed it under one of the rocks in the back of the temple where I guessed the offertory table might have once stood. The Temple of Apollo wasn't much, just a foundation surrounded by fallen columns scattered about like children's building blocks. Weeds and tall grass burned by the sun left no signs of the previous spring rains. The sky had become the ceiling of the temple and as I looked around I realized even the Greeks didn't care about

Apollo any more. If he had really been so powerful, why had people quit worshipping him? Or maybe he'd allowed his temple to fall into ruins to test the faith of his followers. Had the deaths of River and Tom both been tests? Was the trip up the mountain my test? What was I supposed to learn from these tragedies?

As I looked into the blue horizon and reached my hand up to touch the ceiling of the sky, I realized that I had carried my burdens up the mountain just as the slaves had 2,000 years ago. Now I needed to drop them and surrender my life to love. I needed to let Richard into my life and see what would happen even if he were leaving and I might never see him again. I had ignored love and my own feelings of self-worth for far too long. I had allowed other people's lives to take precedence over my own for far too long. It was time I stopped worrying about other people's problems. I dropped my hands and knelt on the ancient foundation of the temple. I bowed my head and surrendered to the tears that flowed from my eyes and the sobs that escaped my mouth, at last releasing the past. When I looked up the black bird circled my head. I fixed my eyes on the horizon and realized I'd been given my sign but God let me discover it myself.

I snapped pictures of every ruin on the mountain and then I trekked back down with a new-found sense of freedom. I felt like I could fly.

When we returned to the hotel and Stephen had gone to his room for a nap, Richard and I went up to the rooftop terrace and watched the sunset. He took me in his arms and kissed me. I lay my head on his shoulders and surrendered as he ran his fingers through my hair.

Richard and Stephen's departure hung over me like a thick fog. I wasn't sure where I was going and especially where *we* were going. Until I met Richard I didn't know that I could feel so attractive or so alive. I'd never even had sex until I was twenty-six because of the constant fear of AIDS. The first two relationships I had had ended so badly that I didn't date or have sex with anyone for a year in between each relationship. The few one-night stands that I had after those bad relationships only made me feel empty and guilty that I had succumbed to sexual need.

Richard was the very first man that I slept next to all night. Little things like when he brushed an eyelash off my cheek sent shivers through my whole body. His hands seemed to carry an electric current, every time he drew them down my back I felt their energy. Richard and I talked constantly and for the first time in my life I felt like someone was actually listening. I listened while Richard described his fieldstone fireplace in the living room, the hardwood floors and his creaking staircase. I imagined lying in his big brass bed feeling the sheets, recently warmed by his body. I daydreamed about my return to the States and the first weekend that we would spend together. I remembered the red, gold and orange maple leaves of autumn. I pictured Richard's farmhouse and the two of us raking leaves. He'd wrestle me into a pile of leaves and kiss me as I inhaled the clean smell of autumn and the soap-fresh smell of Richard's body. Since no one in the hotel knew about Richard and I, he would always sneak up on me and then kiss me. The danger of being caught made me appreciate every stolen kiss.

Every night we lay tangled together covered in sweat not wanting to leave each other's side. Then we'd shower together. He'd wash my back, and gently massage my skin with soap. Warm water cascaded over us while we kissed. When we finished taking our shower he'd fall asleep in my bed. I rested my head on his chest. He glowed in the candlelight. I listened to his heartbeat, and gazed at his face just to make sure he was real.

On our last night together we made love with an intensity that I'd never experienced. I couldn't let go of him. Every time he tried to leave the bed I'd kiss him and lure him back. I could only hope that he'd lose track of time. I needed his heart next to mine; our bodies locked together so that I wouldn't lose the memory. I encircled his broad back, his wide shoulders. I needed to recall how it felt in order to survive the next three weeks until I saw him again. When we finally let go and Richard walked up my bedroom stairs for the last time, the realization of the departure set in. My naked body shook. I held on to the wall for support. I didn't know where any of this was leading. What if I never saw him again? Susannah had warned me about affairs with tourists. Maybe he would forget about me and I'd never feel this way again for my entire lifetime. Richard gave me one last kiss before he opened the door at the top of the stairs.

'Promise me you won't cry when I leave,' Richard said. He wiped away a tear and kissed my cheek. 'We'll see each other soon. You call me the minute your plane lands at JFK.'

'I promise.'

Richard opened the door. 'No getting up to see us off either.'

'Yeah,' I said as Richard closed the door.

After Richard left I couldn't sleep. I simply stared at the clock as one slow minute after another went by. In an hour he would be gone. At 5.30 a.m. I heard the door to his room bang closed and the shuffling of feet down the steps. I pulled on my shorts and ran up to the roof. As the sun rose I watched Richard and Stephen as they walked up the hill towards the waiting cab in the distance. I stared at the trail of dust the cab kicked up and wondered if there was any future for Richard and me. Then I picked up a rag and wiped the morning dew off the tables so that they would be ready for the guests.

CHAPTER 14

'There is nothing permanent except change.'

Heraclitus, Greek philosopher

The turbulence from Athens to New York was so bad that for the first time in twenty years of flying I actually used a motion-sickness bag. I missed my flight from JFK to upstate New York because the customs agent decided to meticulously inspect every suitcase and every item in the suitcases. He added up all my receipts and counted every penny down to my souvenir Greek money while also asking me a million questions. I ended up in a seedy airport hotel.

I called Richard from the hotel room and he sounded surprised to hear from me. Maybe I had woken him up. By the end of the conversation he had agreed to pick me up the following weekend. At least I had that to look forward to.

As the plane made its way to upstate New York I realized that it was ten years ago that I had begun my journey to Hollywood. It was the beginning of November after an early snow that I had packed up and left the sleepy town of New Hartford. It was ironic how my life had taken this huge circle back to somewhere I vowed I would never live again. There would be no ticker-tape parade for the conquering hero. The brief conversation I had had with my father assured me that a huge stack of debt awaited me along with angry calls from creditors, which he and my mother had had to endure in my absence.

As the plane descended I saw the expanse of brightly colored leaves. It looked quite beautiful from the plane. My thoughts were drawn to the movie *Valley of the Dolls*. I had always wondered what happened to the one character that ended up leaving Hollywood alive. The movie ends with her in a sleepy snow-covered town in New England. I remembered it looked like a Christmas snow globe. It was an insular little world. Barren white landscapes with ice and swirling powder-puff snow. The plane skidded and came to a halt. My stomach felt queasy. I was about to find out what happens when you escape from Hollywood.

The car pulled into the driveway of my childhood home. The same two-story house that had once seemed gigantic to me now seemed like a doll's house. When I walked up the stairs to my old bedroom I glanced around and felt like I had walked into a broom closet. The remains of my life in Los Angeles were stacked from floor to ceiling in the empty upstairs bedroom.

'I had to open up the heat vents and take down the sheets of plastic,' my father said as he nodded to the banister where the plastic awaited my departure.

'Really,' I said.

'I save $100 a month not using the upstairs. Your mother spends most of the winter in Florida. I fly down for weekends and school holidays. I have all my tickets for the next six months.'

'That's great, Dad.'

The banter had begun. The awkward conversation that existed between my father and me. I don't know when it started. Maybe we had never really communicated. I just remembered that our encounters had always been dotted with one-syllable responses from me. Everything had become even more awkward when I told my parents that I was gay. They didn't disown me but they never mentioned it again. I guess they figured if they didn't acknowledge what I had told them then it would all go away. Strangely enough, before Richard I felt the same way myself. I could sleep with men and explain it off as a temporary lapse in judgment.

My father had been born, grew up, married and gone to college all within a ten-mile parameter. My mother and father married at nineteen years old and had me by the time they were twenty.

I went downstairs to the dining room and smiled at the barometer that still hung on the wall in the same spot it always had. When I was a child that barometer fascinated me. I used to look at it every morning, afternoon and evening. I was enthralled that the needle could predict a storm, rain or dry weather. I wish God gave you a barometer of your life at birth so that you could be aware when a storm was coming.

My father was as predictable as the four seasons. He did the same job teaching New York State history to seventh-grade students year after year. He got up, started the coffee, took his walk and his shower, and arrived at work before everyone else. Like the sturdy maple tree in the side yard my father was unbendable. I guess there is a certain safety in routine and predictability.

My mother on the other hand was as unpredictable as the barometer in the dining room. She could go from clear skies to tornado in two minutes. She always encouraged my dreams of Hollywood. She always yearned for another life. She never really wanted to be housewife and mother, but there weren't many choices available to her. She tried everything. When she was happy no one could be more fun, when she was miserable she buried herself beneath the blankets.

The sun shone and the leaves were their most brilliant colors on the day that Richard came to take me to his farmhouse. The Halloween pumpkins sat carved on doorsteps, a reminder of the night a year ago that River had died. I stared off into the cornfields with the crows picking away at the scattered ears of corn that had been missed by the farmers' machinery. I couldn't help but think of Iris and the pain that she must be in. My life had changed dramatically in one year. I glanced over at Richard and wondered if he would be my salvation. I was excited to see him but he seemed a little stand-offish. I thought it was the awkwardness of meeting my mother. Richard was physical proof that I was gay. She knew that I was going off with a man. Richard couldn't be ignored. An uncomfortable smile and non-stop talking were evidence of her discomfort. It had been easy to ignore when I was in Los Angeles. She could put it out of her mind.

The trees on other side of the freeway blazed with orange, yellow and red leaves. Richard's farmhouse looked like it had been built for the sequel to *The Bridges of Madison County*. No detail had been overlooked in the restoration. Even the staircase creaked at the right moment as I walked upstairs to drop off my overnight bag. There was the antique four-poster in the bedroom with a rocking chair in front of the fireplace that rocked on the planked floors. There was such beauty in the simplicity of it all. I heard the theme song to the movie *Somewhere in Time* and went downstairs to find that Richard had lit a fire in the fieldstone fireplace. He took my hand and guided me to the rug in front of it. We made love and that should have made me feel better except something didn't feel right. Maybe it was the anniversary of River's death? Maybe it was the bankruptcy? The avalanche of responsibilities had descended upon him and me. We weren't in the middle of the Aegean any more.

We raked leaves and then we rolled around in them. That smell of dry crisp leaves intermixed with the smell of Richard as he kissed my neck, just as I had dreamed, made me forget for a moment the problems that lay ahead. The blue skies and puffy white clouds that rolled by showed no warnings of storm clouds. Richard and I had an early dinner and then had sex before we went to bed. Richard didn't talk that much and neither did I. The only conversations we seemed to have were about Stephen and his worsening condition. Richard's antique bed was small and I had trouble falling asleep. I stared into the fire until I at last drifted off. When I woke up the bed was empty and the last red embers of the fire seemed about ready to vanish. Richard never came back to bed and I fell asleep as the first light crept through the windows.

The next morning the sound of the plumber banging on the bathroom pipes woke me rather than a kiss from Richard. I walked down the stairs in search of him. I found him in the kitchen as he sipped a cup of coffee and read the paper. He was dressed in his jeans and a flannel shirt.

'Sorry about the plumber but he's hard to get. There seems to be a shortage of plumbers.' Richard handed me a cup of coffee.

'When he leaves maybe we can have a little breakfast in bed.' I smiled.

'The carpenter is coming to fix the railing later this morning.'

'Oh,' I said. I wondered why Richard had not just

cancelled our weekend if he had all this going on. This was hardly the romantic weekend I had fantasized about.

Richard took me to lunch before he drove me home. He seemed to want to tell me something but he had a hard time talking. In Greece the conversation had flowed as naturally as the stream on the side of the road. The intervening month since I'd last seen him had created a dam. This was not the man I had met in Greece. As we drove down the thruway the trees seemed more barren than the day before. The wind had picked up in the night and stripped them, leaving them naked of color.

'I wasn't sure how to tell you this.' Richard said, breaking the awkward silence.

Damn it! He must be HIV positive. I knew it. We had never discussed it in Greece. I had been afraid to ask, but I wondered.

'One of my closest friends and his lover broke up when I was in Greece. I kind of always had a thing for his boyfriend and we got together in the last few weeks. I thought you should know.'

'Really.' I didn't know what to say. I just let him go on talking.

'We've been dating and I really like him.'

'That's fine. I understand,' I said. But I didn't understand. I didn't understand why we had fucked in front of the fireplace and in his bed. I didn't understand the tumble in the leaves and the tender kisses. I wanted to open the windows and scream.

'I really like you, Chris, and I just wasn't sure which one of you I wanted. I like you both. I need some time.'

'Well, maybe we should both come up next weekend and you can test us out side by side and see who gives better head.'

Richard's mouth dropped open – he was speechless.

The first flakes of snow swirled by the car. I'm sure it was from the cold shoulder that I gave Richard as I turned and stared out of the side window at the freak snowflakes.

'You don't need time, Richard. I'll make your decision for you. I'm not interested.' I pressed my face against the window and watched as it fogged up. When I was little I used to do the same thing with the big bay window in the dining room and draw hearts and flowers. As I grew older we used to write 'Chris loves Janice' with a heart and arrow on the windows of the junior high. Now I wanted to draw a dagger on the window.

The day after Halloween I called Iris. We were somehow connected by a strange umbilical cord. I had traveled to the farthest point I could to escape her and yet I still thought about her and wondered how she was. Now I could feel her pain clear across the country. It took two attempts for me to finally speak.

'Iris. It's Chris.' I said.

'I knew you'd call. Baby, where are you? I miss you,' Iris sobbed. 'You don't know how hard it's been.'

'I do, Iris. Believe me I do.'

'When are you coming back?' Iris said

'I don't know, Iris. I've committed myself to something here through the spring,' I replied.

'Did you see the *Hollywood Reporter*? I took out a full-page ad in memory of River's death. I had more phone calls from that ad than the one I ran for Kirsten's Golden Globe nomination. I think about him every day. I look around the office and I see that picture of him from *The Mosquito Coast*. He was so beautiful. My baby River.'

'I know, Iris. It must be awful.'

'You don't know. Nobody knows my pain.'

'How's Mrs Phoenix?'

'Her name's Heart now – did you know that?'

'I was with you when she changed her name. It was shortly before River died.'

'Honey, do you remember the time when River came by and you wanted him to do the movie *Sneakers* and you ran to the Mediterranean place and picked up vegan food and we all sat on the back porch and had lunch? It was a beautiful day and we all laughed.'

'Yeah, I do, Iris.' I remembered it very well. That was really the last good time that I had with River.

'Chris, promise me that if I need you – if I get ill or something – you'll come. I'm not getting any younger you know. Pete and I aren't seeing each other now and my son, well, you know how that goes.'

Pete was Iris' on-again off-again boyfriend. I'd never met him and wasn't entirely sure that he even really exsisted.

'Yeah, Iris, I promise. Listen I have to go. We'll talk soon.' I hung up. I needed to get off the phone as I could feel the grip tightening around my neck. What the hell had possessed me to call her? I didn't want to go back there. I'd escaped; I was home free. I looked around the rooms of my childhood and realized that the only thing I had done was walked right back into the oppressive environment of my youth. The place where I hid gay magazines and *The Joy of Gay Sex* in the back of my closet until I was so consumed with fear of my parents finding them that I burned them in the wood furnace in the cellar. I don't know if it was Iris that had cinched the noose or my family. Which was worse? To be gay in Republican, conservative and religious upstate New York, or to deal with earthquakes and Iris on a daily basis?

My mother left for the winter house in Florida. My father was driving her there in her car and when he returned we would be alone in the house for the first time in my life. We were strangers and I felt uncomfortable at the prospect of being home alone with him. The gulf that existed between us had grown so wide it had almost become an abyss. Maybe my mother was right – maybe this was my chance to try to mend things between the two of us.

With the onset of winter I slept fourteen to sixteen hours a day. I woke up about an hour before my father came home from work and went to work at my friend's restaurant. I worked until 10 or 11 p.m. and then I returned home and watched the recaps of the O.J. Simpson trial. When I didn't work I watched the trial with my father. It served as a distraction and gave us something to talk about. We never talked about my past life in Hollywood or the fact that I was gay.

The announcement came out in the paper about my impending bankruptcy. The only way I found out was the carefully folded newspaper that my father had left in such a way that I could not miss my name in print under 'Bankruptcy' with all my creditors listed. God, it looked worse than I ever thought possible.

By December my father had made a rather astute observation. Even though I tried really hard to disguise my marathon sleep sessions he caught on that I wasn't doing anything productive all day. He left an exacta knife, a scraper and a can of carpet glue remover on the dining-room table. The carpet glue was worse than the orange paint on marble I'd scraped in Greece. It seemed that my life out of Hollywood was filled with manual labor. I sanded the floors and then we refinished them. The next project was to repaint the walls in the bathroom and kitchen and tear up the layers of rugs, linoleum and tile.

I had sent Iris a Christmas card and that elicited a phone call from her. I was in the middle of pulling down old wallpaper when the phone rang. I almost missed the call by the time I untangled myself from the mess.

'Honey, it's Iris,' she cooed. 'Thank you for that lovely card.'

'You're welcome.'

'You sound out of breath. Are you all right?'

'Yeah, I was taking down the wallpaper.'

'I didn't know you were so handy. I would have put you to work when I redid the big house in the hills. Anyone would have been better than that man that remodeled my house. Remember him? He and Nancy Sinatra were together. The builder left her and me in the middle of the job saying he had run out of money. I called up Nancy and said, "Honey, you better take the jewelry that Frank gave you and pawn it or my boots are going to walk all over him." Imagine the nerve – leaving me with a house that looked like a bomb had blown up. That house has been such a nightmare I still haven't moved in.'

'I remember. What's up, Iris?'

'Did I catch you at a bad time?'

It wasn't that Iris caught you at a bad time; it just took two to three hours to get her off the phone.

'Did you see *To Die For*? There is talk of Joaquin getting a nomination and then there's Kirsten for *Interview with the Vampire*. She is a shoe in. I've been looking for my dress to wear to the Academy Awards.'

'That's nice, Iris.'

'The reason why I called is because I've heard rumors that you are taking a position with another agency. I said that I couldn't believe that my Chris would do that to me. Would you?'

'Iris, I haven't talked to anyone or met with anyone. I've

heard that people want to talk to me but I haven't been in touch with anyone. You know how Hollywood is.'

'I knew that no one offered you a job,' Iris said smugly.

'Oh, I've been offered jobs, Iris, but I haven't spoken to anybody.'

'Well, as long as you don't work someplace else. I couldn't bear the humiliation after I defended you to everybody and told them that you had a mental breakdown.'

'Merry Christmas, Iris.' I hung up the phone before she could respond. Great that she had let everyone that called know that my reason for leaving Hollywood was because I had a mental breakdown.

It was the longest coldest winter that I could remember. I walked to the mall along the icy highway as the cold wind cut through me. I needed to find another job so that I could afford to rent my own apartment. It was like I'd gone from infancy to puberty in three months. I was headed into teenage rebellion. I wondered what chore would be thrown at me next. My father used to say that we didn't need a dishwasher because he had three of them. He also converted our house from electric heat to wood heat and disconnected the dryer so that we had to drag the clothes down the cellar stairs and hang them out to dry on clothes lines, which were strung up all over the cellar. The feel of those stiff towels, which you practically had to beat to fold, is something I'll never forget. My father could have easily lived in the mountains and been very self-sufficient. It was no wonder I buried my face in magazines and books about Hollywood. The rest of the world was in the twentieth century and he was still back in the Civil War.

My father's next assignment was to paint the two-story house. I painted from 6 a.m. until 1 p.m. and then

I helped my grandmother until I went to work. I cleaned the cellar and the attic and wondered what he could possibly find for me to do next.

In September I'd sent Iris a birthday card and she called me again. 'Honey. That was so sweet that you remembered my birthday.'

'Happy birthday,' I said.

'Oh, these clients are so crazy. You know that crazy mother – the nutcase that peed into the bottles in the dressing room? The fucking bitch left me. Can you believe that?'

'Why'd she leave?' I asked, knowing it was the mother who had protested about not having a private bathroom in their trailer. They had to walk down the hall and use the ladies' room with everyone else. She and her daughter had peed in Mason jars and left them in the dressing room until the janitor said something and the producer called the office.

'She had the fucking nerve to say that I didn't push for her daughter hard enough for the lead in a movie. I booked five kids in the fucking movie and I would have loved to book another one. Honey, I want to push the bitch off a cliff. The casting director told me that the mother listened at the door, and when she didn't like the director's direction, she walked in the room and redirected her daughter *and* the director. The stupid bitch cost her daughter the movie not me. The fucking hell I go through.'

I laughed and Iris laughed. I missed the laughing. I could get Iris to laugh even in her worse moods.

'Honey, when are you coming back?' she said.

'I don't know – my grandmother isn't doing so well.'

'This bitch I have working for me is just awful. She has more problems. The kids need to be picked up. She and her husband are getting a divorce. Then they're not getting a divorce. She's fucking whacked.'

'Happy birthday, Iris.' I hung up the phone, missing her and at the same time really not sure if going back was the right thing.

CHAPTER 15

'They that can give up essential liberty to obtain a little temporary safety deserve neither liberty or safety.'

Benjamin Franklin

Shortly before my grandmother left for Florida I was helping her ready the house for winter. We were sitting and looking at the display of colors on the trees in the first weeks of autumn.

'You know, Chris, I really think you should go back to Los Angeles. You're miserable here.'

'I made a mess of everything,' I said

'No – you gambled and lost. Now go back and throw the dice again.'

I just looked at her, unsure where that had come from. She really hadn't been the most supportive about my decision to move to Los Angeles in the first place. Now she was encouraging me to go back. I really didn't know if I wanted to go back and I certainly wasn't going to ask Iris for my job back. If I was meant to go back she was going to have to ask me.

The escape from upstate New York came in November. It seemed like November was a key month for me to move. One of my oldest and dearest friends, Candi Fifer, lived in Boston. She was the manager of the Boston Ballet ticket office. They needed temporary help for The Nutcracker ballet and it didn't take me long to accept the job and the space on her couch for as long as I needed. This would give me an opportunity to be able to search for a job in the Boston area.

Every lunch hour and every night after work, I pounded the pavement and filled out more job applications and handed out more résumés than I thought possible. Boston sobered me up to the fact that I was branded as a Hollywood agent. No one was interested in me for even the most menial of jobs.

Having been raised in upstate New York, I was more than familiar with the cold and snow but I never encountered as many blizzards as I did in that first two months in Boston. Mountains of snow ten- to 12-feet tall were on the sidewalks and roads. The Boston Ballet never closed and it was my job to reschedule the subscriber tickets. The ballet kept me busy but I wasn't going to make enough money to be able to afford my own place. Without a second job I couldn't live on my own and I didn't want to wear out my friend's welcome.

Iris called me just before Christmas. Every time I sent her a card I received a phone call. The switchboard put her right through and I was surprised when I heard her voice.

'Honey?'

At first thought it was a strange way for a customer to talk to me, but then realized, it was Iris. 'Oh, hi.'

'Baby, you always said that if I needed you that you would come back.' She paused. 'Well, I need you. I can't do this alone and the new girl sucks. I'm going to get my business manager to call and she's going to make you an offer that you can't refuse.'

'Iris, I don't know if this is the right thing.'

'Honey, let's put the past behind us. I can't do this for ever. I only want to do this for another couple of years. It's time to retire soon and then I'll give you the agency.'

There was an awkward silence as I thought about what she had just said. I didn't really trust that Iris would keep her word, but at least it would get me back out to Hollywood. The worst that could happen was that after a year it didn't work out and I would have re-established myself in the business. As the wind blew fresh snow past my window I realized the only choice left was to go back.

'OK, have your business manager call me.'

'Great! I promise that you'll love the deal.'

'One thing, Iris, I want to officially be made an agent through the Screen Actors' Guild.'

'Why does that matter?' The sweet tone had left Iris' voice.

'It matters to me.'

'Fine. Fine.' Iris hung up the phone.

I stared out of the window and wondered how I was going to break the news to my friend Candi. I left the offices of the Boston Ballet, pulled up the collar of my coat and tightened the scarf around my face. The icy snow pelted my head as it whipped by. I realized I finally had a destination and Iris needed me as much as I needed her.

Iris made me start back to work even before I had officially returned to the office. She wanted me to attend the premiere of a client's movie. The client had just recently left the agency. Since it was someone that I had initially brought to the agency I was sure Iris assumed that I could entice him back. She insisted I meet her at her house. The premiere was at 7.30 and when I arrived at 6.15, Iris greeted me in her bra with a towel wrapped around her waist.

'Honey.' She kissed me on the cheek. 'Come talk to me while I put my make-up on.'

I dutifully followed Iris to her bathroom and prepared myself for the ritual that Iris undertook when she had to be seen out in Hollywood. While I hated being late to anything, Iris thrived on being late. In Hollywood, being on time was the exception rather than the rule. The mirror in Iris' bathroom took up almost the entire upper half of one wall. The lights that surrounded the white-tiled double sink vanity made Iris' bathroom resemble a studio dressing room. The drawers were overflowing with brushes, eyebrow pencils, assorted lipsticks, powders and gels. Scattered across the top of the counters were compacts, curling irons, blow dryers, brushes and electric rollers. I stood in the doorway and watched as Iris slammed drawers and then took out this horrible contraption that curled her eyelashes. Then she applied mascara. Iris was meticulous when she applied the warpaint.

'You know Pete and I are finished.' Iris glanced up at me in the mirror.

'You mentioned that.' Her relationship with Pete was on and off again so much it was like a faucet.

Iris paused and stared into the mirror. 'The pain and suffering I went through. Do you know they cut through all the nerves behind your ears and on your scalp and literally pull you skin and cut away the excess?'

I wanted to vomit. The image of Iris' skin being pulled away from her face, lifted and then cut and stitched made me feel strange. 'That must be awfully painful.'

'I have these electric shocks now. The doctor said that it's the nerve endings healing. The itching is horrible.'

'Really?'

'But it was worth it because tonight everyone will see the new Iris Burton.'

'You look fantastic, Iris.' I had to admit that not many woman in their sixties looked as good as Iris. The fact that she had never had a boob job and had tits as perky as hers was miraculous.

'Oh, honey, thank you.' She caressed my cheek with her hand. 'It's so good to have you back.'

I looked down at my watch. It was almost 7 p.m. and she still wasn't dressed.

'Don't look at your fucking watch. You'll make me nervous and I'll fuck up.' She applied some lipstick and then put a tissue up to her lips and pressed them together. She looked at the tissue, applied some more lipstick and then headed to the bedroom, where she had meticulously laid out four entire outfits with accessories.

The fact that she wasn't even dressed made *me* nervous. There was late and there was late, but she was headed towards rude even for LA standards. She put on the black cashmere turtleneck and matching slacks.

'You look so gorgeous, Iris.'

She admired herself in the mirror. 'Oh, honey, do you think so?' She stood in front of the vanity mirror with an amber necklace. Then she picked up a pair of ivory beads so old that they were no longer white but antique white. Iris had the most amazing collection of antique jewelry acquired from her travels around the world. She slipped the gold Rolex with the diamond dial on her wrist. She had been to the safety deposit box. It meant she was pulling out the big guns.

'They all think I'm finished. You're about to watch me play million-dollar Spit in the Ocean.'

'What?'

'Honey, I may not have the clients that I used to have – this business is fucked right now – but I'm not going out without a fight.' She picked her two big art deco diamond rings off the vanity. 'I need you to help me.'

'That's why I'm back, Iris.'

She walked back into the bathroom. I looked at my watch. It was 7 p.m. and with the traffic, we might just make it to a 7.30 screening by 8.30. Iris picked up her toothbrush and I had to wonder why the hell she hadn't done that before she put her lipstick on. Now she would have to fix her make-up. I wanted to scream. I hated being late as much as Iris loved to be late. She talked the entire time she brushed. I barely understood a word that she said. The toothpaste foamed out of her mouth and down her chin. Damn. I wanted to hit the wall. Why the hell was I letting it bother me? We would be late to an ex-client's screening of a movie that we were accidentally sent an invitation to. Who cared?

Iris fixed the damage to her make-up and headed back into the bedroom. She looked down at her stomach.

'I should've had lipo too. I guess I can do that next.' She smiled at herself in the mirror. 'Wait until you see what I did today. I went to the furrier and I took this out of the vault.' Iris pulled open her fur closet where she had her mink-lined raincoats, fun furs, leather and cashmere coats. The really major furs – the lynx, sable and full-length mink – were stored at the furrier's vault along with her famous leopard coat. Iris had the original coat from the movie *The Graduate*. According to Iris, Anne Bancroft had seen her in the coat at some restaurant and fallen in love with it. She said it was perfect for her character in the movie. The production company paid Iris to use it for the filming.

'I'll show them. Those dirty sons of bitches stealing my client. They didn't want the little prick until he landed a big movie. The fucking ingrate.' Iris admired the fur in the mirror. She smirked as she spun around and looked at the back of the coat. I had to say it was impressive – and nobody else at the premiere would have an antique leopard coat. I think it is now illegal to hunt leopard. Only Iris would have a coat that was nearing extinction. She put the amber beads up against the black sweater and dangled her ivory necklace of a carved fist right beside it. Iris had told me it was an Italian symbol to ward off the evil eye.

'Which one – the amber or the ivory?' she asked

'I'd go with the first.'

'You're right.' She dropped the amber beads and reached for her black Chanel bag. 'Fuck.' She glanced down at the nightstand and realized that she had forgotten her good-luck charms. Iris swiftly pulled off the jacket, lifted up her sweater and safety-pinned the charms to the inside of her bra. She was obsessed with that bunch of charms. Once we spent thirteen hours looking for them and they ended up being attached to a bra that the maid had forgotten to take out of the laundry basket. Iris was hysterical until I found them.

'I'm not about to go out without that.' She patted her breasts and looked in the mirror one last time. 'Not bad for an old bitch.' She smiled and then left the bedroom.

I followed her through the living room and out to the front steps.

'Let me get the car out. You wait here.'

I stared out into the ten-foot hedges that surrounded Iris' tiny English rose gardens. The night-blooming jasmine released their scent. Iris had bought this little two-bedroom cottage with a guest house as a temporary residence while she redid her big house in the hills. It was like a doll's house and everything was perfectly manicured. The Christmas wreath was still on the door even though Christmas had long passed. Though she was Jewish, Iris celebrated every holiday. She called the Christmas tree her Hanukkah bush. Iris didn't miss a chance to receive gifts. She made a list out for me every year to inform the clients what she wanted. She had every catalogue carefully marked.

I heard Iris' horn. 'Come on! We're going to be late,' Iris yelled out of the window of her new four-door, black Mercedes that she had given herself for Christmas. I shook my head and looked at my watch. It was 7.15. I had arrived almost an hour ago. We were off just like the old days.

Once I was in the car, Iris used the car phone to check with her answering service – she didn't have voicemail because she always wanted a human voice to answer her phones, no matter what time of the day or night. She proceeded to have a fifteen-minute argument with the service because they let the phone ring six times before they picked up. She then called three clients to let them know that I was back at the agency. She was doing damage control.

By the time we arrived at the premiere there was a traffic jam on Wilshire Boulevard.

'And you kept looking at your watch. Look at this fucking mess.'

I looked down at my watch. It was 8 p.m. We'd be lucky if the movie started by 8.30. That was typical of LA screenings. It was even more typical of people in the business. I'd once been left sitting in a restaurant waiting for a friend for an hour. When he arrived he sat down and ordered a drink as if nothing was wrong. There's always a client or a conference call to blame in Los Angeles.

'Fuck, I forgot to take my handicap sticker from the other car.'

155

'Iris, since when is having a facelift cause for a doctor to give you a handicap sticker? If it were, half of LA would be able to park in the handicap spaces.'

'I didn't get it. I had my son's ex-wife get it for me.'

'You're unbelievable.'

'Listen, have you seen some of those people that get out of the car in the handicap spaces? They are no more handicapped than you.'

'Or you.'

'Drop it.'

Iris cut off another driver and pulled into a parking spot. The driver blew his horn non-stop.

'Fuck them.' She jumped out of the car and ignored the other driver who drove away giving her the finger.

I followed Iris to the elevator doors and she pushed the button. When the door closed she turned around and admired herself in the mirror at the back of the elevator. As the elevator stopped she spun around as if on cue, just as the doors opened, and put the biggest Broadway smile on her face that she could muster. She grabbed my hand and proceeded to pull me into the lobby of the theatre through the sea of blue suits.

'It's Iris Burton,' I heard someone whisper.

'I thought she was out of the business,' another said.

'I thought she was dead,' someone else whispered.

If I could hear the whispers, then Iris could as well. She just gripped my hand and smiled as the sea of suits parted. She acknowledged certain producers and studio heads by nodding in their direction in a way similar to royalty. She squeezed so tight on my hand that I thought for sure the circulation would stop. The client who had recently fired her caught sight of us and went pale. Iris didn't even look at him. This was like taking out an advertisement in the trades. She didn't have to say a word. In the morning the phones would be ringing off the hook. Hollywood is fueled by gossip and all the former clients and managers that I had worked with would know we were back in business. I heard a few gasps from the women as Iris marched through the throng. I had to admit she looked stunning in her leopard-skin coat. She looked like an old-time movie star.

There was an air of mystery around Iris Burton. Greta Garbo had nothing on her. Iris wasn't conventional and she didn't follow rules. She was the first person ever to run an agency from the house she lived in. She had fought all the other agents in the Screen Actors' Guild in court. She knew every person that had filed the suit against her. None of them were still in business. Iris won the suit. She spoke her mind and didn't care whether she was talking to the head of a studio or a famous director. When Iris Burton put her seal of approval on an actor people took notice.

Iris glanced around the lobby and then locked eyes with the former client. If looks could kill he'd have been dead on the spot. Iris would have her revenge. She'd make a remark to some producer, casting director or director and make sure that he lost an occasional job. She would let everyone know that he was an ungrateful actor that had gotten too big for his britches.

We headed into the theatre and Iris looked for the seats that had been reserved for her. They would be marked with a placard.

'There they are, honey,' she said and finally let my hand go.

One of the studio staff approached Iris. 'Can I help you, ma'am?'

'I'm Iris Burton.' She said it loud enough so that people would stare. They did. Our former client walked in with his entourage. Iris called them suits. She plastered another big grin on her face.

The movie began. Halfway through Iris dug her nails into her thigh. That was a clear sign she hated the movie. She leaned over and whispered into my ear, 'It's a pity that that squall didn't suck him up. He sucks.' She glanced in the direction of the former client. 'What the fuck did we lose, honey? He's no movie star.' Iris' whispers were the same level as most people's conversational tone. Before the movie even ended the sounds of people slipping out of the theatre could be heard all around us.

Iris grabbed my hand. 'Not a word out of you until we're in the car. What a fucking bomb,' she hissed.

She pulled me up the aisle like a two-year-old. It was a stampede to leave. Iris was fast and she maneuvered herself through the throng. By the time we hit the lobby, Iris had reached full speed, and I was dragged behind her as she bolted towards the elevators. They were already pretty full. 'Come on,' she yelled over her shoulder. When we reached the elevators the doors began to close. 'Hurry up.' Iris did a dancer's kick with her leg and swung the heel of her boot into the door right before it closed. She stopped the door and pulled at the crack with her hands until the door opened. Iris smiled at the occupants of the elevator and then shoved her way in yanking me in with her. When the door closed there was total silence: the silence in the wake of a huge bomb. However, Iris had accomplished her mission. She had shown the town that she was a younger, thinner and sleeker version of the old legend.

Since my departure from Hollywood two years before, the town had been invaded by suits. The agencies may as well have been Fortune 500 companies on Wall Street and Madison Avenue. They determined talent by use of spreadsheets and box office returns rather than finding raw talent. In the new Hollywood, actors like Marlon Brando, Al Pacino and Robert De Niro would never have achieved stardom. They were not obvious stars. The true mavericks of Hollywood that Iris had learned from did not exist any more. Talent and creativity were no longer a factor. Celebrity was the new gauge of talent in town.

The Aaron Spellings and Lew Wassermans had been replaced by a bunch of MBAs and lawyers who wanted to use their positions as agents to party, travel and get laid. Beautiful women and men wouldn't give these men a second glance in the real world, but if they flashed a card with the logo of a big agency or a studio, the clothes came off and looks didn't matter. It was about power. I respected Iris because she didn't mix her business with sex. She could have had a stable of boy toys if she wanted. Iris lived by rules that were long extinct. She drilled it into my head to never mix business with sex. It always became messy. If you represented someone they had to trust in you or it didn't work. Iris believed that if you were molding someone's career, they had to be comfortable enough to let you guide them without question. Actors were not always the best judge of what project they needed to do. Ego tended to get in the way.

I glanced over as Iris drove the car back to the office. She was vulnerable. It showed in her eyes. This was the first time in twenty years that Iris Burton didn't have a top-rated series on the air or a big teen heart-throb. We had some strong possibilities but nobody was at the level they needed to be to have the respect of the town. An agency needs a star to play ball with the big boys and be offered the great projects. No stars meant that your clients are offered sloppy seconds. Hollywood returns calls when you have what's hot. Iris Burton needed some stars because the fact that she was a legend wasn't going to cut it. She was becoming as endangered as the leopard coat that she wore.

CHAPTER 16

The smell of stale Sherman cigarette smoke surrounded me as I stood in the middle of my old office. Nothing had changed in eighteen months. Now I was right back to where I'd started. Forty feet away across the courtyard, Iris slept. It was 9 a.m. and she wouldn't stir until sometime after 12. As I looked out into the garden the phone rang. I didn't need Iris woken up. No sense having to deal with her before it was necessary. It was business as usual and, as I leaped across the room and picked up the phone, I landed in my old desk chair. It felt good to be back.

'Iris Burton Agency.' It naturally rolled off my tongue like I'd never left.

'Callback for Natasha.' The voice on the other end of the phone said.

'Hello.' I heard another groggy voice on the phone. It was unmistakably Iris' gravelly voice. She was now listening in on the call.

'I have it, Iris," I said.

Hopefully she would go back to sleep. I needed to figure out who was still on the books. I reached over to the bookshelf and grabbed the notebook that contained our current clients. I had heard the rumors from friends; Iris had been hemorrhaging clients in my absence. A quick flip through the notebook confirmed the rumors. There were maybe 12 clients left out of 120. Fred Savage's brother Ben, Joaquin Phoenix, and Kirsten

Dunst were still with the agency but only because they had signed three-year contracts.

Joaquin Phoenix hadn't worked in eighteen months since *To Die For*. Kirsten Dunst wasn't working. She had done a string of movies including *Interview with the Vampire* and *Little Women* prior to my leaving. Since I'd left she'd only done the movie *Jumanji*. Kirsten was thirteen and in the middle of a transition. She was looking very mature. Iris had told me the night before that she was having problems finding work for her as well as Joaquin. He was only getting offered strange and obscure roles. Nobody was pursuing either one of them. I had my work cut out for me.

The kids business had changed. They weren't doing many family movies or television shows. The commercial business, which had once been very lucrative, had been lost in the last actors' strike.

In the corner of the office was a three-foot stack of manila envelopes that contained headshots. I started opening them and sifting through the potential clients. I made a pile of people to call. I tossed out all the clients I wasn't interested in. I doubted that many would still be available based on the postmark.

I heard the rattle of the office door. Iris staggered in still half asleep and cinched her robe shut with one hand so as not to expose herself. The white robe with the blue oriental writing on it was one of the few gifts that Pete had given her, so it bordered on sacred. The belt had been missing for as long as I could remember and the stains and frayed edges were a testament to how much she loved Pete. I think he was the only person that Iris loved, and he was more of an obsession than anything else. Her hair was unkempt and looked like she'd slept in front of the fan. She certainly wasn't the seductress of the prior evening. She'd gone to sleep with her make-up on and it was smeared all over her face.

'Hi, Iris,' I said.

'Honey, you don't know how good it is to see you. I've missed you so much.' She bent over and kissed my forehead.

'Iris, is there another binder filled with the clients' pictures? This one is very empty.' Iris pulled a box of cigarettes out of her bathrobe pocket and opened the desk drawer and fumbled around for a lighter.

'That's it. That's all that's left.' She lit the cigarette and opened the side door to the office. She stared out into the garden.

'Iris, I think we have to start taking on young adults. From what everyone has been telling me that's where the money is.'

Iris turned her head and glared at me. 'I have always been known as a children's agent. That's what people expect.' She sat down in the wicker chair and continued to smoke.

'It's just a suggestion,' I said and sat back at my desk.

The next day I was setting up meetings with new clients and putting out calls to managers. Managers wouldn't usually work with Iris. She had a reputation for hating them. Only when I started working with her did we start to work with managers. I acted as the buffer. Iris did not want to share credit for anything. It had to be her discovery and hers alone. Unfortunately, most of the actors in town now had managers, so Iris was putting the agency at a disadvantage. The client had to pay the manager, not Iris. I really didn't see why it mattered. We needed clients and the quickest way to get them was to call managers. That was what I did. Iris just wanted to be back on top again. She'd come around.

Between the managers and Iris' performance at the premiere, old clients began to call the agency by the end of the week. Clients that had left in my absence returned and Iris didn't say a word. In one month I had taken on enough clients to make it through pilot season.

One of my closest friends was a manager and she had some young adults she wanted me to handle. Iris had vetoed the idea but I had a hunch. We were handling Joaquin and he wasn't a child. What harm would a few more be? I knew that young adults was the way to go. I had talked to enough people in my absence to know that the kids' business had suffered. Iris didn't know who I was submitting and didn't care as long as we made money.

Finally, I read the perfect project for Joaquin. It was called *Inventing the Abbots*. The script reminded me of *East of Eden*. Joaquin met the director in New York in the middle of a terrible snowstorm. The following week they flew Joaquin to Los Angeles to screen test with Liv Tyler and he stayed at a hotel right down the street from Twentieth Century Fox Studios. His contracts needed to be signed before the screen test. Rather than pay for a messenger, Iris sent me over to the hotel.

I was really uncomfortable about seeing Joaquin. It had been three years since I'd last seen him on the set of River's last completed movie *The Thing Called Love*. Joaquin had played basketball outside River's trailer on the Paramount lot. Iris made us all laugh with the story of the bullfighter she dated in Acapulco after her divorce. We watched a rough edit of scenes of Gus Van Sant's new movie, *Even Cowgirls Get the Blues*, which starred River's sister Rain. The scenes we watched were of Uma Thurman in a chicken suit as she flapped around and made chicken noises. Iris had glanced over at me and given me one of her what-the-fuck-is-this looks.

As I walked down the hallway to Joaquin's room, it felt more like I was headed down the plank. I thought of everything that had gone unsaid between us. I still hadn't let go completely of my own guilt. I could not imagine what it must be like for Joaquin. His brother's untimely death was constantly thrown at him by the press. Grief is a private emotion and having the press shove it in your face everyday by asking stupid questions like 'How do you feel about your brother's death?', only made things worse. How did they think he felt? How would they feel about the death of their own sibling? How does someone ever really forget a tragedy like that? With great trepidation, I continued my journey down the hallway to Joaquin's room. I hesitated before I raised my hand to knock on the hotel door.

Joaquin opened the door just as I was ready to knock. He smiled from ear to ear and pulled me into his hotel room and gave me a big hug. The awkwardness that I had anticipated didn't exist. In fact it seemed like I had never gone away. He seemed in good spirits and was excited at the prospect of the screen test. He quickly signed the contracts. There was no mention of what had transpired in the three intervening years since we had last seen each other. About a year before River's death, Joaquin had decided to take the business seriously again after a five-year self-imposed exile at his family's properties in Costa Rica and Florida. He hadn't worked since *Parenthood*. He had screen-tested for several important projects but *To Die For* was his entree back into the business. When Joaquin had finished signing the contracts I went back to the office.

'How was he?' Iris pounced on me when I returned.

'He was fine,' I replied. 'He seemed happy.'

'Did he bring his girlfriend?'

'There was a girl with him. She seemed nice.'

'What did he say? Did he ask about me?'

It was worse than the Inquisition. I didn't understand why she hadn't gone herself.

'I told him that we would have dinner with him later, just as we discussed.'

'Then he did ask about me.' She smiled.

'Yes, Iris,' I replied.

'Let's hope he gets this. He needs a movie.'

'We need a star,' I said.

The next week was incredibly tense as we waited to see if Joaquin would be chosen to play opposite Liv Tyler. It was what he and the agency needed. Iris was extremely anxious but luckily we booked three series with the young adults. I was happy we were doing so well. We only had a few clients but they were working. I had been so busy as I tried to find new clients that I had almost forgotten all about Iris' promise to make me an agent – officially.

My desk chair seemed to be a source of contention because every time I returned from lunch and sometimes first thing in the morning when Iris had been up all night, she sat in my desk chair and made me sit in the wicker chair across from her. It was hard to do my work because everything I needed was on the desk. Usually Iris was in the desk chair because there was some imagined problem or something that she wanted to argue about. It usually had more to do with yet another fight she had with her on/off boyfriend, Pete or her son. Iris would stay in my desk chair until she was damn good and ready to leave. She had her own office in the house, with the same furniture and posters from old musicals like *Cabaret* and *Jerome Robbins' Broadway*, but she rarely conducted business from there. She was mostly in bed or in the kitchen. Iris making her breakfast at 2 p.m. was the norm. She usually buzzed me and wanted me to talk to her while she scrambled eggs and had a bagel slathered in cream cheese.

She was never showered and she usually had on the robe Pete gave her. If Iris had recently seen Pete, she was happy and smiling. If a long period of time had gone by since they had communicated then she would be in utter misery and she would lash out at anyone in her proximity. Many a messenger went running off the premises. He even went so far as to totally ignore her at an awards show where he and one of her clients were nominated for an award. She cried on the phone with me from 1 a.m. until 5 a.m. Her own son had fired her as his agent so many times that I'd lost track.

When Iris told people I was in my office, it meant that's where they could find me. But that didn't mean that the office was mine. I had no input on what hung on the walls or how it was decorated. I tried to leave a bottle of Tylenol and some gum in one of the drawers but Iris complained and my briefcase served as my desk drawer. The accountant that came in on Saturday to do the checks had his stuff in a file box underneath one of the wicker chairs allocated for his things. I felt like I worked in Toys 'R' Us with the gumball machines, a stuffed Mickey Mouse and various toys that were scattered about the office shelves. Iris used them as traps for prospective child actors. If they couldn't focus and pay attention in the office then they would be distracted on the set.

I was a little worried that Iris had not mentioned the paperwork that would officially make me an agent. Any other agency would have done it immediately because they wouldn't want to be left open for a lawsuit. Iris had refused to make me an agent the last time I worked for her even though I closed deals all week long. I needed to confront her about this before it slipped too far away, then she would use her usual excuse that she didn't remember saying anything.

'Iris, we need to talk,' I said.

'Yes,' she said lighting a cigarette.

'The deal we made before I returned was that you would officially make me an agent. Legally. Through the Screen Actors' Guild.'

'I don't see the problem.' She waved her cigarette at me. 'It's a fucking piece of paper!'

'A piece of paper that you agreed to file. Maybe you've forgotten our conversation.' I wasn't about to back down because if I did I'd be sunk in her eyes for ever. With Iris you had to stand up and not back down. That was how she conducted her business even though she hated confrontation. She had drummed it into my head that the people on the other end of the phone could immediately feel your sense of conviction about the client you were trying to sell. Well, at this moment I was selling *me* and without that piece of paper no one else would take me seriously.

'I hate paperwork – you know that.' She stood up and stared at me, insulted. She pushed right by me at the door and, with a final glance of disdain, slammed the gate on the back porch then mustered all her strength to slam the back door to the house. I couldn't let her win this. I followed her to the house but when I reached the door it was locked. She was unbelievable. I went back to the office and got the key. I unlocked the door and when I entered the kitchen she stared into the refrigerator. I closed the door behind me.

'I'll do the paperwork, Iris.'

She slammed the refrigerator shut and reached for her pack of cigarettes. 'It's a piece of paper. Jesus fucking

Christ, Chris! Don't you trust me?' She turned her back on me and lit her cigarette on the gas burner.

Whether I trusted her really wasn't the issue. Trust really wasn't a word that pertained to Hollywood and its occupants. The word meant something everywhere outside of the area of Hollywood. Iris didn't trust anyone – not even her own son – so why would she trust me? And vice versa? If she trusted me she wouldn't monitor my phone calls and check every paper and appointment for a mistake. It was funny that she would use that word in regard to our relationship. I had to play this one very carefully. This had to benefit Iris or it wouldn't work.

'Hold on, Iris. Hear me out. Let's pretend that you go away and I have to negotiate a deal on behalf of a client. The client books the job and then they decide that they don't want to pay the agency.'

'I'm listening,' she said in a patronizing tone.

'If I'm not a sub-agent under your license the client could refuse to pay. They could be on a series for seven years and you wouldn't make a dime, Iris. Just think about that.' I opened the kitchen door and she puffed on her cigarette. Let her stew on that for a while. I closed the door and she didn't say a word. I went back to my desk.

An hour later Iris walked back into the office. 'Get the fucking papers,' she snapped and slammed the office door on her way out.

Joaquin booked *Inventing the Abbots* and he moved out to Los Angeles to shoot the movie. Early word at the studio was that there was great chemistry between him and Liv Tyler. I was happy that he was working and turned my attention to finding work for Kirsten Dunst. She was in the 'in-between' phase – in-between a child and a teenager – which was the worst place you could be whether you were well-known or not, as film work was scarce. That was the reason that Joaquin had taken all those years off. TV seemed to be the best option, but convincing Kirsten's manager of that was not an easy task. Television networks and studios love to put movie stars in their shows. It elevates the material to another level. Movie actors use television to do projects that the studios feel don't have a wide enough appeal. They can also try out different roles that the public wouldn't necessarily pay to see them do. Kirsten needed to show people that she had matured. A mini-series was offered to her and I was able to convince Iris and Kirsten's manager that this was exactly what she needed.

The shoot for the mini-series was located out of town. Iris made it a point to visit certain clients on location since she could write the cost of the trip off her taxes, so she decided to watch Kirsten film the mini-series. I was a little concerned because a sleepy town in Northern California was not London or New York. Iris was not a small-town girl. I looked forward to a blissful three days without Iris' physical presence. However, even when she was out of town she called as much as five times a day: she checked sometime in mid-morning to see that I had arrived; she called before lunch to make sure I didn't leave early; she called one hour after lunch to make sure that I didn't take a long lunch; and she called fifteen minutes before I would leave and talk to me for an hour or longer so that I didn't leave the office until 8 p.m. The only chance that I had to take a long lunch was if she was in transit because Iris would never spend the money to use the plane phone. Unfortunately Northern California was only an hour flight.

When Iris arrived on location she hadn't been there an hour before I received the first call.

'Honey, it's Iris! Forward the phones to the service. I need to talk to you.'

I wondered what could have happened already that required me to forward the phones.

'You have no idea what a dump this place is. The towels are so stiff I may as well use Brillo pads and the toilet paper is as rough as sandpaper,' she ranted. 'How do they expect me to stay here? I just can't have this. You need to do something.'

'Calm down, Iris. That's the only hotel in town. Kirsten and her mother are staying there. Maybe you could go buy your own toilet paper.'

'I should spend *my* money? Can you imagine the toilet paper that they sell in the stores here? Honey, they probably scrape their asses with bark. I should have never agreed to come to this stinking shit hole, what was I thinking? I'm sure I'll get stuck picking up the dinner check as well. Good old, pick-up-the-check Iris.'

I moved the phone away from my ear and just let her go. When she went on a rant it was just better to let her go until she wore out. I found it funny how Iris carried on about picking up checks. Iris *never* volunteered to pay, which is why I stopped going to dinner with her years before. She was never discreet about picking up the check. If I wanted to pick up a check I slipped off to the bathroom and discreetly gave the waiter the credit card so that there wasn't a scene at the table. With Iris, it was a Mexican stand-off to see if someone else would pick up the check before her. Iris even expected me to pay when she'd asked me to dinner. Twice she'd ordered five soups to go and I had to pay for it. Somehow I managed to calm her down.

Three hours later I received another frantic call from her. 'Oh my God! Honey, forward the phones. Something horrible has happened to me!' Iris was hysterical. My guess was that someone had ordered wine and she was stuck with a whopping dinner bill. Iris hated when someone ordered drinks and she had to pay. But when she was with someone who was picking up her check she ordered two appetizers, an entree, dessert, coffee and sometimes a drink.

'I can't believe what just happened to me. In my whole life I never thought I'd see the day. Oh my God! Oh my God!' She was hysterical.

'Iris, just calm down and tell me what happened.'

'I went to dinner with Kirsten's family and her manager.'

'Yeah.'

'Oh my God, I can't believe this happened to me.'

'Iris, just tell me what happened.'

'When I came back to my room, I opened the door and this fat pig of a man was fucking this woman. I thought I had the wrong room. The woman screamed. The man jumped up. I screamed and closed the door. It was horrible. Then I looked down at the key and the number on the room. It was my room. So I opened the door back up. The woman had pulled a sheet up and the man was standing over her naked and it wasn't a pleasant sight. He had this big beer belly and was all hairy. He looked like a fucking ape. Then, I noticed my suitcase on the floor where I had left it. The woman said, "Honey, we don't have much time," to the man. She was a fucking hooker! Can you believe it? The hotel must have let them use my room.'

'What did you do?' I had to hold back the laughter.

'I picked up the woman's dress off the floor and threw it in her face. I told her and the big prick to get the fuck out. Then I picked up the phone and called the front desk and asked for security. They told me they didn't have any security. They were renting my room out to hookers while I was at dinner.'

'I don't think so, Iris.' I held the phone away from me and laughed.

'Wait, it gets better. I called the front desk and told the woman I wanted new sheets and towels. This bitch has the nerve to tell me –' Iris took a drag from her cigarette. '– the fucking nerve to tell me that there is a water shortage and they only change the sheets every three days. I'm supposed to sleep on sheets that someone else has fucked on.'

'That's crazy.' I couldn't wait to hang up the phone so I could laugh.

'I told this bitch that I wanted new sheets and towels immediately. I didn't care if she had to personally take them out to the river and pound them on rocks and air-dry them. Water shortage, for Christ's sakes, they've had rain for days. Now I want you to call the producer of this piece-of-shit mini-series and tell him I want my linens changed.'

'OK, Iris.'

'Fucking hookers. Now I can add madam to my fucking job description.' She hung up the phone.

I called the producer. Maybe he could give Iris *his* sheets.

CHAPTER 17

'Those who are enjoying something or suffering something together are companions. Those who enjoy or suffer one another are not.'

C.S. Lewis

Iris walked into my office one day and made a proclamation. 'Honey, I want you to call every client in the agency and tell them that every month they need to either bring in or send in a roll of fax paper. Give them the model number of the fax.'

'What?' I replied

'Am I speaking French?'

'Iris, you can't do that.'

'I most certainly can! Do you have any idea how much money we waste having their fucking lines sent here?'

'We will lose clients. None of the other agencies do that,' I tried to reason with her.

'I don't give a fuck what anyone else does. Just fucking do it!' She slammed the door and left the office. I reluctantly called all the clients and they laughed and thought I was joking. Enough of them actually brought in a roll of fax paper that she didn't say anything for quite a while. That's when I started to spend my own money to copy scripts, FedEx and messenger clients' scripts. If we were going to remain competitive and not lose clients, we had to provide the services that other agencies provided.

It was a new business and everyone had to play the game. Iris had stopped calling to try to get appointments when she found that no one cared who she handled any more. Hollywood had become a business and was being run by people who had MBAs or law degrees. These people had to be shown spreadsheets, graphs and pictures. Creativity and former track records didn't mean anything to them. This new breed had to have concrete proof. Iris didn't want to accept the new Hollywood so I just didn't tell her. I am sure that she knew what I was doing with the stamps but we never talked about it. I told her the messenger was to pick up scripts.

The rumors persisted about Joaquin and Liv having a romance. I had dropped off several scripts for him but he hadn't liked anything. I didn't know if he even read them. But I didn't want to push things because I didn't know where I stood with him. Then I read this script called *Scream*. I am not a big fan of horror pictures but I loved the script. I told Iris about it.

'This agency does not do horror films. Never have. Never will. All that blood is disgusting.'

'But, Iris, it's really good.'

'I don't care if they dig Alfred Hitchcock up from his grave and he directs it. This agency will not do a fucking piece-of-shit horror film.'

'It's going to be a hit, Iris.'

'I don't want to hear it.' She hurled the script into the garbage and trudged out of my office slamming the door.

The next project I found was a script that my friend told me about called *Boogie Nights*. I was familiar with the director's work and knew that this was a special project. It was one of those scripts that came along every once in a while and made stars. I called Joaquin and rushed the script over to him on the set on my way home from work. Iris had been out of the office for the day at her business manager's and obviously was deeply involved in something because she never checked in. One of the producers of the project had been involved in River's last uncompleted film *Dark Blood*. I couldn't wait to tell Iris the good news but it had to wait until she got up. I eagerly watched the clock and finally at 2 p.m. I buzzed her bedside phone. I figured that she had to be up.

'Iris,' I said sheepishly into the phone. 'Iris.' I raised my voice an octave.

'Hum,' she moaned.

'Iris, I found Joaquin's next film.'

'What?'

'I found Joaquin's next project.'

'I heard you the first time. Why the fuck are you bothering me now?'

'I just wanted you to know that I dropped it off at his hotel last night.'

'You did what!' she screamed. 'How dare you do that without asking me. This is my agency. Joaquin is my client. Did you see him?'

'No, Iris. I dropped it off. Did you want to pay for the messenger?'

'He can come and pick it up. Why the fuck should I pay to deliver scripts?'

'Because that's what agencies do for important clients, Iris.'

'What the fuck is it about? Give me a quick summary.'

'Young man leaves home in Orange County and stumbles into the world of porno films and becomes a huge porno star and then falls prey to drugs and alcohol. It's a great part.'

'Are you fucking insane! First horror films and now you want to put Joaquin in porno films?' She slammed the phone down. I could hear her cursing as she plodded out of her room and through the house until the kitchen door swung open. She walked out onto the back porch and clutched the top of her robe.

'It's bad enough that his brother did that piece-of-shit movie *My Own Private Jerk Off*, and died of a drug overdose. Now you want his brother to do a fucking *porno!*' She banged her hands on the porch railing and her robe flew open.

'Iris, it's not a porno! You have to read it. It's wonderful and the characters are so well developed. It's brilliant. This guy is a good director. I have seen his work.' I left my desk and took a copy of the script and placed it on the railing in front of her. 'I'm telling you, Iris, this script is great.'

She flipped through it and looked at the last page. 'Jesus Christ, this thing is long.' She glanced down and noticed her robe was open again and clutched it.

'But it's amazing. I know that Joaquin could get an Oscar Nomination for this.'

Iris pulled a cigarette and lighter out of her robe. She took the script into the house. A half-hour later she came back out on the porch dressed in a sweatsuit carrying the script.

'I'm going to go get something to eat.' She drove off. On the rare occasions that Iris read anything she did it at Canters, the Hamburger Hamlet or Norm's. They were all diner delicatessen-style restaurants. Joaquin called while she was out and asked me to set up the meeting with the director. He had liked the script but he also was nervous about the subject matter. I really didn't find it offensive at all.

Two days later Joaquin met with Paul Thomas Anderson at Dan Tana's, a New York-style Italian restaurant in West Hollywood not far from the office.

Joaquin came away from the meeting interested but still nervous. The producer called and told me that the director was definitely interested in Joaquin. Iris, Joaquin and I had a conference call and no amount of persuading on my part could convince Iris, never mind Joaquin, to do the project. I was really upset when we had to pass. Mark Wahlberg ended up accepting the role. Joaquin would later regret that decision.

A great part came up for a young teenage girl on *ER*. This was a great opportunity for Kirsten to be on the number 1 show in the country. All of her scenes were opposite George Clooney. The problem was convincing Iris and Kirsten's manager to let her do a television show and audition for the part. They finally came around to my view after days of arguing the merits of such a high-profile project, despite the low pay. But it was still more money than not working and having people still see you as a little vampire.

It was around that time that I ran into Thora Birch and her parents at a premiere. Iris was out of town on a vacation. We had made Thora the hottest little female actress in the city. They had fired us while they were in London filming *Patriot Games*. I remember calling Iris at her decorator's after Thora's father had called.

'Iris, Jack Birch just called from London.'

'I'm busy picking out carpeting so this better be good,' she snapped.

'Well, Iris, first of all the beds in their rooms weren't made when they returned from set today.'

'Do they think that I'm a fucking maid?' she screamed.

'That's not all, Iris. They are angry that we didn't take into account the fluctuation between the dollar and the pound when we negotiated their per diem.'

'Get that fucking prick on the phone,' Iris yelled.

'I'm not finished, Iris.'

'There's more?' She hit her hand on the wall. 'Tell me quickly so I can get that bastard on the phone.'

'They are upset that Harrison Ford's dressing room is better than the one they are in.'

'*What*?' I heard the phone drop to the floor.

'Iris,' I called out. I hoped that she hadn't collapsed.

She picked up the phone and was breathing heavily. I heard the click of her lighter and then she inhaled and exhaled. 'You get that mother-fucker on the phone. You conference him in to the call. Get him on the phone now! I'm going to kill that son of a bitch!'

I called the Birch's hotel room in London and put Jack on the phone with Iris.

'Jack.' She paused for a second. 'It's Iris. I understand you have problems.'

'Hi, Iris' he said shyly. He was hardly the raving madman he had been with me earlier. People were terrified of Iris. 'Well, our beds weren't made when we came back to our rooms today.'

'CHRIS!' she screamed into the phone.

'Yes, Iris,' I said.

'Book me a flight to New York and then book me on the Concorde so I can get to London as fast as possible. If we're lucky I can make your beds tomorrow morning. I'm not a fucking maid, Jack. Nobody negotiates the fluctuation in foreign currency in a contract. As far as Thora's dressing room, when she can open a movie as big as Harrison Ford then I'm sure the studio will be happy to give you Disneyland as a dressing room.' She slammed the phone.

Iris called me right back. 'Someone is trying to steal her.'

Iris was right. The next day they fired us and went to ICM. Fortunately for us they had just signed a new contract with the agency so they couldn't make a move without paying us. Plus we had her locked up with option pictures at Paramount and Disney. We informed ICM of that fact the very next day. ICM immediately fired the Birches. They then went to William Morris.

Thora had met the producer David Geffen when *Interview with the Vampire* was still in the very early planning stages but then it was postponed. When we took on Kirsten Dunst after Thora left, I knew from the minute I met her that she could get the part of Claudia. She looked like a china doll and that's what they wanted. Thora had a more rural beauty, which is why she was perfect for the remake of *Little Women*. Thora had the role but in the end her agents out-priced her and I scooped up the part for Kirsten too. The Birches fired William Morris and went to UTA. Thora was now plagued with the same problem as Kirsten, except Thora had huge breasts.

At the premiere, the Birchs complimented me on what was happening with Kirsten's career. I knew that they wanted to come back to the agency.

They called two days later and we all had dinner together. I convinced Iris that we should take Thora back. She was a totally different type than Kirsten. Iris was concerned that Kirsten's mother and manager would have a problem with Thora being with the agency. I pointed out that Robert De Niro and Al Pacino had the same agent. Iris pointed out that they didn't have mothers and fathers meddling with their careers. The transition from child actress to teenage actress was a tough one.

I had very little time for a social life because I was cooped up in the office all day and rarely met anyone accept the postman, UPS man and the FedEx guy. I was right in the middle of West Hollywood – the fabled gay Mecca of the world – and I was without any dates. I'd actually given up after Richard. On my way to work I'd exercise at a gym and on occasion I would have an encounter in the steam room. Intense staring and a grope would lead to a quick run to their apartment where we would have a quick and heated encounter before I went to work. It would all lead to nowhere because they always seemed to have boyfriends. It further entrenched the idea in my head that I didn't need a boyfriend because he'd be groping someone in the steam room, just like these guys. I had become a cynic about love.

I would go out to bars with friends but that would usually lead to a one-night stand. It was probably my fault because I didn't have the energy or patience to give anything to another person after dealing with Iris and the clients all day. My dreams of romance had gone out of the window with the Danielle Steele romance novels that I'd stopped reading ten years before. One man that I had an encounter with became irate when I wouldn't let him spend the night after sex. He called me 'the most self-contained man in LA'. He followed that with, 'How could you have been as passionate and intimate with me as you just were and then kick me out of bed at 3.30 in the morning?' I responded, 'I have trouble sleeping with strangers.' It seemed stupid that I could have sex with a stranger but I couldn't sleep with one. I was really afraid to let anyone get close. Los Angeles is a place where everyone seems to want something, especially if you're in the entertainment business.

Joaquin still wasn't being sent scripts to play leading men. We needed to have people see him as a big movie star on the cover of magazines. It came to my attention that they were deciding on who would be the next Prada model. Prada had made it a point to take respected actors like Willem Dafoe and John Malkovich and make them the focus of their marketing campaigns. They didn't want real models. They wanted anti-models. They had decided to go younger for their next campaign, so I sent Joaquin's pictures off to the advertising agency in New York that had been awarded the Prada account. Within a very short while we had word back that Joaquin had got the gig. Unfortunately I had forgotten to take into account that Joaquin is a vegan and doesn't wear leather. Prada is primarily a leather-based company with shoes, bags, luggage and belts making up the majority of their collection. I thought we were going to lose the campaign until they agreed to shoot Joaquin from the ankles up.

Iris didn't need to have her arm twisted to take another trip, so I negotiated that Prada pay for Iris' plane ticket to Milan and her expenses. Joaquin took Liv Tyler with him, which was the first public acknowledgement that they were a couple. When Iris arrived in Italy, she wasn't in the room more than a minute when I received the phone call from her.

'Call me back in the room.' She slammed down the phone. It would have been helpful if she'd told me the room. She sounded pissed and I couldn't imagine what could have happened between the airport and the room to annoy her. I dialed the hotel's number.

'You should see this fucking closet that they call a room! They had fucking ironing boards set up in here when I walked in. What the fuck do they want me to do? Work off the plane ticket and the room by ironing dresses for the runway models? I yelled at the bellhop but he just tossed my suitcases in the room and looked at me like I was insane and left me with these ironing boards. The son of a bitch can't speak English. Nobody understands a word I'm saying. Now you get that bitch on the phone in New York and straighten this out. They may as well have put me in a fucking coffin. I can't breathe in this fucking room. I haven't even seen a bathroom, maybe they expect me to bang on the door of the room next to me and ask if I can take a shit. Hold on let me look around and see if there's a chamber pot.'

When Iris was like this, nothing could be done. She wouldn't let anyone get a word in edgewise so it was best to just let her go off until she was finished. I called the advertising agency in New York to see what I could do. They called back and said that the hotel was full. There was a convention in Milan. There were no other rooms, at least for the night. I really didn't relish having to tell Iris the news. She called me back again several hours later and was even more furious.

'I just saw Joaquin and Liv's room. It's like fucking Versailles compared to mine. Honey, Liv Tyler's ass couldn't be cleaner. I get ironing boards and they get fruit and flowers. We went over to the Prada store and they're ripping things off the racks to give to Liv. I couldn't even get a Kleenex to blow my nose. They *give* Liv the fucking clothes. Little old Iris gets a fucking 20 per cent *discount* . . . I did buy a beautiful tan cashmere coat . . . but they are giving Liv everything! You can forget about getting anything. Why they asked for your sizes and mine, I'll never know.'

'I don't know what to say, Iris. Liv is a movie star. We don't land on the covers of every magazine.' I tried to be practical about it.

'I don't care. If he hadn't brought her then I would be getting all the free clothes. This sucks!' Iris slammed the phone down.

This was not going to be easy. Iris liked to be the star and if anyone eclipsed her . . . well, look out. The next day was worse.

She started, 'I had to sit around all day and wait for

the fucking car because Liv decided to be chauffeured around while Joaquin was at the photo shoot. I didn't want to sit there all day while they took his picture. I want you to call and have them give me a car for tomorrow because *I* want to be chauffeured around Milan. Do you understand me?'

Iris was worse than any of the clients. I wondered what she would complain about next. In the meantime I had found a couple of good films for Joaquin. I wanted to talk to Iris about them but I couldn't get a word in about business.

'Honey, forward the phones right away. This is a nightmare. They were taking me to the shoe and handbag showroom today and then Liv decided to go. Well, I can guarantee you *she* isn't vegan because she was stocking up on shoes and handbags like there was a leather shortage. I managed to buy a few pairs of shoes and get a few pocketbooks after she had first crack at the purses. Joaquin didn't even think about getting you anything.'

'That's really fine, Iris. I don't think the world will end if I don't have a pair of Prada shoes,' I replied.

'They couldn't care less that I'm here. Joaquin and Liv are all in love and I sit in my room alone. I feel like a mother on a honeymoon.'

I didn't know what Iris wanted me to do but mercifully the photo shoot was finally finished so maybe she would give me some peace for a few days. I was having enough problems with running the office. The project that I had found for Joaquin was *U Turn,* to be directed by Oliver Stone. Joaquin didn't like it but after several weeks of phone fights he agreed to come to LA to audition for the movie. His scenes were really funny and he would be acting with Claire Danes and Sean Penn. His character was called TNT. I really didn't like the script but Joaquin's scenes would lighten up his image. He flew out and had a taxi drop him off at the office. He would literally only be in town for twenty-four hours so Iris had agreed to let him stay in her house since she was away. I drove him to all his auditions as Iris has instructed me to do. She didn't let anyone drive her cars.

A manager from Minnesota sent me a picture of a great-looking nineteen-year-old guy. He had only done local theatre and she wanted him to come out to Los Angeles for pilot season. I took one look at his picture and told her that if he could speak, she needed to send him out on the next plane to LA. She informed me that he was going to college in New York and wanted to know if I could handle him there. I told her I had no problem with that and sent his picture over to the person in charge of casting for one of the networks. She would be going to New York in early fall to scout talent for the new pilot season. A few months later she called me when she was leaving for New York to set up a meeting with my client, an actor I'd never met. His name was Josh Hartnett.

The casting director called me from New York after she had her meeting with Josh.

'My God, Chris, have you met this boy Josh?'

'No,' I replied thinking that maybe there was something wrong with him. It was not unusual for an actor to doctor up their photos. 'What's wrong?'

'Well, he's more incredible in person than the picture if you can believe that.'

'Are you interested?'

'He's not right for *Dawson's Creek*. He's not innocent enough. He's more smoldering. But you have a winner. This boy is a star.'

Well, I was happy to hear that but with Josh in school it would be a little hard to get him working. As luck would have it, he decided to take the semester off and move to LA for several months to see if he could land a series or a movie. The young adult department was doing very well, in fact it was doing so well that we had to keep a watchful eye on the larger agencies that we quickly dubbed 'Poachers!'. I had heard from Joaquin, as well as Kirsten's manager, that agents had approached them from bigger agencies. The one great thing about handling kids was that we'd never really had a big problem with poachers. Nobody would leave the best children's agency in the business to go to a second-rate agency. The big agencies didn't want to have to deal with the mothers. It was also a relief that the young adults had already been through puberty, braces, pimples and growth spurts. With the 'uglies' behind them, if they were doing well, chances are they wouldn't have to worry again until their mid-forties.

The Iris Burton Agency didn't provide tickets to baseball games, tables at exclusive restaurants and premiere tickets to big movies. Neither Iris nor myself wore black suits with black sunglasses at premieres. I hated to go to premieres because Iris drove me nuts, following me around the event with her eyes and interrupting me every time anyone started to talk to me. I respected the fact that Iris didn't use tickets to events to try to steal other people's clients. It was only the big agencies that picked up other agencies' clients after someone else had expended money, time and energy. In the old days actors stayed with an agent and an agency sometimes for their entire career. That wasn't the case now. Hollywood had become a part of the TV channel 'clicker culture'. Actors kept clicking to another agent at the slightest lull in their careers. As our clients did better and better, the wolves circled.

The holidays approached and I dreaded them as always because Iris would be in a melancholy mood, due to the fact that years ago her mother had died right before Christmas. She mourned until well after New Year's and usually made a pilgrimage out to Forest Lawn. I usually took as much of my vacation time as possible during the Christmas holidays, just to escape her. But I couldn't escape Iris' Christmas rituals.

They started right after Thanksgiving. Iris would head downtown and go to the wholesale market and buy gifts for the selected clients. If someone had made her money they received a gift. If they had not she felt that her annual Christmas party at a miniature golf course and arcade was enough.

Iris would buy various studio executives, directors and special clients like Joaquin a gift from David Orgell's in Beverly Hills. The casting directors and anyone else that Iris felt she had to acknowledge received donations letters. I dreaded that project more than anything else. Iris was sent a donation card from a charity one year and she had the brilliant idea that rather than spend $25 a card and have the organization do it, she would run off her own letters and have me stuff Christmas cards that she bought on sale after the holidays. Then I had to lick (yes, it was the days before self-sticking stamps) at least 1,000 stamps. In between my other duties I licked and stamped. Then there was the wrapping of the clients' gifts. I would spend two or three nights after work until 3 or 4 a.m. wrapping while Iris figured out who was deserving of what gift. She had an attic full of gifts that had been given to her that she always tried to regift. As the holidays approached any basket of goodies that was sent to the office was immediately taken to her manicurist, banker, hairdresser, massage therapist, gardener, maid and postman. Then I had to check and double-check to make sure exactly how many people would be attending the party. The clients dreaded the outing as much as I did. Iris always threw some kind of tantrum. I drove way out to the arcade in the Valley, parked my car and waited for ten minutes before I walked into the throng of mothers and kids. Iris was always an hour late anyways so I didn't care.

'Chris.' One of the clients banged on my window.

'Hey. How are you?' I glanced at the large package from Tiffany's that she held.

'Can I put this in your car? It's Iris' Christmas present. I know that you'll only have to drag it out later.' She smiled.

I opened my trunk, which caused ten other mothers to jump out of their cars and head towards me with gifts. They loaded up my trunk with presents for Iris and me and then I headed into the noisy arcade. Clients and mothers ran towards me and tried to get my ear before Iris showed up. They didn't want to be caught talking to me in front of Iris. She'd think there was some conspiracy or that the conversation was about her. The arcade owner jumped on me immediately and wanted to know if he should give the kids tokens and I told him I didn't care. Iris strolled in an hour and ten minutes late to her own party, in one of her Christmas sweaters with bows, ribbons and lights on it. She had on earrings that looked like Christmas lights and red boots.

'Chris . . . Chris!' she yelled as she walked down the aisle. It was too late to hide – she had seen me. The mothers who had been talking to me scattered.

'Yes, Iris?' I called.

'I had a horrible fight with Pete last night. He was supposed to come.'

'Iris . . . Iris.' A six-year-old boy who was a client

pulled at her hand. 'The man won't give us any more tokens until you say he can.'

Iris shot me one of her looks that made me want to go jump in the reservoir that was about a mile away. 'Why don't you go ask you mother for some money to buy tokens?' She smiled. 'Why are they giving out tokens anyway? I told them not to give out any fucking tokens until I got here. Do I look like a Rockefeller?'

'Iris, you are an hour late. What was I supposed to do – have the kids sit in a circle and sing camp songs? I don't know the words to "Kumbaya" any more.'

'How dare you defy my orders?'

'It's only tokens, Iris.'

'Tokens I have to pay for!' She stormed down the aisle, looking for the arcade owner.

God, how many of these bloody Christmas parties would I have to endure? I don't know why she organized them, other than she wanted to get presents to put under her tree. She would head to the wholesale florist downtown and fill her car with wreaths and poinsettias to decorate a house that didn't have any Christmas visitors. On top of everything, Iris was Jewish.

'Chris ... Chris!' She must have grabbed the microphone from the arcade owner because now my name was being broadcast all over the arcade and miniature golf course.

'Yes, Iris.' I only had to get through a few more days and then I had a vacation.

'Look around this room. Do you recognize all these faces?' Her voice boomed around the arcade.

I glanced around. 'I recognize some of them.'

'Well then, who the fuck are the rest of these pigs eating pizza and soda that I am paying for? I want you to go out there and find out who the rest of these people are and if they aren't with the agency I want you to start collecting one dollar a slice from them. If they have a soda it's two dollars.'

She was interrupted by the cantina owner, 'Ms Burton, someone wants to take home a pizza and they said you would pay for it.'

Iris' face turned beet red and I wanted to head for cover. She stammered and couldn't do anything except sputter out a few specks of spit. 'What the fuck is going on here! Maybe I should open the event up to all the orphanages in Los Angeles. I'm not Mother fucking Teresa of the free pizzas. Show me the mother. Point her out to me now!'

I turned to leave.

'Chris!' Iris yelled. 'You're coming with me.'

The arcade owner guided us to the woman. Iris tapped her on the shoulder.

'Yes.' The woman turned around.

'Who the fuck are you?' Iris snapped.

'I beg your pardon,' the woman said.

'Did I offend you, lady?' Iris said

'Well, your language is vile.'

'Your manners are vile. You wanted to order a pizza to go on me and I don't even fucking know you. That is vile.'

'Well, we came with one of your clients. They invited me and my five kids but two couldn't come because they were sick.'

Iris' eyes bulged out of her head. 'Get the fuck out of here this instant. The fucking nerve! How many other people are eating on me?' She turned to me. 'I told you to tell them only the clients. I'm not feeding their whole family. This is out of control.' Iris went over to the arcade owner and the concession stand and told them that everything down to a glass of water had to be approved by her or she wasn't paying for it.

I fantasized about the two weeks in Florida at my grandmother's house, walking on the beach.

Joaquin went off to film *U Turn* while we waited for *Inventing the Abbots* to come out. The early buzz was that Joaquin was amazing. The Prada campaign would also have Joaquin in all the big magazines. A script was sent to me called *The Yards*. They hadn't yet locked in their financing but the director had done a really interesting independent movie. I loved the director's previous work. *The Yards* was a movie about the sins of the father being delivered upon the children. It was also a story of redemption and Joaquin's character was coming back home after a stint in prison. I sent him the script.

Joaquin had decided to move out to LA for a while and he rented a guest house on the property of one of Rudolph Valentino's homes; Liv moved in with him. It seemed more like a small house than somewhere for guests to me. He was two blocks away from me in the Hollywood Hills and five minutes from his sisters.

Joaquin's mother, Heart, came out for a visit. It would be the first time I had seen her since River, Samantha Mathis, Mrs Phoenix and I all went to the screening of *The Thing Called Love*. Again I felt awkward and nervous at the thought of seeing her, but Iris was out of town and we all had a wonderful meal. She was happy with the progress of her children. They were all doing well.

Joaquin liked the script for *The Yards* and decided to meet the director. After the meeting he agreed to attach himself to the project and was lined up to play the juicy role of Leo Handler. The producers went to work finding someone to play opposite him for the role of Gutierrez. Benicio Del Toro was mentioned. He was hot from *The Usual Suspects*. Unfortunately, even when you put the two together they didn't equal financing. Neither one of them had proven that they could open a picture. Miramax Films became involved with the project and structured a more formal deal with us for Joaquin. *The Yards* was definitely going to take time to get off the ground.

Kirsten was doing terrifically. The *ER* episodes opened doors and within a very short time she did several television movies and small independents. She was working her way back up the ladder. She had to prove to Hollywood that she could make the crossover. I was having no luck with Thora Birch. I managed to get her a few guest spots on television. Her parents kept making comments on how great Kirsten was doing. I hated to admit that Iris had been right about the Birches. She didn't believe in taking people back once they'd left.

Iris continued to travel. She was in Paris, London, Rome, Saturnia in Italy and New York. As always she had problems with the hotel rooms, the toilet paper and the fact the people did not speak English. She bought three needlepoint handbags in Paris and had a big drama because she thought they were $200 each and they were actually $2,000 each. She had fights with American Express and the shop in Paris and eventually lost her American Express card over the incident.

My big problem was that Iris had made no further mention of making me a partner or retiring. She had lured me back with all these promises and now they were pretty much forgotten. I was really tired of running her business, and making the agency a great deal of money while still being broke all the time. I was paying expenses and there was no reimbursement for them. Iris and I had a huge fight every time I brought up the services other agencies provided for their clients. We were in the midst of a huge transition in the business. The big agencies snapped up anyone that even had a line in a feature film. If they had a television series the agents lined up around the block. The new agents didn't know how to develop talent, they only knew how to steal it. They dangled lavish offices and masses of people in suits to provide the illusion that they did something.

I was living from check to check. I decided to confront her after she returned from her stay at the exclusive Golden Door Spa. Iris had gone there every year since as far back as I could remember. It was her birthday present to herself. Barbara Walters, Candi Spelling, Barbara Davis and wealthy women from all over the country booked themselves in for a week of massages, facials, hiking, swimming and gourmet diet food. Of course Iris didn't hike at sun up or sun down but she did love all the treatments. I figured when she returned she'd be in a good enough mood for me to bring up the fact that I had been back almost two years and nothing had changed. I really regretted not having everything put into writing by her business manager. I waited two days and then I approached her while she was having her breakfast at 3 p.m.

I buzzed the intercom to her room. 'Iris, I need to talk to you.'

'Talk,' she barked back.

'Could you come out here?' I said.

'Why?' Her voice registered suspicion.

'Because it's easier for me to write appointments and answer phones out here.'

She walked into the office, cigarette in hand. So much for her promise to quit smoking. 'Yes?' She stared right at me.

'Iris, when you asked me to come back to LA, you said that you were going to retire.'

'Retire? I'll never retire. Why should I?'

'You promised to make me a partner. You told me that you were tired and that you only wanted to do this for two more years and then you'd make me a partner. That I'd be making a percentage of the bookings.'

'Did I?' she said in a patronizing tone as she took a drag on her cigarette and gave me a steely-eyed stare. She walked over to my desk and exhaled her smoke right in my face.

'I have a very good memory, Iris. You're always saying how I never forget anything. While we're on the subject, you made me an agent and you continue to call me your secretary and it really bothers me. You seem to know how to call me your associate or agent when there's a problem. Why is it so difficult for you to treat me with respect? I'm far more than a secretary, Iris, and even they make more money than I do.'

'This is about what I *call* you?' She took another drag of her cigarette. 'What would you *like* to be called?'

'I'm the one that started the young adult division, Iris. We wouldn't have a business if I hadn't persisted. The kids sure aren't working.'

'I did quite fine my entire life without you as my *secretary*! I'll do just fine when you go back to wherever the fuck you came from!'

'Fine with me. Good luck keeping the clients when I'm gone again.' I grabbed my keys and my briefcase and strode out of the office. For once I was the one slamming the door. I slammed it so hard that the vertical blinds came crashing down to the floor behind me.

I was walking down the driveway when she yelled out to me. 'Nobody walks out on me! You son of a bitch! Get back here!'

I continued to walk to the street, jumped in my car and sped down the street before she could even make it to the end of the driveway. I raced home. When I walked in the door the phone was ringing off the hook. There were already eight messages. I sat and listened to the phone ring and ring for an hour until I finally picked it up. Iris told me how much she loved me. How much she needed me. She offered me a $200 dollar a week raise. She promised she'd make me a partner soon. She'd even announce it in the trades.

The partnership advertisement never ran. Iris called me her associate for a few weeks as a compromise and then she slipped right back into referring to me as her secretary. I had received a raise but I was slowly coming to the realization that I was a prisoner of my own fear. I was too afraid to move on There was some sort of bond between the two of us. It was as though she had me under some strange spell. Maybe I understood the wounded person that lay beneath that tough exterior. Iris was extremely vulnerable although she covered it well. I was just as damaged as she was. Iris somehow managed to make me feel more insecure than I already was. I didn't really know how other agencies operated. I needed to find a way to break the cord that bound us together. I needed to get stronger than Iris in order to break away from my prison of self doubt.

CHAPTER 18

'A new nature is being not merely made but made out of an old one. We live amid all the anomalies, inconveniences, hopes, and excitements of a house that is being rebuilt.'

C.S. Lewis

Josh Hartnett came to LA in late January after only a few months at college. By the end of his first week of auditions he'd received ten callbacks to meet with producers and directors. Every casting director called after his auditions and raved about how amazing he was. I still had not met him in person. By his second week in Los Angeles we had interest from several series. Josh needed visibility so I picked the series that had the most chance at critical acclaim and the least chance of making it more than half a season.

Kirsten had generated enough heat that we were able to attach her to two movies *Dick* and *Drop Dead Gorgeous*. We waited for both the producers to put their funds in place. Kirsten was in the same boat as Joaquin. The studios wouldn't lay out the money to finance their projects unless someone else was attached. *Inventing the Abbots* did not come out with a bang. It bombed at the box office. The studio really didn't do a good job marketing the movie.

A good script was sent to us called *Clay Pigeons*. Unfortunately, they were searching for financing and would have to come up with more high-profile names to satisfy the financiers. It was the same story every time we found a quality project. If Joaquin wanted to do a horror film, money could be found. But nobody wanted to do an intelligent, good script. We were in a holding pattern everywhere we turned.

A manager sent us two sisters, Haylie and Hilary Duff, that she wanted us to represent. I took the meeting and was having a tough time deciding what to do. The older sister, Haylie, was a good actress but she was heading into that tough thirteen-year-old bracket. She was very mature for her age. The little girl was adorable and was in the perfect eight- to ten-year-old bracket. The mother seemed like she would be overprotective. After all these years I had a good barometer about mothers. Iris didn't care who I took on as long as they worked, so she rarely took meetings with the new clients. It was a much faster process if Iris wasn't in the office.

With the Duff sisters though I needed Iris' advice and would have to risk one of her three-hour monologues. There was something about Susan Duff that I didn't like. Iris would use any new, captive audience to tell the old story of how she won the Most Beautiful Child in New York contest when she was nine. The trophy sat tarnished in the corner of the office – a testament to Iris' fading beauty. The picture of her taken at the time shows a different person, a child full of innocence. What had happened in between had jaded Iris to such a degree, that no matter what anyone did, she wouldn't let them in. She had supported her family as a dancer on Broadway until she moved to Los Angeles and screen-tested for a movie at Paramount, *The Vagabond Kings* by Michael Curtiz. Jack Lord and Leslie Nielsen had flown out on the same plane with her. She didn't get the part but was put under contract at Paramount. She worked as a dancer in the Dean Martin and Jerry Lewis comedies and danced in *The Ten Commandments*; that she dated Gene Kelly, Donald O'Connor and Steve McQueen. I knew the stories by heart. This is the abridged version, Iris made it much more elaborate. However, I hadn't heard the stories in a while, so rather than risk a bad experience I buzzed Iris.

'Iris, I need you to meet somebody.' I smiled over at Mrs Duff.

'I'm not dressed,' she snapped.

Mrs Duff glanced down at her watch and was probably wondering why Iris wasn't dressed at 4:30 p.m. Susan Duff could hear everything Iris was saying so I needed to get her off the speakerphone.

'OK, I'll send them in to you in fifteen minutes. That's how long that conference call to Steven Spielberg should take.' I figured I'd give Mrs Duff something to take note of. Steven Spielberg was a code that meant I wanted to get someone out of the office or off the phone.

'What's wrong with them?'

'Iris, they're sitting right here in front of me. They're just adorable. They can't wait to meet you.' I smiled over at Susan Duff. She shifted nervously in her chair. I continued to smile.

'You come in with them. If you're sending them in to me then you have a problem with them. I know you.'

'OK see you soon, Iris.' I hung up the phone.

Iris had pulled herself into one of her cashmere sweatsuits and pushed her hair into a cap. I ushered the Duffs into Iris' living room. This was a rare occasion, as Iris didn't like people to see how she lived.

As I passed by her in the kitchen she grabbed my arm and whispered in my ear,

'There'd better be a good reason for this. I was cleaning my closet.'

Then she plastered on a big smile and strolled into the living room. After a half an hour the phone rang and Iris and I both jumped up to answer it. I beat her to it.

'Honey, do you need me?' she called out from the living room.

'No,' I replied.

'Are you sure?' I glanced at her. Iris winked.

'It's about Joaquin.' I called back.

'Excuse me.' Iris smiled sweetly until she turned and faced me. Once in the kitchen she squeezed my hand and whispered, 'What's the problem? The kids are cute.'

'I don't like the mother.'

'She has a manager, we won't have to deal with her,' she snapped.

'I don't know, Iris, there's something.'

'Are you suddenly a junior detective?'

'Fine, Iris, we'll take them but if I have any problems, you deal with them.'

Iris was becoming more difficult every day. Her diabetes was not good. The exercise and required three meals a day with snacks that her doctors suggested were ignored. She felt that a visit to her plastic surgeon was easier. Iris treated herself to liposuction, a tummy tuck and a chemical face peel as a birthday present instead of her normal visit to the Golden Door Spa. There was a problem because she had to lower her blood sugar levels in order for the doctors to operate. I never saw Iris eat the proper meals so diligently. She made fruit and vegetable drinks with her juicer and steamed vegetables. Iris could do anything she put her mind to, which is why I thought it was crazy to slit her stomach from one end to the other and have the fat sucked away. If she took care of herself all year like she did before the surgery then she wouldn't have needed it at all. It was just easier to vacuum and peel the fat and years off her body.

Joaquin had only been on location for a few weeks when he called the office and asked about hiring an entertainment attorney. I presumed Vince Vaughn had made a case for his lawyer because he mentioned her name.

'Iris, we need to find an attorney for Joaquin.'

'He's just talking. He won't hire an attorney,' Iris said. She disliked managers and attorneys about equally. They both had a tendency to take clients and bring them to their agent friends at the bigger agencies.

'If we don't take control of this situation and he finds his own attorney we'll be left out in the cold,' I reiterated.

Iris raised her eyebrows and didn't speak. She lit a cigarette and stared out into the garden. 'You might be right. Who do you have in mind?'

'Someone new who needs the business. He works at the same law firm as Vince Vaughn's lawyer. He can be controlled.'

'All right. Let's call Joaquin together.' Iris reached for the phone and I dialed Joaquin's cell phone. Together, Iris and I convinced Joaquin to go with the lawyer we had chosen. If he had gone to a lawyer we didn't pick, we would have been kicked to the curb.

Iris headed to her adventure with the plastic surgeon's knife. She had booked herself into a place called the Hidden Gardens to recover. It was a well-staffed medical hotel. I was really thankful because I really didn't want to be a nurse. It would be bad enough when she finally came home.

She called me two nights before the surgery. 'I just had a Reuben sandwich with extra Thousand Island dressing, potato salad and a piece of cheesecake. If they are going to suck out the fat I may as well enjoy myself.'

'Nice,' I responded.

'I really want you to be there. Promise you'll come see me after the surgery. You know how much you mean to me. I don't have anyone else.'

'I'll be there, Iris,' I agreed, reluctantly.

As promised I showed up at the Hidden Gardens. I hated hospitals but this place looked like a $2,000-a-night suite at an exclusive resort. She had a huge bedroom, a sitting area, a table and chairs looking out into lovely gardens. The bed was dressed in the best of linens. Iris was sitting up in a chair sipping juice through a straw. She looked like someone had taken a blowtorch to her face. It was bright red and was oozing some sort of liquid. She was wrapped in gauze from below her chest to her privates. Tutankhamen had nothing on Iris.

'How do I look?' she asked, wincing in pain.

'Great . . . I guess. I really don't know how you're supposed to look.' If Frankenstein was the look she was going for then she had accomplished it.

'I lost ten pounds.' She smiled as she patted her stomach. The room smelled of antiseptic. That smell always made me nauseous.

'Do you need anything? Because with this traffic it will take me forty-five minutes to get back to the office. I'm sure you need to rest.'

'What's your hurry? I'm the boss.'

'It's not that, Iris. I have a good deal of work to do.'

'I'm telling you to stay. You can check the service from here.' She glared at me.

I was being held captive. I glanced at the phone and prayed that it would ring. She had a son who rarely called or visited. Her boyfriend Pete was a mysterious phantom that no one had ever met, which made the clients and me wonder if Iris had made him up. I needed to pray really hard for the phone to ring.

Josh Hartnett's TV series, *Cracker*, came out to great reviews and lousy ratings. By December I knew that the show would barely make it into the New Year as the ratings kept slipping lower. Josh received good notices. When it was announced that Jamie Lee Curtis would be reprising her role in the twentieth anniversary of *Halloween*, I read the script. I hate horror films but this one seemed really good for Josh. He could definitely play Jamie's son. I called the casting director and pitched Josh. He set up a meeting for him with the producers. They fell in love with him. The movie would start filming shortly after Josh finished *Cracker*. Now all that was left to do was tell Iris.

'What the hell is wrong with you?' Iris bellowed, waving her cigarette at me.

'This is with Jamie Lee Curtis, Iris.'

'Do you have an obsession with horror films?'

'It's not my obsession, Iris. It's the public's obsession,' I retorted.

'I never did horror films and I'm not going to start now.'

'You never handled young adults either,' I snapped back.

'I hope you know what your doing, mister.' Iris lit another cigarette.

'Miramax certainly does because they want to do a three-picture deal with him. He'll be tied up to us for the next three films no matter what happens.'

Iris raised her eyebrows and inhaled her cigarette like she'd just had the best sex of her life. 'Do it!' she said.

We ended up with four pictures from Miramax because they decided to push the shooting schedule of teen horror movie *The Faculty* to accommodate Josh. We took Josh to Joaquin's publicist and lawyer before he even shot a single bit of footage. We needed to protect our interests and take control of the situation. Josh was potentially more lucrative than Joaquin because he had the looks of a classic leading man. In the new Hollywood, it was necessary to protect and guard our clients from the onslaught of overeager college graduates who needed to make points in order to gain the respect of their colleagues in the big agencies. Even I received phone calls at home and was given messages by casting directors that the big agencies would like to hire me. What they really wanted was for me to leave Iris and bring the high profile clients with me. As much as I didn't appreciate how Iris treated me, I wasn't cut out to be a member of the boys' club. The one reason why Iris and I worked so well together was because most of the time she left me alone to do my thing with the clients. She never told me that I couldn't take on a client. She really didn't care who I handled as long as the agency made money. The big agencies required a whole team of agents to approve new clients.

My personal life continued to be non existent and even the one-night stands from bars were becoming a dangerous proposition. People were forgetting about AIDS and I found myself lecturing about why we needed to use condoms. I was mystified myself because there wasn't a cure and after my volunteer work with AIDS patients, there was no way I was going to have unsafe sex.

One night I had gone out to a bar with a friend and met a really nice guy. We talked for hours and when my friend wanted to leave, the man volunteered to take me home. I thought he was really nice.

When he dropped me off I thanked him and suggested that we exchange numbers. Of course neither one of us had paper or a pen. He walked with me up to my apartment. I really wasn't concerned. I opened the door to my apartment and grabbed a notepad and pen from my desk. By then he was already inside. He closed the door and locked it.

'Strip,' he said.

'Excuse me?' I said.

'You will refer to me as "sir" or "master".'

'Like hell I will. Get out!' I walked towards the door.

He grabbed my arm and twisted it behind my back so hard I thought he was going to break it. I struggled to get free but he was really hurting me.

'Let go, you asshole.'

'I told you to call me "sir" or "master".' He slapped my face and he shoved me to the floor. He took off his shirt. I had no idea in the bar how muscular this guy was. He had on a long-sleeved dress shirt and his muscles didn't show. I was in deep trouble.

'Where's your bed, slave?'

'In there.' I pointed. It wasn't like I lived in the Hearst Castle.

'I thought I told you to call me "sir" or "master".' He yanked me up from the floor and pulled off my shirt. 'If you won't take off your clothes then I'll do it for you.' He dragged me into the bedroom and pushed me face-down onto the bed. He yanked off my pants. 'Now are you going to call me "master"?'

I didn't know what to do. But I wanted this bastard out of my apartment. He didn't know about the entrance to the apartment off the kitchen.

'Yes, sir. Could your slave get you a beer?'

'That's what I like. You know who your master is now. Get me that beer, slave.'

I walked out of the bedroom and into the kitchen and was out the door and down the steps, naked, before he could figure it out that I was gone. I rapped on my neighbors' door. He took one look at me and grabbed a blanket from his couch. I explained what happened and banged on my apartment door until the man finally opened it.

'Get out!' I said.

'I was just role-playing.' He smiled.

My neighbor stood next to me with his phone in hand. 'Leave or we'll call the police,' I said.

'OK. Chill out. I guess you're not into rough sex,' he said.

'I never said I was. Maybe you should ask before you pull this shit with the next guy you meet.'

I had narrowly escaped a horrible experience. I would never take anyone home from a bar again. Nor would I go home with them. This was a definite wake-up call. I wondered what it was about me had made this man think that I wanted to role-play being raped. I wondered if I had somehow sent the wrong signals. The hook-up game was becoming dangerous. My unwillingness to become close to anyone since Richard was not such a wise idea any more. I knew that I needed to start to trust relationships again, but trust was not something that came easy in Hollywood. Hollywood was about pretending and everyone seemed to do it to get what they wanted. There was something deep inside of me that didn't feel I deserved love. Somewhere in the middle of all the chaos I really needed to start to look at where my life was headed. Every time I looked at Iris, I caught a glimpse into what Hollywood had done to her.

Kirsten's manager decided to show his client just how useful he could be by cutting the Iris Burton Agency's commissions. He informed me of his plan first in order to gauge how Iris would react. How the hell did he think Iris would react? I'm sure he wouldn't have liked it if his commissions were cut. Iris would flip out and I'd have to calm her down and convince her to accept the deal. We needed Kirsten. One of the agents that was after Kirsten must have suggested this because they thought Iris would refuse the deal. Iris probably would have, but I wasn't about to let that happen. The manager said that unless we took their deal Kirsten would go to a bigger agency that would. It was highway robbery and he knew it. I knew the big agencies sometimes dropped commissions in order to entice a certain client into leaving their current agent. I had even heard that one agency took no commissions for a year just to prove to a client that they could do a better job. It was all about having high-profile actors on the roster. It was also about stealing from rival agencies. The Iris Burton Agency was back on top again but that left us open for attack. I was left with the unpleasant task of telling Iris.

'"I'll never leave you, Iris,"' Iris said with a sneer. 'You sat at the table with us when we celebrated Kirsten booking *Interview with the Vampire*. Boy, how people forget. You know it's the fucking manager behind this. I *hate* fucking managers! Now you see why I hate them,' Iris howled.

I wouldn't let her even answer the phone until I had calmed her down or she'd blow the whole thing.

'Come on, Iris, what's the big deal? Kirsten is never going to make a million dollars and we only have to cut commissions after she makes one million. We have nothing to worry about. It's going to be pretty tough for her to make a million dollars with what she's making per picture.'

'Don't patronize me. They wouldn't pull this shit with

a big agency. If this gets out then everybody will want me to cut commissions. That son of a bitch. I told you I hate managers.'

'Iris, what do we have to lose by playing along with them? If we don't agree they will leave and we'll lose everything.'

'I know you're right but I don't like how that asshole has backed us into a corner.'

Iris signed the paper that Kirsten's accountant had drawn up and threw it at me as she left the office. 'Fax it to the fuck.'

CHAPTER 19

'Love having become a god, becomes a demon.'

C.S. Lewis

Iris was on again with Pete. I swore she made up the stories about him. She always said that he was coming to some event or another but he never showed up and she would have some feeble excuse. Iris' laments to Pete would take up hours at a dinner and on the phone. Pete had a Svengali-like hold over Iris that was unbelievable. She didn't drop anything for anybody but if her private line lit up then she lit up too. They would go months without contact and she would curse him and their relationship but when he called she was a different woman. Iris used to stalk Pete when she didn't hear from him. She lured me to dinner a couple of times and I ended up driving to his various haunts until 2 a.m. I wasn't the only one that Iris took on her searches for Pete. I had clients and managers tell me about being dragged on one of Iris' midnight runs.

'I know he's in there fucking that doctor's wife.' She stared intently at the door to the townhouse in Hollywood. 'That's his fucking car.' She burst into sobs.

'Maybe it's not his car, Iris. Maybe he sold it.' I said.

'It's his car. I saw him walk into the house last night.' She hit the steering wheel of her black Mercedes. 'Why was I cursed to love this man?' she sobbed.

'Iris, come on.' I patted her arm. 'He's not worth it.' What do you say to someone who has abducted you and forced you to stalk her boyfriend who you are not sure even exists?

'I gave up everything for him and after all the humiliations I thought we would spend our twilight years together. He said we would buy an RV and travel the country.'

There was no way that Iris Burton was going to travel the country in an RV. She could barely handle a three-star hotel let alone life on the road. Iris liked spas, massages, furs, Prada and luxury. She could pretend that she could live in an RV to anyone but me. I wanted to laugh. What would she do with her furs? I stared at the front door to the townhouse and wondered how long Iris would last until she grew bored.

'Don't ever leave me, Chris. You're the only loyal man I know.' She grabbed my hand and held it.

My God, I was doomed. She'd stalk me until one of us died, just like she did with Pete. I knew everything about him, perhaps too much. Pete was a trumpet player. He and his brother had recorded with Frank Sinatra and played Vegas in the fifties and sixties when nightclub acts were big. That's how they met. Her first and only husband, Sid Miller, had worked with singers arranging their musical numbers. He partnered Donald O'Connor in an act and also worked with Judy Garland and Marilyn Monroe. Iris met him through Donald O'Connor while she was filming *The Ten Commandments* on the Paramount lot.

When Iris met Sid she was fast approaching the age when dancers and actresses who hadn't made it needed to find a wealthy husband. Sid Miller fitted the bill. He was a thirty-nine-year-old wealthy bachelor. Iris married him and became a Hollywood wife. She joined the country club and played golf. She threw lavish parties at their house in the Hollywood Hills, which had once belonged to a silent film star. The old screening room was where she had located her first office. I worked there the first three years I knew Iris. There was still a hole cut in the wall where the projector had once been located. There was also a hole in Iris' birth control, as she became pregnant not long after they were married. This did not please her husband. According to Iris he never wanted to have a child so she made it happen by putting a hole in the birth control device. Even with her son, Iris was still required to travel with her husband to Vegas and New York.

In Vegas Iris met Pete. He was recently divorced from a very wealthy heiress. Iris and Pete began what she referred to as a 'backstreet romance', Iris fell head over heels in love. When Sid took her out to the San Fernando Valley with the intention of buying her an estate, Iris had other ideas and right in front of the real estate agent she told Sid she wanted a divorce. When she told Pete she thought he'd be thrilled. Iris had never been more in love. Her divorce dragged on for years and when Pete realized that Iris wasn't going to be a wealthy divorcee, he ran off and married Betty Hutton. Ironically Betty Hutton had once been the star of the Paramount lot. Iris arrived at Paramount just as Betty Hutton was let go from her long-term contract.

'He left me flat and went off with Annie Get Your Gun,' Iris said repeatedly.

But even after he married Betty Hutton, Iris and Pete continued their affair. When Betty went broke and the government chased after her and Pete for the back taxes, Pete split from the marriage. Iris thought that Pete would finally marry her, but she didn't plan on Edie Adams. Edie's husband Ernie Kovacs had just died and left her a very wealthy widow. Pete romanced Edie, who was a working actress, and she paid off his huge tax bill when they were married. Iris was once again left holding the bag. She continued to see Pete on the side while he was married to Edie, just as she had when he was with Betty Hutton.

Once Edie was running low on money Pete was ready to skip out again, but before he could he had a heart attack. Edie frequently called Iris, looking for Pete. Betty even hid in the bushes outside Iris' house one night and jumped out waving a gun at her.

'Betty, you haven't done *Annie Get Your Gun* in years. Put it away. He's not worth it,' Iris said.

Iris loved to tell me that story. I laughed every time.

After a year of silence the private line was ringing again and Iris rushed to answer it. They would usually talk for three- to four-hour stretches, which I loved because I could get my work done. Depending on how the call went Iris would sneak off. She wouldn't even call on her car phone to check in. When she returned from one of her meetings with Pete she would look like a blushing bride. It was usually close to dusk when he called. One day she came back to the office with her hair all wind blown and a few leaves dangled from it. She was all disheveled. She walked funny and carried one of her boots. I looked down at her feet. The other boot was stuck on the wrong foot.

'Honey it was awful!' Iris was breathing heavily as she dragged herself across the room and lowered herself into the chair across from me.

'What happened?'

Her shirt was untucked and her pants were unbuttoned. 'Oh my God, I need some water.' I ran into the house and grabbed a bottle of water. She gulped it down and slowly stopped hyperventilating.

211

'Pete and I were up at the dog park. He was walking his dog so we agreed to meet there. He was getting frisky with me.' She blushed. 'The sun was going down and then my pants were going down. I took off my boots. Honey, the park police showed up! I pulled up my pants and was trying to get my boots back on but in the rush I grabbed the wrong boot. By the time I realized what I had done my foot wouldn't go any further down. The fucking boot was stuck on the wrong foot. I went limping off half undressed. I didn't want to be caught in a compromising position.'

I started laughing hysterically.

'What's so funny? I could have been arrested. I can see the *Variety* headline: AGENT FOUND INDECENT WITH PANTS DOWN IN PARK. You have no idea how hard it was to drive the car.'

Soon we were both hysterically laughing. With Pete back, there would be more rendezvous and more tearful three-hour-long phone calls when they broke up. I might even end up meeting him. Pete was right up there with Santa Claus and the Easter Bunny.

It was announced that Sofia Coppola was directing her first feature film. The movie was based on a book called *The Virgin Suicides*. I managed to get a copy of the script from a friend. When I finished reading it, I was determined that Kirsten Dunst would play the role of Lux. I had a huge argument with Kirsten's manager over the role. He thought that it was too mature a part for her. I disagreed and said it was exactly what she needed. I wasn't about to let this one go by the wayside. I hadn't fought hard enough for other projects, but this script was too good. Iris was in Hawaii so I decided to go over the manager's head and call Kirsten's mom. I hadn't played that card since the days of *Interview with the Vampire*. It did the trick because Kirsten's manager called and told me to set up the meeting. Sofia was heading to Toronto to go location scouting, so it was arranged that she would meet Kirsten there as she was currently on location filming *Dick*.

I brought up Josh Hartnett to Sofia's casting director and she was interested in meeting with him. I called Josh and convinced him to take the meeting. He hadn't even read the script. He flew to New York from Texas were he was filming. Kirsten's meeting with Sofia went well. They offered her the part but they had no money. Kirsten's manager went ballistic on me and hung up the phone saying that they would not do the project unless there was more money. I was backed into a corner. The only thing left to do was for them to come up with more money; Kirsten's manager wouldn't budge.

Josh had an offer by the week's end. There wasn't anything that could be done about him getting more money. He didn't even have a film out in the theatres yet. Sofia Coppola apparently donated her salary to Kirsten because she wanted her so badly. Her manager was appeased but when I told him that Josh had booked the movie he flipped out again.

'He'd better keep his zipper up around my Kirsten,' he said and hung up the phone on me. It was always difficult to have two clients on the same movie. Kirsten's manager didn't even know Josh. Why would he presume that he would try and sleep with Kirsten? She was a minor.

With the announcement that both Kirsten and Josh had landed the two leads in *The Virgin Suicides*, the sharks started to circle. Other agents made phone calls to Josh while he was on location filming *The Faculty*.

Kirsten's manager was being called, and she and her mother had been approached. They all told me what was happening. It put me in an awkward position because if I said anything to Iris her paranoia would kick in and she would think I was somehow involved in some plot to steal the clients. She wouldn't take the news well anyway. They were warning me of what I knew only too well. Whether Iris wanted to accept it or not, the big agencies provided the perks that actors loved. They were like car dealers who threw in free stereo systems, spoke wheels and unlimited oil changes. These agencies only wanted celebrity clients so they would go to any length to get them. Tickets to sold-out Broadway plays, tables at exclusive restaurants and meeting with A-list directors were the lollipops that were dangled in front of these actors. Iris had a track record and had guided a large percentage of young Hollywood to great success but that didn't matter in the world of the new super agencies. What Iris did with the clients was learned from fifty years in the business. Iris may not have had the best bedside manner but she did know what she was doing. She believed in finding the right project that meant a good script, great director and the right studio. The new agencies promised nonstop work. But for the most part it was crap work. Once in a while they were lucky but they didn't guide careers, they ruined them. Iris wouldn't throw people into projects she didn't believe in. She was from the old school. She wasn't about to change, which I respected, but how do you explain all that to a bunch of kids who only saw their other actor friends being lavished with luxury? We were headed for shark-infested waters, that much was clear, and I didn't know what to do about it except sit back and let it unfold. Iris was sitting in Hawaii enjoying the latest of her carefree vacations. The business was changing and I feared Iris wasn't going to change with it.

When Iris returned home I decided to have a talk with her about selling the agency. She had certainly made it clear she wasn't going to make me a partner. I just wanted a gracious way out so that we could remain friends. The last thing I wanted to do was to hurt Iris.

'Iris, we need to talk.' I went into the kitchen where she was running vegetables through her juicer.

'What about?' She fed a carrot into the grinder.

'We have a problem,' I said as she shoved in an apple. The juicer made an annoying whiny sound and then spit out the pulp and seeds.

'Agents have been calling Josh down in Austin.'

Iris didn't respond. She just pushed a stalk of celery through the grinder. 'Yes. What else?' She picked up another carrot and forced it in. The machine whined and spat out some more skins. She had this dazed, almost demonic look on her face, similar to Jack Nicholson in *The Shining*.

'They're after Kirsten too.'

'Which motherfucker is trying to steal from me? I want names.'

'Does it matter who they are? We are sitting ducks, Iris. Those agencies have offices all over the world and more staff than the President of the United States. They prey on these actors. They find out their weaknesses and they lure them away,' I replied.

Iris just kept grinding her juice. Then she suddenly flipped off the machine with a carrot still half out of the machine.

'Iris, it was bound to happen.'

'I had agreements with those motherfuckers that they wouldn't touch my clients.'

'Well, Iris, the people you had agreements with have long since retired. It's a new town.'

'Don't try to tell me the game.'

'Hey, I'm just letting you know that we are on shaky ground. If you want my opinion you should sell to Endeavor. They're new and they have a shortage of actors. They have writers and directors but not many actors. You said you wanted to retire.'

'Are we back to this again? Have you been approached?'

'For Christ's sake, Iris, don't get paranoid! I couldn't give a shit about working in another agency. If I were plotting to overthrow you I certainly wouldn't fucking tell you what I was doing. I would walk off like a thief in the night with the Rolodex, like everyone else in this fucking town.'

'I will not sell this fucking agency! Do you understand?' She flipped the juicer back on and shoved a celery stalk in and watched as it was devoured. She didn't look at me. I had been dismissed. She could ignore me but that wasn't about to change the inevitable. She needed to sell now while she still had something to sell.

Joaquin and Iris' decision not to do *Boogie Nights* came back to haunt them. When the movie came out Mark Wahlberg was the talk of the town. The producers of *The Yards* offered Mark the role of Willie Gutierrez, opposite Joaquin. A week later I received a phone call from Joaquin telling me that the director, James Gray, had called him and asked him if he spoke Spanish fluently. Since there are no lines in Spanish in *The Yards* I was immediately suspicious. The next call Joaquin received from the director was to ask him how he felt about the Willie Gutierrez role. The director thought it would be more challenging if Joaquin played that role instead of playing Leo Handler.

I smelled a power game. My instincts were totally right as Miramax retracted the offer for Joaquin to play Leo Handler and offered him the role of Gutierrez. Mark Wahlberg's agent showed him what they could do. They flexed their muscles and sent an overt message to the agency and Joaquin. They had the power because they had a certified box office star. The power in Hollywood was all in the weekend box office. Our hands were tied. We either accepted the offer or we were out in the cold. Mark Wahlberg's agency offered up their clients Charlize Theron and James Caan. Joaquin had no choice but to accept the other role. Iris needed to merge now more than ever. They were circling from all sides.

'Those fucking bastards.' She slammed open my office door. 'Those miserable cocksuckers. They're trying to steal Joaquin. I'm not stupid. Aren't they the same agents that are after Josh?'

'They're not the only ones, Iris.'

'Is that supposed to make me feel fucking better?' She kicked my garbage can, sending papers flying. 'Get my lawyer on the phone. Let him make some inquiries about selling this fucking rats' nest before it's too late. I can't believe these people are trying to steal what I've sweated over. How dare they? How fucking dare they!' She marched out of my office and slammed the door, sending the blinds crashing down.

The inquiries were made and Endeavor was very interested in the idea. The head of the agency took Iris to lunch. I saw a ray of light that this might be my way out. I had promised Iris I would help her for a couple of years after I returned and we were almost finished with our third year and still she didn't show signs of wanting to retire. Iris was pushing seventy and she still hadn't made me a partner. The talks hit a snag when Endeavor informed Iris that they wanted her to continue working at home. They wanted me to come into their offices and be the liaison between Iris and them. Apparently they had done their research and heard of Iris' legendary three-hour-long phone conversations. They didn't need her grandstanding at a staff meeting.

I was uncomfortable with the plan all the way around. I didn't want to work with Iris, I wanted out. Putting on a suit and tie and heading into an office on Wilshire Boulevard held no appeal to me. I just wanted to do my work with my clients and not be involved with Iris' health problems, her boyfriend, maid, gardener and son. Casting directors were constantly telling me of openings at other agencies and I did take several meetings, but the thought of meeting quotas and stealing clients from other agents just didn't appeal to me. If I couldn't meet my quotas then I'd be out in a second. Iris never really put overt pressure on me to bring in more commissions. These bigger agents demanded more and more deals. Was it best to put up with Iris and her diabetes-affected mood swings or move on?

Endeavor wanted a commitment from me of at least two years to help make the transition with the clients a smooth one. Iris really couldn't sell the agency because if she did all contracts were null and void. She stood to lose a good deal of money because we had a lot of clients on series. Iris knew that most of the clients had an allegiance to me since I dealt with them on a daily basis and they rarely, if ever, talked to her. She had never met or spoken to some clients that had been with us as long as three years!

Then I accidentally overheard Iris talking on the phone. She was talking to a manager right in front of me and then she excused herself and placed the phone on the chair. She was taking the call in the house. She usually called and told me to hang up the phone but she forgot, I was busy giving out appointments and didn't notice. My phones stopped ringing and since Iris spoke so loudly I heard what she said.

'Do you know who is holding up the deal with Endeavor?' Iris hissed. 'Chris! He wants to be paid the same salary as other agents. He doesn't want to be an assistant or to be called a secretary. Who the fuck does he think he is?'

I heard the voice on the other line say, 'Iris, he runs your entire company. Everyone knows that. He does the deals. Finds the clients. Gives out the appointments. Frankly I don't know how he does it all so well. He doesn't even have an assistant.'

'This is the Iris Burton Agency! It's my fucking name on the door. I'm killing this fucking deal with Endeavor!'

Iris had made my decision for me. I knew at that moment that I had to find a way out of this situation with her. I had been more than loyal to her. I went out of my way to be nice and nothing could break through that tough shell that mistrusted everyone. I had given her no cause to not to trust me. I simply wanted what she had promised me. I realized that I had no easy escape. I had to find a way out on my own.

Iris damaged herself badly by pulling out of the deal with Endeavor. She had announced the merger to all the clients before she had finished the deal. She had talked incessantly about all the benefits the clients would have. When she pulled out it ruffled a lot of feathers because she had made the move seem so desirable. She had held out the lollipops of the directors, writers, and producers who were represented by Endeavor. She had told everyone that they would be packaged into projects.

When she pulled the plug on the deal she had nowhere to go and no one she could blame. The clients were even more tempted than ever to leave now that they knew about the benefits of a bigger agency. We were sitting ducks and I just sat back and waited to see who would be the first to leave.

Iris made further problems by backing out of a promise. She and Kirsten's manager had agreed to throw Kirsten a sweet sixteen party. Since Kirsten had been up in Toronto filming for most of the year and would be there on her birthday, her mother decided to have the party in Toronto. When Kirsten's manager called to go over the details with Iris, she said that she had changed her mind. She hung up the phone and turned and gave me a vile look.

'Why the fuck should I pay for her birthday party? They shafted me out of 3 per cent of my commission.'

'Iris, you haven't given up a dime. She hasn't even come close to making the amount of money that entitles them to drop the commission.'

'I don't care. It's the idea that they tried to screw me. I don't give a shit about her birthday party. I'm not flying up there. I'm not sending a gift. I don't give a damn.'

'Iris, if she was with a bigger agency they'd find a sponsor for the party and pay for the rest themselves.'

'I do my job for her and if she's not happy then let her go to a big fucking agency. I don't want to hear another word about it.' She trudged out of the room. There was no reasoning with Iris once she'd made a decision. She was furious. I knew that they were getting ready to leave the agency.

Iris was becoming more erratic and difficult to deal with by the day. I went to lunch one day and when I came back to the office, she was already buzzing my phone non-stop. When I picked it up she screamed into the phone. 'Where the fuck have you been?'

'At lunch. I go to lunch everyday at this time,' I defended myself.

'You left without even checking to see if I was alive. I was lying here in a pool of blood.' She screamed so loud that I held the phone away from my ear.

'What are you talking about?'

'I rolled out of bed and banged my head on the nightstand. I was unconscious in a pool of blood and nobody even knew it. I could have been dead.' She sobbed into the phone.

I really didn't know what to say. Up to this point it had never been part of my job to go in and take Iris' pulse. I guessed from then on I would add that to my duties before I went to lunch. She screamed at me if I woke her up without a really good reason. I really had no idea what had gotten into her or why she had fallen out of bed. The agency was now becoming a nursing home.

I read in *Variety* that Brittany Murphy landed the role opposite Kirsten in *The Devil's Arithmetic*. Brittany was with ICM, and one of the top six agencies in town. Brittany was one of the casualties when I left Iris after River died. We had shepherded Brittany's career all the way to her career-making role in *Clueless*. She fired Iris shortly after the movie opened. Now she would be working with Kirsten Dunst. Brittany and Kirsten had once shared the same manager. I called Iris' attention to the article in *Variety*.

'You're so negative,' Iris snapped.

'Iris, ICM will be FedExing scripts and sending fruit and flowers to location. Maybe you should fly over and visit.'

'Are you fucking insane? What the fuck am I going to do in fucking Lithuania? I don't even know where it is. I can't even imagine what the hotels are like.'

'Maybe you should send flowers.'

'I'm not doing a damn thing.' She left the office as usual because she didn't want to hear what I was saying.

Iris didn't want to hear about emails or computers either. Hollywood was slow to embrace the computer age but when it started to take hold it was like a wildfire. Iris, of course, didn't want to spend the money for a computer so I was forced to buy a laptop and a printer so that I could do my work and keep us somewhat competitive. Iris could not have cared less what I did as long as it didn't cost her any money. She had no idea how much money was coming out of my pocket to keep the clients happy. I was constantly copying and delivering scripts. When I went to lunch with a client I picked up the check. When they had birthdays I would buy them a gift. It was the cost of doing business. Iris didn't see it that way. She taught me a big lesson by not catering to the clients. It was the small things that they noticed: a birthday card, lunch and a phone call. Clients needed to know that you cared. Iris didn't see it that way. She thought the client owed her.

Iris decided to go in for another tummy tuck. I was amazed considering the amount of pain she had been in after the first one. The recovery took months. I had to run around the house picking up phones because Iris needed constant help. She couldn't carry the groceries, take out the garbage or even tie her shoes. She was beyond miserable. Iris learned a hard lesson about liposuction. When they suck the fat away from one area you can gain it in other places especially if you don't change your eating habits. Iris was also freshening up her prior facelift with injections of fat cells into her wrinkles.

A month before the surgery she went in to have her blood-sugar levels checked. She called me from the car, sobbing hysterically into the phone.

'Iris, what's wrong?'

'My doctor just yelled at me because my blood sugar is so high. He said he won't let me have the surgery unless I can lower my blood-sugar levels.'

Iris hadn't exactly been following a diet for a diabetic. Midnight visits to Jewish delis for Reuben sandwiches, potato salad and cheesecake were not on any diabetic diet that I knew of. I had no idea what Iris ate when I left but I would always have some idea the next morning based upon how long she slept and how miserable she was. When Iris was good she was terrific. When she was bad it was a living hell being around her.

'I have to get this diabetes under control. I'm going to be good. You wait and see.'

While Iris was off having plastic surgery or taking her trips to Italy, Switzerland, Hawaii, Austria, Budapest, Israel, Prague, cruising the Mediterranean, Tahiti, New York, Las Vegas, or various spas I was handling the business and the 120 clients. It was actually a relief to have her out of town because then I didn't have to worry about her moods on top of everything else.

With so much responsibility it was no wonder that I woke up one morning at 2 a.m. with severe pains in my stomach area. I had never experienced pain on that level before. I thought it was gas or an appendicitis attack. The pain only seemed to get worse so I showed up at my doctor's office at lunch doubled over in pain. Iris was out of town again so I had to schedule tests early in the morning or at lunch. After a series of tests I had to be referred to a specialist. My blood pressure problems weren't enough. Now I had something else to add to it.

Joaquin finished *The Yards* and then I read the script for *Return to Paradise*. There was a great part in it for him of a man wrongly accused of selling drugs who gets a death sentence because he is in a foreign country. His friends fly back to try to help him. It was another situation where the script wasn't spectacular but the part Joaquin would play was outstanding. He needed flashy parts in order for Hollywood to take notice of him. The movie would star Vince Vaughn, which thrilled Joaquin because he had loved working with him on *Clay Pigeons*. They ended up on the cover of the *Vanity Fair* Hollywood issue, under the banner 'The Next Hot Wave'. Joaquin was finally on a roll.

All the activity finally generated interest from the studios and Joaquin was offered the film *8MM* to be directed by Joel Schumacher. The movie was going to star Nicolas Cage – an actor who really had the Midas touch at the box office. What Joaquin desperately needed was to be in a movie that would open big. The studios were interested in how much a movie grossed in the first weekend. It was not a script that I loved – the subject matter of snuff films wasn't exactly pleasant. Joaquin's character would be Nicolas Cage's guide into the seamy world of fetish films. Kirsten was also up for the movie at one point and then they cut the part because they were afraid to have someone underage in a film about pornographic movies. Joaquin was also just beginning to make money after twenty years in the business.

Josh Hartnett came back to LA after his back-to-back movies and went right into Warren Beatty's new picture *Town and Country*. Josh had landed his fourth major movie without one film released in the theatres. Thanks to his publicist the industry was already talking about him. It was solely based on the hype of what was coming.

Kirsten went off to Lithuania in late September. Iris did not go. She didn't want to go and no amount of persuasion could make her. I felt something bad was about to happen which is why I kept trying to get Iris to spend some time with Kirsten and her mom. Because of her manager we really had very little contact with them except at mandatory functions. Another major lesson in being an agent is to keep contact with your clients. That check-in phone call or trip to a location is really important. Kirsten's manager informed me that Brittany Murphy's agency had sent Kirsten a fruit basket and a bouquet of flowers. They were also sending her scripts. They were trying to show Kirsten and her mom how much better they were than the Iris Burton Agency. Kirsten and her mom really had nothing to do in Lithuania so they hung out with Brittany Murphy and her mother. We were in deep trouble. Agencies operate in the same way that cults do. They use the existing members to recruit.

'Fuck that.' Iris slammed her frying pan on the stove.

'Iris, you didn't pay for the sweet sixteen party. You didn't go up there to visit her. You haven't seen them in a long time.'

'Don't tell me how to run my business! Don't you dare send anything and say that it's from this agency.' She banged the vegetable steamer on another one of the burners.

'Iris –'

She cut me off. 'Fucking fruit baskets. They should be sending me fruit baskets for all I've done for them.'

*   *   *

Sure enough, I received a phone call on Thanksgiving weekend at home and was told that Kirsten would be leaving the agency. They wanted to let me know that it had nothing to do with me and that they appreciated everything that I had done for Kirsten, but that they really didn't want anything to do with the Iris Burton Agency. They had seen what a big agency could do. The manager was giving me fair warning for what I would be in for. An hour later I received the call from Iris.

'Those miserable ingrates. I hate fucking managers.'

There would be no living with Iris now. I was thankful that I would soon have my two-week holiday break. One client down, two more to go. This was going to be a huge financial blow to Iris as Kirsten's star was on the rise. Iris would still have been making huge sums of money on Kirsten if the merger had gone through. The Iris Burton Agency had just been successfully attacked. With Kirsten's defection the rest of the agencies would come at our star clients hard. The first blow had been struck, and now the vultures were circling. There was no turning back now. It was only a matter of time before the whole thing would crumble.

CHAPTER 20

'It's not a question of God "sending" us to Hell. In each
of us there is something growing up which will of itself be
Hell unless it is nipped in the bud. This matter is serious:
let us put ourselves in his hands at once – this very day,
this hour.'

C.S. Lewis

'Go to lunch now!' Iris barked into the phone.

'Why? It's only 11.30?'

'Just go to lunch! Forward the phones to the service,'
she bellowed into the phone and hung up.

The skies had poured buckets of rain on us all morning
and had not stopped. I was suspicious because Iris never
wanted the phones forwarded to the service if one of
us was in the office. In all the years I'd known Iris, she
had never demanded that I go to lunch. If anything she
sabotaged my lunch break so that I never left on time.
Hollywood went to lunch between 1 p.m. and 2 p.m., so
it was pretty safe for me to go then because I wouldn't
worry that Iris might piss off a client or a casting
director. Iris wanted to answer the phone to assert that
she was still around but the problems developed because
she really didn't want to be bothered with work. She'd
forget to tell me that a casting director had called back
or that a client had confirmed an audition. If her son
or Pete called, the office might just as well have been
closed to anyone else. I had trained the clients not to

227

call between 1 and 2 and the ones that hadn't listened never called again if they had a good dose of Iris. She either talked your ear off or was gruff and rude. There was no middle ground with Iris. No one that knew her wanted to get her on the phone unless they had time to kill. Iris always complained to me when I returned from lunch that there had been a bunch of hang-ups. I knew the hang-ups were people who had forgotten what time it was. Casting directors, producers, directors, and clients hung up when they heard Iris' distinctive voice. They would call back and continue to hang up until they got me. The only way I knew this was because they told me. There was definitely something suspicious about her sending me to lunch. Maybe she was secretly interviewing people for my job. That was fine with me. Just like everyone else I never knew where I stood with Iris. It was either 'honey', 'sweetie', or 'Chris, what the fuck are you doing?' Either way, rather than face Iris' wrath I took an early lunch.

First though, I needed to go in the garage to retrieve my umbrella. Iris hated wet umbrellas in the office. I shot out into the rain and opened the garage door, retrieving my umbrella from inside. All at once I heard the garage door closing behind me. It happened so quickly that I couldn't get out before it closed, locked. I was trapped. There were no windows or other likely escape hatches. It had been a carport that was illegally turned into a garage. I tried lifting the door but it wouldn't budge. I pounded on the door and screamed out Iris' name for about ten minutes. The rain drowned out my voice. She was never going to hear me. I sat down frustrated on the trunk of Iris' gold Mercedes convertible. I wondered how long it would take for her to realize that I was missing.

Shit! I paced back and forth across the garage. I wondered if the car was unlocked. I went around to the driver's side door. It was open so I pulled the door handle and sat down in the car. I may as well be comfortable. Twenty minutes later, I stared at the dashboard and then realized that Iris had a car phone. I picked up the phone but it didn't work. The car had to be running for it to function. Then I remembered that Iris sometimes left the keys under the seat. I groped around and sure enough I felt the keys. I turned on the ignition. The lights on the phone lit up. I dialed the office line and then immediately hung up, realizing that I had forwarded to the service. I dialed one of the other lines that didn't go to the service. The phone rang and rang. I held the phone and listened to it ring for ten minutes. What the hell was she doing that she wouldn't pick up the phone?

I waited a few minutes and then dialed again: the same thing. I wondered if Iris had fallen in the shower or had rolled out of bed again and was lying in a pool of blood. I could see the headlines in *Variety*. Legendary agent Iris Burton found dead in a pool of blood, killed by her associate Chris Snyder, who apparently then committed suicide in Burton's gold Mercedes. It probably wasn't wise to leave the car running that long in a closed garage. I turned off the ignition, waited ten minutes and then tried the private phone. Somebody finally picked up but did not speak. I only heard the sounds of a shower running. I hung up and tried another line. The same thing happened but Iris yelled out, 'Pick up the fucking phone, Pete!' I could hear the sound of the shower.

'It's your phone, Iris.' It was a man's voice.

I hung up the phone and dialed again. I let it ring a few minutes.

'What!' Iris screamed into the phone.

'I'm locked in your fucking garage is what, Iris!' I screamed back.

'How the fuck did you do that? Pete, Chris is locked in the garage,' she whispered.

'I don't know, Iris, I thought I'd try to be Houdini today and see if I could escape from a locked garage. Tomorrow I think I'll try locking myself in chains. Just get me out of here.' I hung up the phone.

I waited but the door didn't open. I started the car again and dialed the house.

'Honey, the power just went out. Pete, how are we going to get him out of there?'

'Maybe we should call the fire department?' Pete said.

I looked up to the heavens, praying to God to let me out of this hell and that's when I saw the red cord dangling from the ceiling. How had I missed it before? I bet that released the garage door from the mechanism that opened the door. I yanked the red cord and I was able to lift the garage door right up.

'How the fuck are we going to get him out, Pete?' Iris was standing in the kitchen holding a towel in front of her. A man with grey hair was standing next to her wrapped in a towel. They were too busy arguing to see me. I just walked down the driveway to my car. I certainly wasn't going to go and introduce myself to the famous Phantom Pete when he was naked. The fact that I had actually had a Pete sighting after all these years was miraculous. If Pete existed maybe Santa Claus and the Easter Bunny did too.

Joaquin went off to Thailand to film *Return to Paradise*. Liv joined him for part of the trip. When they returned to Los Angeles they rented a house high in the Hollywood Hills off Nicholas Canyon. Iris and I were invited to lunch over the weekend because Heart Phoenix was in town with her daughter, Liberty, and Liberty's new baby. He was almost a year old and his name was Rio. They had named him after River. It was a windy February day and we had been blasted with driving rainstorms all week. Iris asked me to drive because she didn't want to have her Mercedes splattered with mud. The roads were narrow and the remnants of mudslides were evident as we drove further up into the hills. There were streams of water coming down the roads.

'Where the fuck is this place?' Iris bitched.

'I've no idea. I'm just reading the directions.'

'Keep your eyes on the road. I should have cancelled. I could be killed.'

The wind grew stronger and the road became narrower the further up we went. I wished I had a Range Rover or a pickup truck instead of my Ford Escort. Banks of mud drifted into the road like snow as I pushed onwards up the mountain. The further up we went the fewer houses there were.

I still felt awkward in Mrs Phoenix's presence. I wished Iris had cancelled. It was so uncomfortable to pretend that nothing had happened between all of us. I felt as if everybody had taken part in the same nightmare but only I remembered what happened. The rest of the group had some how managed to erase all traces of the nightmare from their thoughts. I was sure that they all remembered but they each held on to their own part of the nightmare and refused to share it. The fact that Rain and Joaquin were in town celebrating their birthdays the night River died would haunt them forever. The same night, Mrs Phoenix was on a flight headed out to Los Angeles to deal with issues that should have been addressed a year before. Iris never wanted to listen to me or any of the others who had tried to warn us. I wished I had spoken out sooner and louder. I wrestled with this all the time. But I still didn't know if certain things were just predestined and that River's death wasn't the catalyst that woke up a good many people. I changed my whole life because of River's death. I would have never left the States to live in a foreign country. I guess I could look at River's death as a tragedy or I could find the good in it. I tried to find the good in it everyday because finding the bad really hadn't netted me anything.

It would have helped immeasurably if the participants of the tragedy shared with each other. The fact that River's name went unspoken by all of us was the true sin of the tragedy. The mere mention of River created awkwardness. It's tough to explain but I guess pretending that someone didn't exist was a good deal easier than taking blame.

A lot of my guilt had to do with responsibility, and as I worked with new clients I wondered how responsible I was for them. I really had to find a gauge to work with the new clients so that I wouldn't feel guilty every time one of them went down the wrong path. I was still learning about my responsibility to clients and I had several that I was concerned about, including Joaquin. His behavior was very erratic at times. I really had a hard time understanding him, although I cut him a good deal of slack because of what happened to River. But he was stubborn when it came to his behavior and who he let into his life. I don't think Joaquin ever let anyone in. He kept everyone out so that it seemed like there was a thousand miles between his feelings and the person he was with. Similar to my family, he was here on earth but he wasn't living. He didn't enjoy life and he certainly didn't enjoy a profession that gave such amazing creativity and freedom. He seemed to hate acting and everything that it embodied, yet I watched him time and again pour out his raw emotion up on the screen. He was like a big gaping wound that just oozed pain. I hadn't once seen him appear happy on screen or in real life. He might laugh at a joke and smile but there was always something that he held back. I think it was the horror of what his life had been. It made me squirm sometimes just to be in his presence because I never knew how I would be greeted. At least with Iris the pendulum only swung to one extreme or the other and once I had a handle on the mood of the day I could cope with her. With Joaquin you never knew what would happen and that was part of the allure. The caretaker in me couldn't help but be a magnet to his need. You wanted to pour as much love as you could in his direction and hope that he would heal. With River we could chalk a good deal of the blame on the irresponsibility of youth. We had all done stupid things when we were younger because we feel like we're invincible. With Joaquin he was way past youth and the signs he was exhibiting spelled disaster.

'Watch out!' Iris yelled as a huge bank of mud slid in the road. I swerved to avoid getting stuck. 'We should turn around,' she said.

'We're almost there,' I replied.

I looked over at Iris and wondered how much she thought of River. I'd watch her sometimes. She would just stare off in the garden with a forlorn look. River had been the crown jewel of her agency. He was what she had worked so hard for. River gave her respect and power. He was what made her different from all the other children's agencies. She had stars before but they were the stars of *Teen Beat* magazine that lasted until the issue hit the garbage bin. River was a certified Oscar-nominated star. River gave her an entree into a world that she had wanted to be part of her whole life. Iris had grown bitter after River's death. It was never the same, as much as I tried to rationalize that she was just having a bad day, week or month. It had started to stretch into 'Iris is having a bad year.' There was really nothing I could do about how she felt. Like Joaquin, she wasn't about to reveal how she felt to me or anyone else. I wonder if it was thoughts of what could have been that drove her so crazy. There had been rumors that River was leaving the agency shortly before his death. We never talked about River. It was always bleak on the anniversary of his death. The fact that it fell on Halloween made it hard to forget. It also was peculiar that Halloween is all about masks and disguises. River had taken his mask off and exposed who he was for the entire world on Halloween while the rest of us continued to wear ours.

'I had better things to do today besides have lunch way the fuck out here,' Iris said.

'Iris, we all have better things to do – this is business.'

'I'm sure they won't have anything that I like to eat. It's probably all vegan.'

'I'm sure it is. I know you'll be fine once we get there.'

'I'm diabetic. I need to eat at certain times.'

I knew that but I also knew that Iris didn't heed the doctor's warnings or the eating schedule that he told her she needed to be on, unless she wanted to make a scene. She clearly wanted attention today. I should have packed a lunch for her. I should have thought to bring her a snack and some water but it was only a twenty-minute ride.

It was difficult to have lunch with people when you had to avoid certain topics of conversation. It was even more difficult for me because I was the person that everyone came to and griped to about the other person. Iris would inevitably make sarcastic comments about everyone at the lunch when they were out of earshot. Those same people would make comments about Iris. No one would ever really say what they really wanted to say to each other. That would be too easy. I was left holding the bag, sympathizing with everyone. If we had all talked before River died, the pieces to the puzzle would have been put together before it was too late. Together we had all the pieces. Now we stood separately with our heads in the sand. I felt like I was in a bad horror picture and that ultimately I knew where it would all lead, but I was too afraid to say anything or drop my mask for fear that I would be ridiculed.

When we finally reached the house I knew why Joaquin had chosen it, the view was spectacular. The house was perched on its own mountaintop with nothing but spectacular views of hillsides, the city and the water-soaked skies. The sun broke through on occasion. The wind whipped up and we walked up to the house.

'He may as well have rented a fucking house on the moon,' Iris cracked.

'I didn't even know this place existed.'

'Leave it to Joaquin.' Iris shook her head.

In the end we had a pleasant afternoon with the Phoenix family. Iris still bitched all the way home that there wasn't enough food and that she didn't like what they did have. What could have been a dismal day turned out fine because I decided I wasn't going to let anyone bother me. Whatever problems existed between all of us were overshadowed by the fact that there was a new one-year-old baby stumbling around, just beginning to walk. It diffused a tense situation. Babies have a way of bringing hope. Children are unwritten tablets, and the optimism of the future is a powerful tool in diffusing the unpleasantness of the past. It helped me realize that there is a cycle to life and that we could have a clean tablet at any time just like a child if we choose to release the past. I looked at all the people that surrounded me on the mountaintop and realized that they all carried a past that they could not change into the future. That seemed to cloud what they did because they never tore out the old pages and started again. It was really easy to keep retracing the past with a pencil because it was safe, it was already written. Blank pages scared me, which is why I went back to Iris. She was safe. I had traced, sidestepped and long ago figured her out. I knew the map to the landmines. Forging ahead without Iris meant that I might step on some buried landmines and be maimed. I looked out across the Los Angeles basin and realized that there was a whole city of opportunities in front of me, but I had to be willing to take risks. I didn't really need to escape from Hollywood. I just needed to find a way to work within the structure of a city built on a major fault line. I needed to allow myself to be healthy and strong.

My body still rebelled, despite the trainer, yoga and blood pressure pills. I attacked the stress from every angle. The yoga somehow began to give me a strange sense of empowerment that I hadn't felt in a long time. I had switched prescriptions so many times that my medicine chest was beginning to look like the local pharmacy. So many of the pills prescribed for my blood pressure made me lethargic. I had to concentrate on moving each leg just to walk. I collapsed into child's pose, which is a resting position in yoga, so much that I really got the knack of just letting go of the burdens I carried all day. My new doctor was incredibly supportive, as was my acupuncturist. I felt safe enough in their offices that I could actually drop the mask enough to allow myself to feel. Not only was I crying in my yoga classes, I had begun to cry the entire time that the acupuncture needles were in me. It wasn't that the needles hurt at all, but they were releasing stress that I didn't realize was there.

The pains continued in my stomach. The doctors kept prescribing antibiotics for infections but none of the tests showed what was wrong. The stomach specialist finally ordered a colonoscopy. It was a good thing I had fought Iris to provide health insurance because my medical bills were headed into the $25,000 range.

There was no way to do it and go to work afterwards so I scheduled it for my lunch hour. I would have to take half the day off which really irritated Iris. She said I was a hypochondriac, which was funny coming from her. I had a friend drop me off at work. I would then walk the five blocks to Cedars Sinai hospital. I would have another friend pick me up at the hospital and drive me home.

When I arrived at the office, I knew that I was in trouble because Iris was sitting in my desk chair. The fact that she was up at 9 a.m. spelled trouble. That meant that she had had a bad night and would want to talk all day about whatever had made her unhappy. She flipped through my notebook of clients' appointments. I sat down across from her.

'It's over between me and Pete,' she sobbed.

'I'm sorry, Iris.'

'There's nothing left between us. He's got some other bitch. I haven't heard from him in two weeks. I'd just bought him $200 worth of vitamins. You know he has prostate problems.'

'I'm sorry.' How did Pete's prostate problems affect their relationship? I really didn't want to even ask.

'I'm alone. I'm all alone. Last night I went to Canters and I was a bad girl. I had a Reuben sandwich, French fries and a piece of cheesecake. I don't care if I die.' She sobbed.

I looked at my watch. I had two hours before my procedure. Did they have to pick this day to break up? I had fasted for several days and spent all last night on the toilet after drinking some hideous concoction that made me want to vomit. Just then one of the client's managers walked in. Iris continued to sob.

By the time two hours had gone by I'd accomplished not much of my work and Iris was still a basket case. But it became worse because she started to nod off. She had overdone the sugar. I was sure she hadn't had breakfast or taken her diabetes pills. I looked at the manager unsure what to do. She volunteered to take me to the hospital.

Iris' head popped up. 'I'm taking him to the hospital'

'I can walk, Iris.'

'I'm taking you and that's final.'

There was no sense arguing with her. I'd just have to let her take me. How much trouble could she possibly get in driving a few blocks?

We left the office with plenty of time to spare. The driveway was very narrow, which made it difficult to get in the passenger-side door. There was a row of hedges that went all the way down the driveway. Iris had a hard time backing up the car, which is why she usually left it at the very end of the driveway. She motioned for me to get into the car but there wasn't enough room and I didn't want to be accused of scratching the car.

'I'll wait down here,' I hollered to Iris.

'Yeah, yeah,' she said as she fumbled to get the key in the car door. Iris didn't look good. The midnight run to Canters hadn't done her any favors. I noticed one of the local papers lying on the driveway. It had been there for days and no one had picked it up. If I threw them out Iris would yell at me. If I put them on the table in the house Iris would yell at me. I just left the damn things in the driveway.

'How long are you going to let that paper lie there?' Iris glared at me before she stepped into the car.

The woman could not be pleased. I wondered what had brought about her latest break-up with Pete? I leaned over to pick up the paper. In the split second that it took for me to bend over I heard a loud explosion. I looked up and it took me a moment to realize that Iris' car was no longer in the driveway. Where the hell had she gone? Then I noticed the smoke coming out of the garage and the hole in the garage door. Holy shit! Iris had crashed her car through the garage. I ran up the driveway. When I reached the door smoke was pouring out of the garage. I stepped through the hole and saw that the tires were still spinning. I couldn't see Iris. I needed to turn the car off.

Shelves and shrubbery behind the garage had luckily stopped the car from going into the neighbors' backyard. When I opened the car door Iris was slumped over the steering wheel.

'Iris . . . Iris . . .' I shook her. Then I reached over and turned off the ignition. I hoped she hadn't had a heart attack. Suppose she was dead. I shook her again.

'Iris . . . Iris . . .' I didn't know what to do. Then she started to moan. Thank God she was alive.

'Huh? What?' She lifted her head. She looked stoned.

'Iris, are you hurt?'

'I don't understand.'

'Come on we have to get you out of here.' I guided her out of the car. At least she could walk. That was a good sign. I smelled gasoline and realized that the whole place could go up at any minute.

'Come on, Iris. Hurry.' I pulled her across the garage

and out of the hole in the door. I opened up the house and brought her into the living room. She still didn't know what happened. I grabbed my cell phone out of my bag and dialed her business manager. I explained the situation to her and then called one of our client's managers on the house phone and told them to talk to Iris until her business manger could show up. I also called the fire department. I needed to get to the hospital. I had fifteen minutes until I was due to report to the room for my procedure.

When I reached the hospital my side ached and my head throbbed. Iris called my cell phone right before I went into the procedure. She still didn't understand what had happened. I was going to be totally unconscious for the procedure. When the doctor arrived she smiled down at me as I lay on the gurney.

'Are you ready, Chris?'

'Please give me the needle and put me out.'

Three days later the test results showed that I had diverticulosis. The doctor said the condition is prevalent in the elderly. The stress was doing this to me. I knew it.

Liv Tyler had flown to London to do a movie. I found out from Joaquin's publicist that he was in London with her but sometime shortly after the trip, Joaquin and Liv broke up. Of course I had to hear about everything from his publicist. It was always the same, we were the last to find out anything.

While we waited for Josh Hartnett's movies to come out, he read for a part in *The Patriot*. He didn't get the film and we sat and waited for something else to come along. He ended up testing for a movie called *Here on Earth*. The studio was hot to get Josh on the buzz that had been generated. His screen test did not go so well though – he and the director did not see eye to eye. They were having a hard time finding the other male lead. Then an article ran in *Variety* that the studio and the director had a falling out. I called up to see if they would be interested in Josh for the other role. I had always liked the other role better. Josh took another meeting with the director and was off to Minnesota to film for the summer.

Halloween H20: 20 Years Later came out that summer and did incredible business at the box office. The industry took notice of Josh Hartnett. When *The Faculty* came out, Josh's manager was plagued by calls from other agents. At times I would rather have not known who was after Josh. It just put more pressure on me and quite honestly, I didn't need any more pressure.

Iris flew to New York for a screening of one of Joaquin's movies. She was having serious trouble with her health. Her sciatica was acting up and she was having trouble walking. She called five times a day to tell me how miserable she was. Hilary Duff's movie *Casper Meets Wendy* was also having a launch party but it was straight to video. I pleaded with Iris to stay in New York and go see the movie. She stayed after I talked the film company into picking up her room bill.

'You would think that she was the next Shirley Temple,' Iris said on the phone from New York.

'I told you I had a bad feeling about her, Iris.'

She's going to fire her manager because she doesn't feel that the manager got her enough press.'

'That's not her job, Iris,' I said.

'Tell that to Mrs Duff,' Iris said.

Now I'd really have to deal with Mrs Duff. This wouldn't last long – she was way too demanding. Within a few months we parted ways with the Duffs. I couldn't have been more relieved.

I continued my yoga and writing classes and took great pleasure in the fact that I was getting better at both. I was feeling a little more grounded. I noticed that certain yoga poses and certain writing exercises would bring me to tears. I was very emotional and raw. It could have been the fact that I had so much pressure on me. But I still felt aimless. I felt like there was something missing from my life. I had tried going to church. I had stopped hanging out at bars after the last incident with the crazy man. I felt very lonely at times. There was no one to turn to at the end of a difficult day. I found it hard to meet people because I was cooped up in the office all day. I had flirted with Iris' neighbor who was a retired teacher. We went to a couple of movies, had lunch a few times and had several sexual encounters. Then we agreed, because of the proximity, it might be best to stop before things went too far.

Mentally I was becoming stronger with regard to dealing with Iris. I really put my foot down about going to dinner with her or seeing her on the weekends. I was trying hard to distance myself from her. She was suffocating enough the five days a week I saw her. I couldn't add weekends and evening to the mix. The more in control I became, the more Iris called me her secretary. It was some kind of huge control thing with her.

Josh Hartnett booked two independent movies: *Blow Dry*, which shot in England, and *O*, a contemporary version of Shakespeare's *Othello*. Josh had not really wanted to do either project. *Blow Dry*, I reasoned, would get us out of one of the options with Miramax. *O* was a really great acting role for Josh and would surely be at all the film festivals due to the controversial subject matter. Miramax shafted us and said that they wouldn't allow *Blow Dry* to be used as an option picture because they were splitting the production with someone else. Iris didn't want to start trouble with the Miramax people so she told me to shut up. We had been royally screwed. A bigger agency would have stood their ground. *O* was an independent but Miramax picked it up when they heard Josh was in it.

The early word on *The Yards* was not good. The rumors were that they wanted to do extensive re-shoots on the film. That proved problematic because Charlize Theron, Mark Wahlberg and Joaquin had other commitments. Considering that a film with no special effects usually shoots in eight to ten weeks, there had to be huge problems. Now that Joaquin had a few decent films under his belt, he thought the red carpet was going to be rolled out for him. He was making the mistake that a good many actors make. They forget that they are actors. Directors want to see the actor performing the role. If an actor wants to play different roles, then they really have to prove to everybody that they are believable in it. I didn't like the fact that Joaquin was being fed information by his friends in the bigger agencies. Especially since they were telling him about films that he wasn't right for and didn't have any chance of being offered, no matter who he was. Joaquin didn't want to audition any more and he felt he had earned the right not to.

Actors spend their entire career proving themselves by doing different roles. A director is not going to hire the actor unless they can do the role. It would be easier for me if everyone were just offered everything. Unfortunately, Joaquin thought that other agents could just hand him a career and an Oscar. That was never going to happen.

American History X was another film that Joaquin didn't like and didn't want to do. There was a small window over the course of the weekend when there were some problems with the director, studio and Edward Norton's representatives. They wanted Joaquin to meet the director. He and Iris didn't understand the script. I thought it was a brilliant script that was sure to get several of the actors nominated for the Academy Award. I was vetoed and no meeting took place. The opportunities were there: Joaquin just wasn't taking them.

Jude Law, Edward Norton, Ben Affleck, Matt Damon, Mark Wahlberg and Leonardo DiCaprio were the top actors on the scene, and really tough competition. The choice roles were going to go to all of them before they would even consider Joaquin. It boils down to who has the bigger box office potential. No agent in town could have secured the roles that Joaquin was longing for. He had made the choices not to do the roles that would have put him in contention. Now we would have to sit and wait and hope that everyone on the list ahead of him passed on the projects that we wanted.

I had read about the movie *Gladiator* in *Variety*. It seemed like a great project and I was fascinated with Ancient Rome. I had checked on the project early on and had heard that Edward Norton was the frontrunner to play the role of Commodus. I didn't think we had the slightest chance of nailing down the role for Joaquin. However I received a phone call from Ridley Scott's casting director, Lou DiGiaimo, asking where Joaquin was. As luck would have it he was in Los Angeles. Lou said he wanted me to pick up the script for *Gladiator* and that Ridley Scott wanted to meet Joaquin on

Monday. Ridley's production company was two blocks away from the office. Iris was out of town again, so I forwarded the phones and went down the street to pick up the script.

I read the script as I walked back to the office. I was thirty pages in when I called Joaquin and told him to come over immediately to pick it up. I had read the scene where Commodus kills his father and knew that this was a project that could snag him an Oscar nomination. Russell Crowe, who I thought was a brilliant actor, had signed on to star as Maximus, the gladiator of the title. In the time that it took Joaquin to show up at the office I had read the entire script. I hadn't been this excited about a project since *Interview with the Vampire* for Kirsten Dunst.

Joaquin raced over on his brand new Ducati motorcycle. I made him sit down and read the scene between Commodus and his father. He looked up and smiled at me. I pointed out several other scenes. We were both grinning by the time he left the office. I called out to Joaquin as he climbed on his motorcycle, 'If you can nail this part you'll get an Oscar nomination.' He smiled and put on his helmet.

Joaquin met with Ridley Scott and the meeting went well. He read some of the scenes for Ridley. I received a call from Lou DiGiaimo, he said that Ridley wanted to put Joaquin on tape for the studio. Ridley Scott had a vision. He could see Joaquin in the role but he couldn't get the studio on board. After the screen test the word came back that they were having problems buying Joaquin in the role. The studio had the hots for Jude Law. He had *The Talented Mr Ripley* coming out and everyone was talking about his performance. The one thing in our favor was that Jude Law's agency wanted an offer. They didn't want him to test for the role.

Ridley pushed for a full screen test in period costumes so that he could prove to the studio that Joaquin was the right person for the job. The screen tests would be in London. Jude Law's agents continued to give everyone a hard time about him screen-testing. It was a case of hold out and they'll give you the part. Since Ridley was with Jude Law's agency, it really wasn't a wise choice. Joaquin had worked with Ridley Scott's company on *Clay Pigeons*. There was an allegiance to Joaquin on Ridley's part.

After the screen test the studio still refused to give the role to Joaquin. There were all kinds of problems that had nothing to do with him. The studio was afraid to spend over $100,000,000 on a movie with two actors who really hadn't generated that much box office in lead roles. Up to this point Russell Crowe was a respected actor but he hadn't proven himself at the box office. Joaquin certainly hadn't proven himself. They wanted some guarantee of a return on investment and they were worried that the subject matter wouldn't be of interest to the general public. There was talk that the plug would be pulled on the movie. Universal stepped in and agreed to split costs with DreamWorks, lessening the amount of money they would have to put out.

Co-productions were starting to take place amidst all the studios because nobody wanted to be out of pocket for the entire cost of a film if it bombed at the box office. Now it's the norm when you have a big budget film to split the costs, especially of these 'epic' films. It was the most prolonged wait for any client to be given a part after a screen test I've ever known. They were also having trouble agreeing on who would play Commodus' sister. Ridley Scott wanted Danish actress Connie Nielsen but she was also an unknown commodity in the United States.

There was still talk of Jude Law. Somebody at one of the studios didn't like Joaquin. This is when I finally dragged Iris into the battle. People were afraid of Iris. Nobody wanted to start with Iris because she would wear you down after three hours on the phone. It was time to wind Iris up. I explained the situation to her. She lit cigarette after cigarette while I explained what had been happening. When I was finished she smashed her cigarette in the ashtray.

'I want you to start dialing the phone and I don't want you to stop until I have talked to every person involved in this project, including the janitor at the studio. I want to know who has the problem with Joaquin.'

'OK,' I said.

'Get me someone now!' Iris lit another cigarette.

By the end of the day I had placed calls to every relevant person at DreamWorks and Universal, including Steven Spielberg. He had always hired Iris' clients since she had found Henry Thomas and put him in *E.T.* River Phoenix had done an *Indiana Jones* movie. We had four kids in the movie *Hook*. Iris made her point. We never did find out who the opposition came from but by the end of that week Joaquin Phoenix was offered the role of Commodus.

The situation between Iris and me was becoming more and more tense as our top clients became more successful. She began to talk to the managers more. I had always been the one that dealt with them in the past. Now Iris made it known that if the managers had any problems, they should talk to her about them and not me. Well, that was not a good idea because the only thing that managers wanted was more auditions for their clients. None of our clients went without auditions. After a year most of the casting directors were very familiar with the clients. If they didn't do a good job it was difficult to get them back in again.

It really wasn't my fault if the clients weren't prepared and didn't audition well. One of the managers took Iris up on her offer and called her because she felt her clients weren't getting enough auditions. She wanted feedback. I called up the casting director to get the feedback on the client in question.

'Hold on let me look at my notes . . . He fucking sucked,' the casting director said.

'Excuse me?' I said.

'He fucking sucked. That's what I wrote, Chris'

'Thanks,' I responded.

When I informed the manager of what the casting director said her response was,

'What does that mean exactly?'

'I think it's pretty clear. He sucked. How many more ways do I have to spell it out to you?'

I don't really know what was so hard for her to comprehend. That wasn't good enough? She told Iris that I didn't like the client. That I had it in for him.

'What's your problem? Why are you giving the managers a hard time?'

'Excuse me, Iris. I'm giving the managers a hard time? I think it's the other way around.'

'You're not getting the clients enough auditions is how I hear it.'

'That's bullshit, Iris, and you know it. The appointment sheets sit in this binder and you pore over them every night.'

'I do no such thing.'

'Iris, my chair is warm everyday when I sit down at 9 a.m.'

'I want you to keep these managers happy.'

'I'll tell you what, Iris, why don't you start getting

appointments for these clients and see just how easy it is, especially when they receive feedback that they *fucking* suck? You just don't want to upset Josh Hartnett's manager. Out of the twenty people we have with her, only three of them are halfway decent. The rest of them *fucking* suck! What the fuck do you want me to do?' I grabbed my briefcase and stormed out of the office. It was bullshit: the tension was becoming too much. The managers were starting to use the interest from other agents to try to put the squeeze on us for more auditions. I needed to find a way out of this situation and fast. I could feel my head pounding. My blood pressure was through the roof and I had an ache in my side from the diverticulosis.

CHAPTER 21

'Be extremely subtle, even to the point of formalness. Be extremely mysterious, even to the point of soundlessness. Thereby you can be the director of the opponents fate.'

Sun Tzu, *The Art of War*

While they were trying to work out the re-shoots on *The Yards*, I talked to the person in charge of development at the production company. We were having a casual conversation about the amount of lousy scripts we had to read. I said that I hadn't read a good script in so long. She accommodated me by sending over a script called *Quills*. It was based on a play about the Marquis De Sade. She sent it just for my pleasure. The script was brilliant. It was the best I had read in years. They had Philip Kaufman attached to direct the film with Geoffrey Rush already attached as the Marquis. Kate Winslet would also star in the movie.

I called the development person up and asked who was playing Coulmier. She said that no one had been signed but that they were interested in Jude Law. What a surprise! I pushed the issue and said that I wanted to speak to the producer. He was one of the producers of *The Yards*. I asked him why he hadn't thought of Joaquin for the role? He told me that the studio would never buy Joaquin with a cast of English and Australian actors. He also didn't think Joaquin was right for the role. I argued that he was. I challenged him. I made a bargain that if I could get the studio to approve a screen test for Joaquin, that he wouldn't block the meeting with the director. He agreed, probably thinking I didn't have a snowball's chance in hell of getting the screen test.

I called the head of casting at the studio and asked her why they weren't considering Joaquin for the role of Coulmier. She said that she loved Joaquin but he wasn't right for the role. I disagreed and asked her to at least let Joaquin test for the role and prove everyone wrong. She had another film that she wanted Joaquin to do and the director wanted to meet Joaquin badly. I agreed to get Joaquin to meet the director if she would at least let Joaquin read for *Quills*. She accepted my deal.

I immediately sent the script to Joaquin and he agreed that it was amazing. He really didn't want to do back-to-back pictures. He would have to shoot *Gladiator*, do the re-shoots on *The Yards* and then film *Quills*. Joaquin was not like other actors who bounce from film to film. He liked his time off. But this was a once-in-a-lifetime opportunity. He agreed to take the meeting with the director of the project even though we had no interest in the project. Then he was off to film *Gladiator*. Word was circulating around town that Jude Law's agents wanted a straight offer for him to do *Quills*. Even then they were not guaranteeing he would do it, because it was a favored nations deal. Every one of the main actors would be making the same low salary. His agents didn't want to lock him in for such a low rate. They were waiting for a big studio payday. They were stalling. If Jude had committed to the picture there wouldn't be this long drawn-out dance. They would all have to take huge pay cuts. True to her word, the casting director arranged Joaquin's meeting. She gave me twenty-four hours to find a way to get Joaquin to London to read with the director.

This posed a big problem since Joaquin was already filming *Gladiator* in Malta. The casting director knew this, which made me even more determined to get him there. She gave me my chance because she knew that it was an impossible task. I called the line producer to plead my case. They were filming in the Colosseum so he promised to let him out for the day on Monday. Joaquin had a fit that he had to go to an audition while he was filming but I didn't give him any alternative. I told him the plane was waiting and that the producer had the material he would be auditioning with. I had already faxed it to Malta. Joaquin was off to his screen test.

On Tuesday of the next week we had an official offer for Joaquin to play the role of Coulmier. I was thrilled beyond belief. Iris however, was far from thrilled, especially when she heard the money that they were offering.

'Are you fucking crazy?' she screamed at me.

'Iris, this is an incredible film.'

'I really don't care if it's *Lawrence of Arabia*, his price just went down to what he started at.'

'Iris, for God's sake, everyone is taking a pay cut. Kate Winslet makes a hell of a lot more than Joaquin Phoenix.'

'Do whatever he wants. I don't give a fuck. Nobody has any money any more.' She marched out of the office and slammed the door.

Joaquin finished *Gladiator* without the Agency being called about any problems, which was a relief. Joaquin had some down time before finishing *The Yards*, and was set to start *Quills* in London right after. About a month before filming Joaquin called the office and told me that he wasn't doing *Quills* – he wanted out of the project. I thought he was joking. This was the role of a lifetime. He started ranting and raving about not wanting to work, that he was tired and he couldn't take it. This was a nightmare. It was shades of River all over again. I buzzed Iris and quickly put her on the phone to hear what Joaquin was saying. He ranted for an hour. There was something wrong with him and I was not going to go through this again. I called his mother. Joaquin needed professional help. His mother, Iris and I talked. Joaquin had been very depressed in the last year. He sometimes didn't return calls for a week at a stretch. When he did call back he mumbled and was incoherent. We had a long talk with Mrs Phoenix and suggested that she try to find out what was bothering him.

When she called back, Mrs Phoenix informed us that Joaquin didn't want to do the film. We already knew that. She was supposed to try to get to the bottom of his problems. I had to explain to her what a blow this would be to his career. He was knocking at the door of major critical and financial success. He had to do this film. It wasn't like we were shoving him from film to film with only a couple of days off. He had months before he had to work. He wasn't carrying the picture. It was Geoffrey Rush's movie, not his. Heart understood the predicament and talked to Joaquin. Her solution was to join him on location in London. She would spend time with him during filming. His sisters, Summer, Rain and Liberty with her two children, all agreed to take turns being with Joaquin during filming. Since it was London, Iris also agreed to go over and do her part. I think if the location had been Lithuania, she would have made other plans. She called me twice a day from London. She was having problems with her sciatica and was miserable.

'I don't know why the fuck I came over here. Nobody calls and invites me anyplace. I'm alone most of the time.'

'How's Joaquin?' I said cutting her off. Iris could go on for hours about a pimple.

'I don't know what the hell is wrong with him. He is so moody,' Iris said.

'It's what he's not saying, Iris! It's what none of us talk about,' I yelled.

'What's that?' Iris yelled back.

'You know what it is, Iris. It's the same thing that I think about everyday. It's about River. God forbid that we should even utter River's name. That we should admit to feeling guilty about what happened. That maybe we didn't act soon enough!'

'Now you're Sigmund fucking Freud. Is that what you study in those fucking retarded classes you take every Thursday? Are you studying to be a *psychologist*?'

'Really funny, Iris. Don't change the subject. There is probably more to all these rumors than we know. Just like with River, Iris. We've been ignoring everything anyone says with regard to Joaquin. We just say he's quirky. Well, it's more than quirky! the walks around and says that he sucks and he's going to ruin people's movie. I have never met anyone with lower self-esteem than Joaquin.'

'Enough! I don't want to hear any more!' She slammed the phone down.

Iris could keep slamming the phone down but whatever problems he had weren't going to disappear. Joaquin wasn't about to share his problems with anyone. He hadn't up to this point. I doubt anything was going to make him start now. I just prayed that his family's presence in London would help to get him through this movie. Right after he finished filming he would have a long break because there were no other projects in the pipeline. Hollywood was waiting to see what Joaquin would do in these next three movies. His career swung in the balance of the box-office receipts and reviewers.

Two months after his return we had a call from Twentieth Century Fox wanting to know if Joaquin would be interested in being in the movie *X-Men*: apparently Dougray Scott had to back out at the last minute because *Mission Impossible II* was way behind schedule. Joaquin had been a fan of the comic books since he was a young boy. Even despite the problems that he'd had with *Quills,* he was still considering doing the movie. At the last minute he decided that it was best he not take on such a physically demanding role. But at least we had protected the agency by letting him know there was interest in him. That way he couldn't come back and say we didn't know about projects. What most actors don't realize is that the higher you go up the ladder, the more control the studios have. They are ultimately the ones paying for the movies. They have the last say.

It was announced that *The Virgin Suicides* would be screened at the Sundance Film Festival. Hollywood flocks to Sundance every year at the end of January. It becomes party central. Josh's manager asked if I was going. I doubted Iris would want me out of the office. If anyone would go it would be her, but Iris didn't do well in the snow. In the end, of course, Iris went to Sundance with Josh's manager and publicist. They shared a condo together.

While she was at Sundance I heard that they were still looking for the lead in *Pearl Harbor*. Joaquin had been in consideration for the role at one time but he didn't have the best meeting with the director Michael Bay. Just like *Gladiator*, Disney was giving the producers a hard time about the budget. They didn't want to shoulder the responsibility of a $125,000,000 budget. They had offered the female lead to Gwyneth Paltrow, who turned it down. Then they went to Charlize Theron. Neither one of them accepted the role.

Then they tried to find an A-list actor to play the male lead. They had very little luck. The movie was really all about the special effects. It was a director's picture as opposed to an actor's picture. We had Josh go in and read for the movie but they weren't quite sold. The casting of all three of the leads was taking on the hype that had gone with the casting of *Gone with the Wind*. The director and producer liked Josh but he hadn't proven that he could draw in the kind of box office that was needed to make a return on their investment. They had locked down one A-list actor – Ben Affleck – who had worked with Jerry Bruckheimer and Michael Bay before on *Armageddon*. He agreed to play one of the leads. Ben made the studio feel more confident to move forwards with the picture but they wanted the budget cut to the bare bones.

Josh was flying into LA to watch a screening of *Here on Earth*. I was to meet him at the screening since Iris and Nancy were in Sundance. Josh would join them there the next day. We heard that he was going to be on the cover of *Interview* magazine. We decided to send the magazine over to Jerry Bruckheimer and Michael Bay to prove to them that Josh was headed towards the A-list and that they should grab him. Josh also had the same law firm as the producer Jerry Bruckheimer. We pushed from every angle.

The screening of *Here on Earth* proved a big disappointment because they had cut away all of Josh's really good scenes. I was really embarrassed since I had been so hot on the script. But how was I to know that the good scenes would end up on the cutting-room floor?

*   *   *

'Honey.' It was Iris. I looked at my bedside clock: it was 2 a.m. 'I just ran into Kirsten Dunst at the screening of *The Virgin Suicides*. She was hugging me and kissing me. It wasn't her and her mother that wanted to leave, it was that fucking manager.'

'What did you think she was going to do, Iris, make a scene in a public place?'

'You're so fucking negative!' she yelled.

'Is this what you called me about at two in the morning – to tell me that Kirsten is coming back? I really don't think it's going to happen. So let's move on to something important. How was Josh in the movie?'

'Honey, he's a star. He's sexy and he has this scene . . . Oh, honey, the way he walks. He has this swagger. The boy is sexy.'

'Is it worth trying to get scenes over to Jerry Bruckheimer?'

'Definitely.'

'Fine, I'll call the studio tomorrow and see if they can put some of Josh's scenes on a reel.'

'You can't believe how much my legs are killing me. I had to buy new boots my feet were so swollen.'

'I'm really sorry to hear that, Iris, but I have to get some sleep. I have to work tomorrow.'

'What the fuck do you think I'm doing up here? Do you think this isn't work?'

'Iris, if you want to start a fight wake up somebody that's right in your condo. I'm tired.' I hung up the phone.

As soon as Josh booked *Pearl Harbor* Iris informed me that I wasn't allowed to talk to him any more. She and his manager would be the only two people that talked to Josh. Josh apparently was uncomfortable dealing with me. Iris was up to her old tricks. Now that he'd booked the biggest movie of the year, he was her client.

I really didn't care any more. I was slowly sliding back into old habits. The migraine headaches continued. Excedrin Migraine was always in my briefcase. I was using them more than I probably should. I was feeling anxious and the panic attacks had started again. They would hit me with very little warning. I became adept at heading to the bathroom and pulling the car off to the side of the road. I would patiently wait until they subsided.

Sexually I had discovered a new and safer way to have meaningless sex. I was introduced to the world of bathhouses. I had read about bathhouses in gay novels when I was younger but they seemed like sleazy disgusting places. Then one of my friends took me to a place called the Hollywood Spa. It was like a gym and had lockers, a steam room, a hot tub, a sauna and rooms that you could rent if you wanted to have sex. There were also video rooms that played pornos or common areas that played regular movies. There was a cafe to buy food and beverages. I was really surprised at how clean the place was. I had had this image of a seedy filthy place and it was really clean and nice.

It was just like a bar except the 'merchandise' was on display. The only garment allowed in the spa was a white towel. I was quickly sucked into this new world and enjoyed the fact that nothing bad could happen to me there. There were lots of other people around. The Hollywood Spa in the Valley even had a sundeck with lounge chairs. I had a great time talking to people on the rooftop terrace. Most of the people were there for one reason and one reason only: to have anonymous sex. For some reason people opened up to me and I quickly learned that half the men at the Spa either had boyfriends or wives. When I was in the bathhouse I temporarily forgot the world that I was a part of. I didn't have to explain who I was or justify my existence. Doctors, prominent attorneys, agents, publicists, musicians, chefs, singers, gardeners and cement workers dropped their watches in a safety deposit box and became a different person. Within the walls of the bathhouse people were free to be themselves. It was amazing to meet somebody on the way out of the bathhouse because the minute they had their street clothes on their whole demeanor changed.

For a brief period of time in the confines of the bathhouse, I didn't feel worthless, like Sisyphus – rolling a rock up a hill, only to have it roll back down once I had reached the top and then starting all over again. I knew that the situation with Iris and the clients was only temporary and that I was building strength and gaining wisdom every time I rolled the rock up the hill. Soon enough I'd be able to push it to the top and it would easily roll down the other side. I wasn't ready yet. I wanted to leave Iris so badly that I could feel the breeze of freedom right outside my office door. With every yoga class and acupuncture treatment, just like Sisyphus I was building my biceps and my strength to endure my escape.

Just when I thought I couldn't endure Iris one more day, she made it impossible to leave. I had just been offered another job running a new division of a very big agency. The money was really good and I had turned them down twice in the last year. I finally agreed to a lunch with the owners of the agency. I agonized over the idea of leaving Iris. The lunch went well until the very end.

'So, Chris, how much money does Iris Burton make?' one of the owners asked.

'I really have no idea. I have nothing to do with filing her taxes,' I replied.

'How much money do you anticipate bringing in to the division, based on your experience with Iris?'

'I really don't know.'

'Well then, how many clients will you be bringing with you?' He smiled like he was possessed by the devil himself.

I felt really uncomfortable and regretted even agreeing to the lunch. When Iris asked me to come back to the agency she had gambled that I could make things happen again. She gambled that I could put the agency back on the map even though I had been out of commission for almost two years. Nobody would have given me a shot but now with the success of the young adults I was being seen as a viable candidate. Guilt kicked in. I couldn't screw over Iris.

I was on my way back from my summer vacation in Italy with my great-uncle, when I checked in with Iris at the Miami airport. Iris dropped an unbelievable bomb-shell in my lap and announced that she had to make payouts from her pension plan in another year because she was turning seventy. She had always been disgruntled that she had to include me in the pension. The charter agreement had been drawn up when she was running the business alone. Had she had to take employees into account she would have never structured the pension in the way it was.

She put me on the phone with an actuary handling her pension who informed me that my lump sum payout would be $72,000. I wanted to scream and jump for joy. As soon as that money came in, I was leaving. The very day that I had the check in my hand was the day that I was going to hand in my notice. There was a light at the end of the tunnel. I had something to look forward to. I had to get strong. I had to work on my writing. Most of all I had to plan my escape so that Iris didn't know that I was depending on that money. If she had even a whiff that I would leave when I got the money, she would stall until the day she died. I called the agency that I had interviewed with and told them that I wasn't interested in leaving. I was going to finish out my time with Iris until I had the pension money no matter how rough the waters. The money was my freedom and I took it as a sign.

Joaquin finished *Gladiator* while Josh prepared to start filming *Pearl Harbor*. They still hadn't found the female lead for the movie. We had one of our clients up to screen-test but the shit hit the fan one Friday afternoon. I was sitting at my desk and I heard the fax machine go off. I went over to retrieve the fax and saw that it was from Miramax Films. They were exercising Josh Hartnett's option to do a movie called *Get Over It*. That script was a piece of shit. I had read it and passed on it a year ago. What the hell was going on? I had told Josh's attorney to make sure that he informed Miramax that Josh was doing *Pearl Harbor* and would be unavailable for several months. That was the proper protocol with options. We had a major problem because the attorney hadn't followed proper procedures.

Iris, as usual, wasn't in the office. I called Miramax and they stood firm on their decision. Josh's lawyer whined to me that he thought since Disney owned Miramax and *Pearl Harbor* was a Disney film, he didn't have to send the letter. Knowing how possessive of those options Miramax was, he should have just followed procedure. There was more to this whole thing than Josh. It had been announced six weeks ago that he had been cast in *Pearl Harbor*. If Miramax wanted Josh they would have exercised his option then. There was information that we didn't have.

By the end of the day I had all the answers. Miramax wanted Kate Beckinsale for a movie with John Cusack called *Serendipity*. Apparently her agents had done everything but close the deal. When the *Pearl Harbor* casting dragged on and had seen every girl between the ages of eighteen and thirty-five that they could find, Kate Beckinsale's agent decided to throw her into the ring even though she wasn't really available and had committed to a Miramax film.

Well, as the saying goes, people want what they can't have. Michael Bay and Jerry Bruckheimer wanted Kate Beckinsale but so did Harvey Weinstein. And when two of the biggest titans in the film world want something, they will go to any means to get it. Harvey Weinstein figured if Jerry Bruckheimer wanted to take Kate Beckinsale from him, then he'd take Josh Hartnett from Jerry Bruckheimer. Harvey Weinstein had the legal means to do it thanks to Josh's attorney. One little paragraph would have stopped the whole thing. Harvey Weinstein now had the legal right to exercise his option and sit on Josh until he was good and ready to use him. We were also in breach of contract for not sending the proper letter to Miramax. I hated option pictures for this very reason. It hardly ever happens but you give a club to a titan and they're going to start swinging at anything in their path. My head started to throb.

The interesting thing about this situation was that Jerry Bruckheimer had a first-look deal with Disney. Disney funded Harvey Weinstein's company. Nobody at the studio was going anywhere near this mess. Even they weren't going to wrangle with this. Iris didn't want to hear about it and refused to make any calls. I called the head of casting at Miramax and pleaded with her to intervene. This was not fair to Josh. We had done nothing wrong. If they had wanted Josh, why didn't they offer him the project months ago when Kirsten Dunst had been cast? Iris was bitter over Miramax using Kirsten because she wasn't being paid for the project. Kirsten's manager had turned down the two-picture deal with Miramax that Iris had wanted.

It was a waiting game. The tension was worse than any I had encountered. Josh's whole career was riding on other people who really didn't care what happened to him. They just wanted to win. Josh was simply a pawn in a much bigger game. It was finally all worked out that the Miramax film, *Serendipity,* would be pushed to facilitate Kate Beckinsale doing both movies. However, we would suffer the consequences by being slapped with another option picture with Miramax. It was looking like Josh would be under option to Miramax forever.

I went into the kitchen to try to talk Iris into doing the right thing. 'Iris, you really should call Harvey Weinstein. This option is not fair. I don't see Kate Beckinsale get slapped with an option picture.'

'Do you think Josh and his manager are going to be loyal to me?'

'This is unfair, Iris. If they were dealing with CAA, they wouldn't allow this to happen,'

Iris slammed the drawer shut. She had just taken out a knife. 'You're right, I *am* going to call Harvey Weinstein. Why should I let them do this to me without getting something from Miramax?' She had this big grin on her face.

'What are you up to, Iris?'

'Put in a call to Harvey Weinstein and then go to lunch.'

I called Harvey Weinstein and he called back before I

left for lunch. I knew Iris was up to no good. She didn't make these kinds of calls unless there was something in it for her.

When I returned from lunch she was all smiles.

'Well, I don't have to worry about my hotel room in Cannes.'

'What did you do, Iris?'

'I took care of Iris. Miramax is picking up my hotel room for my entire stay at the Cannes Film Festival as long as I can get Josh and his stupid manager to agree to this picture option.'

'Iris, this is so wrong.'

'I'm looking out for me and don't you dare tell that manager of Josh what I did. Understand?'

'Do you understand that you just sold Josh Hartnett for $1,000,000 a picture when he'll be worth $5,000,000 after *Pearl Harbor* comes out? Do the math, Iris. A $400,000 difference in commissions to you, for a lousy business expense of $2,500 that you can write off.'

'Honey, there is no guarantee that he will stay with this agency. Let Miramax pick up the check for little old Iris. Fuck them!'

I left the kitchen disgusted that I was a party to such an abortion of agenting. Iris had turned into Emperor Nero. She was going to destroy herself. She was setting herself up for a huge fall. I was only glad that I would be long gone before Josh figured out what she had done.

I plotted my escape every day. The first thing I did was to stop re-signing clients with the agency. I didn't want anyone stuck with Iris when I left. Whenever the clients renewed their agency contracts they always asked me if I would be there for another year. I had always said yes before. Now for the first time I had to admit that I couldn't guarantee that I would be with the agency for another year. The minute that pension money was in I would be gone. The clients didn't want to re-sign so I just let the contracts lapse. Iris hated paperwork. She didn't type or use the computer so she didn't do anything with the contracts. I didn't want to be responsible for anyone being stuck with Iris after I'd gone.

Cannes ended up being Iris' downfall in more than one area. When an agent goes to a film festival the clients expect the agent to take care of business so that they can do the promotional work they are required to do. Film festivals are work for the actors. They don't have time to frolic and have fun. Iris always wanted to be taken care of. She expected everybody to include her in every activity. If she was left out of something or a limo didn't pick her up she became a sulky child. The Phoenixes had their hands full with Iris. Iris had her hands full with me.

I had been desperately reading piles of scripts trying to find another project for Josh – specifically one that would enable us to burn off one of the horrible options that we were saddled with. I really liked the script for *Queen of the Damned*, which was based on an Anne Rice novel. They had originally wanted Joaquin but I thought that given that River was signed to do an Anne Rice novel before he died it may be odd and a little unnerving given Joaquin's current state of mind. I wanted to pass on the project without even telling him but the fact that agents from the big agencies went out of their way to try to make us look ineffective, I had to send him everything. Joaquin was looking for an excuse to leave us. The bigger agencies were really gunning to take him now that he had finally broken through with studio films. When we flew under the radar with independents, they didn't care. Now Joaquin was on the A-list and everything we did became their business, because we took jobs from their clients which cost them commissions and also made them look bad with their clients. They had to muscle us out of the business or the illusion that they had created would be smashed. Anarchy would reign in Hollywood if the big agencies didn't control the studio films. Iris and I had proved that a two-person office could compete with huge companies with thousands of employees worldwide. Not a good message to have out there because actors were easy marks for tall tales.

Joaquin had suddenly become adamant that he shouldn't audition any more. He forgot that auditioning had put him in the place he was in. The agents from the other agencies filled him with candy-coated stories and Joaquin bought the stories hook, line and sinker. He had never given me such a hard time. These agencies were playing hardball and they worked it from every angle. Iris was never someone who refused to let the clients audition. Iris was competitive and had a killer instinct. If someone had talent Iris believed that they could beat out the less talented actors. Joaquin had talent to spare, so the fact that he was actually questioning the two people that believed in him the most disturbed and unsettled me. The last two movies Joaquin had been cast in were because another actor's representatives gave the director and the studio a hard time.

Joaquin was in the self-sabotage mode. He wasn't at a point at not having to audition. An actor has to constantly prove himself.

Joaquin came into town to do a press junket for *Gladiator*. We received a call from his publicist that he was refusing to leave the room and meet with the press.

I buzzed Iris. 'Iris, wake up! Wake up now! We have a huge problem.'

'What the hell do you want? I'm sleeping!' she yelled back.

'You need to get dressed and go over to the press junket for *Gladiator*. Joaquin won't leave the room.'

'Why won't he leave the room?' she snapped back.

'I really don't know, Iris. But you need to go over there right now!'

'Why don't you go? I'll watch the office.'

'Oh no you don't, Iris. He won't listen to me. The publicist asked for you. Not me.'

'Why does he have to pull this shit?' She slammed down the phone.

I never really knew what the hell had caused the incident. Iris said she talked to him for a while and he finally went down to talk to the press. But not before he had kept everyone waiting, including all the gossipy publicity people who worked for Universal and DreamWorks.

I had managed to get Warner Bros. interested in Josh Hartnett for *Queen of the Damned*. Another project came in called *40 Days and 40 Nights*, which was a comedy and would be a good change of pace for Josh. Again his manager didn't understand the script because it was a black comedy. Iris was at Cannes so it was left to me to discuss the project with Josh. He decided to take the meeting with the director after I talked to him.

The film *40 Days and 40 Nights* was set up as a co-production with Universal and Miramax. I feared that Miramax would pull the 'We don't own the whole picture so we don't want to use our option,' line again. I was more than prepared for them this time. They were ready to make an offer to Josh. I had left the *Queen of the Damned* people on hold temporarily. Miramax and Universal decided to make Josh an offer. That's when I said to just exercise his third option picture. Miramax didn't want to do it. So I said we were going to move on to the other project.

'What the hell are you doing? I was just cornered by Harvey Weinstein,' Iris called me annoyed from Cannes.

'I'm just taking care of business.'

'Why the fuck do you care about those options? I like them. It protects me.'

'This isn't supposed to be about protecting you. This is supposed to be about protecting Josh. He was screwed with *Blow Dry* and *Pearl Harbor*. This is a Miramax film and they can just use one of the options or Josh is perfectly happy to do *Queen of the Damned*. So you go and talk to your *good friend* Harvey and fix it.' I hung up the phone on her.

The phone rang. 'How dare you!' Iris screamed into the phone.

'How dare you let Miramax screw Josh again?' I screamed back.

'They are paying for my trip.'

'I'm perfectly aware of that. It's wrong!'

'Don't lecture me! When Josh leaves the agency at least I'll have something!'

'How do you know he'll leave, Iris?' I said.

'They all leave!'

'Well, until Josh Hartnett stops paying us 10 per cent I plan on making sure that he is properly represented.'

'Aren't you just Mr Goody Two Shoes?' Iris said mockingly.

'Just fix it, Iris, or I'll let Josh and his manager know who really is the queen of the damned!' I hung up the phone again. At this point I really didn't care if she fired me. I was sick of being a part of her selfish bullshit.

After all the drama, one day later Miramax exercised the third option on Josh for *40 days and 40 Nights*.

Gladiator opened and was a huge smash hit at the box office. Joaquin landed the cover of *GQ*. Everything was going in the right direction. I waited for the phone to ring from the studios with multi-million-dollar offers. When I picked up *GQ* at the newsstand I was mortified by what I read. In the article Ridley Scott said, referring to Joaquin, 'He's kind of a wounded individual.'

His best friend and Summer Phoenix's boyfriend, Casey Affleck said, 'I've been on planes with him, and I don't really want to look at him either, because he sits down and drinks sixteen shots of whatever he can find and pulls his shirt over his head and stays like that for the rest of the flight.'

James Gray the director of *The Yards* said in the same article: 'Joaquin is willing to put himself into the most troubling and personal and exposing of places, which is all you can ask from an actor. Frankly it's very difficult for me to work with him – I'm not comfortable with torture.'

The article painted a portrait of someone who wasn't easy to work with. An interview on *The Tonight Show* made things more difficult when Joaquin acted weird and pretended to not know where he was. Both the *GQ* and *The Tonight Show* combined threw a wet blanket over any offers coming in. Joaquin was in a movie headed to make more than $500,000,000 and no offers were coming in. I had to go out and solicit work for him. It was as if we were back to square one. All the years of hard work and careful planning had been ruined in a single week. I knew that if he didn't have a picture by June we'd be sunk. The agencies were circling and preparing for the kill. I could smell the blood. The

Phoenixs had made several unsettling comments about Iris' age. They kept saying how old she had become. They didn't like having to take care of her.

I faxed Iris the *GQ* article in Paris. I didn't want there to be any surprises and I wanted to prepare her that she wasn't coming home to the million-dollar offers that she had expected. I would rather she blow off her steam in Paris than come back to Los Angeles and take it out on me.

Iris called me later in the day. 'What the fuck is this shit you sent me?'

'It's Joaquin's *GQ* article, Iris.'

'I know that but what the fuck were these people thinking? They've fucking ruined my chances of making money.'

'Iris, nobody is interested in him. There have been no offers. I almost called someone and asked them to call me back, just to make sure the phone was working.'

'I can't believe James Gray . . . and what the fuck was Casey thinking?'

'I have no idea, Iris.'

I knew exactly where we where headed with regard to Joaquin so it was no surprise to me when he showed up in the office the beginning of June. He had been on every studio project that was casting. CAA kept putting their higher profile clients up against Joaquin just to stall any interest in him. CAA was out for blood and they were hitting Iris every way that they could. Joaquin had decided to spend a month in Los Angeles and I knew that he was taking meetings. Gossip travels like wildfire in Hollywood.

'Chris, I need to ask you a favor.' Joaquin had been sitting in front of me chain-smoking. I was sure that

I would die from lung cancer from the second-hand smoke of Iris and our clients.

'What's up?' I said.

'I need you to help me get Iris through something.' He lit another cigarette.

'What?'

'I'm leaving the agency.'

'CAA?' I said.

'How did you know?'

'Joaquin, I'm not an idiot. They've been after you for years through Casey. I knew it was coming for three years. Iris didn't help with her performance in Cannes. I heard all about it from your mother and sister. They kept repeating how old Iris had become.'

'She was so difficult. I need you to help her through this,' Joaquin said, truly concerned for Iris.

'You'll have to tell her,' I said.

'I know.' He lowered his head.

When Joaquin came back the next day he was white. I hadn't slept because I knew what would happen when Joaquin announced his defection. I knew that Iris was totally oblivious to what Joaquin was up to. I announced Joaquin's visit to Iris. He shuffled into the house like a little boy headed to the principal's office. I followed close behind. He was lucky. It would be over for him in twenty minutes. I'd have to live with her miserable demeanor until the day I left the agency. That day would arrive with a check from the pension plan. Iris would recover from a tummy tuck more quickly than she would from Joaquin's defection. In her eyes she would be humiliated in front of all the people she had told that Joaquin would never leave her.

Joaquin blurted out that he was leaving. Iris stared at him like she wasn't hearing anything he had to say.

When he was finished she was silent. When Iris is quiet it's dangerous. He gave her a hug. She was frozen and stiff as if she had just heard that someone dear to her had died. She didn't respond. I think she was in shock. I waited for the eruption as Joaquin left the room. The silence continued. That horrible, eerie silence that follows an earthquake. Her eyes held all the rage. I didn't know what to do. She just stared.

'I'm finished,' she said. Then stared.

'You're hardly finished, Iris. We have other people working. Josh is actually worth more than Joaquin.'

'How long do you think it will be before they convince him to leave?'

'Iris, you really should sell while there is still something left.'

'You're just a bundle of positivity.' She lit a cigarette.

'Iris, I'm only offering a suggestion.'

'I didn't ask for your fucking advice. Just call my lawyer.'

'Fine, Iris.' There was no sense arguing with her. She wasn't rational on her best days. Hopefully, she would finally understand that she needed to sell what was left of the agency while there was still something to salvage.

I called her lawyer and she told him to get in touch with Endeavor and set up a meeting. They were definitely interested but Joaquin had been taking secret meetings before he came into the office. He had made his choice but Iris wanted to try to sway him to go to Endeavor because she could get more money with Josh and Joaquin as a package. Endeavor was hungry to dethrone CAA, they would pay for talent. CAA didn't have to because they already had Joaquin and been hard at work to get Josh. Joaquin had nothing to complain about as far as his career management. He was unwilling to see that his poor public relations skills had been the culprit. He thought he could give ridiculous interviews and talk show appearances and have people take him seriously. Joaquin thought CAA was the easy answer. To pacify Iris, Joaquin agreed to take the meeting with Endeavor. The meeting with CAA was set first. Iris didn't realize that she had lost control of Joaquin. She still thought she could have it go her way.

The day after my return we had our first meeting with CAA. I actually bought a suit to go to the meeting. I hadn't worn a suit in all the years I had known Iris. It felt so awkward walking into the foreboding atrium of the CAA building. It was all marble with a huge vaulted ceiling and museum-quality artwork strategically placed.

'It's like a mausoleum,' Iris said.

She was right. I'd never walked into a place that made me feel so uncomfortable and intimidated. Above us people used walkways that surrounded the building to walk from one office to another. They all looked incredibly chic. That kind of Prada/Gucci chic, lots of black and grey. I wanted to disappear into the marble. I was in a Brooks Brothers pinstripe suit. I thought I looked nice until I saw how these people were dressed.

'Here lies Debra Winger.' Iris touched a piece of marble and shot Joaquin a glance. She was making a point. Now that she was face to face with Joaquin's decision the pain was all over her face. We were escorted up a couple of flights of stairs to a conference room. When we entered, four agents were already seated at the table. They awkwardly shook our hands. They must have wanted Joaquin badly because CAA didn't ever split clients with other agents. They usually pillaged the best clients from smaller agencies. This was as unusual to the CAA agents as it was to us.

They stalled the meeting with idol chit-chat until another agent joined us.

'Sorry I'm late.' He looked at Joaquin. 'Nicole said to say hello.' He was referring to Nicole Kidman. It was a slick move. He was basically giving Joaquin a heads-up that she thought it was great that he was meeting with her agents. Iris dug her nails into my thigh but she kept a big proud smile on her face.

When they had finished the sales pitch the room went silent. Joaquin was sitting next to his lawyer on the other side of the table smiling. The CAA agent asked if we had any questions. Iris pinched me.

'I have a question.' Everyone looked at me. 'Joaquin is under the impression that he won't have to audition if he is with CAA.'

'Well, we don't encourage auditions.'

'I asked if he would have to audition.'

Another agent responded. 'We usually get offers for our clients.'

'Isn't it true that Heath Ledger auditioned several times on Shekhar Kapur's *Four Feathers*?'

There was total silence and furtive glances amongst the CAA contingent.

'I just want Joaquin to have the whole picture. I mean you do tend to bandy about the word "packaging" like most people use the word "hello". Now back to the question. Did Heath Ledger have to audition for *Four Feathers* or not?'

'Well . . ."' one of the agents said.

I cut him off. 'I just want Joaquin to have the big picture, to know that movies won't be just landing in his lap.'

Iris patted my thigh under the table and smiled like a Cheshire cat as she stood up.

'Well, that's about all for today, boys. We have other meetings.' She walked out of the room.

Joaquin's lawyer looked mortified. Joaquin awkwardly

shook hands with everyone. We all walked out of the conference room and made pleasantries with the exiting agents. This was going to be a bloody takeover. It was more than obvious that nobody in the room liked each other. This co-representation was not something any of us really dealt with.

The next day we had a meeting with Endeavor, which was much more friendly because they were trying really hard to impress Joaquin and Iris. She wanted Joaquin to end up at Endeavor because if he went to CAA then they would be the ones in command. Strategically Endeavor was better – Iris could call the shots. Joaquin had made up his mind he was going to CAA before he even told me he was leaving the agency. A good deal of the agents at Endeavor had come from either CAA or ICM. Iris and I also took another separate meeting at UTA. We all had lunch at the Four Seasons. Iris held my hand and leaned on me as we walked out of the third and final meeting. I just wanted this all to end so that I could get Iris settled and be on my way to a new life.

My blood pressure was through the roof again. No amount of yoga, walking or pills would lower it. I just pushed through. I received a phone call about a script for Joaquin. The casting director told me that she had called repeatedly for a week. Every time she got Iris on the phone she started to sob about Pete and Joaquin. Iris was distraught and the casting director couldn't even discuss her business. She stopped calling and figured she'd wait a week until I returned from my vacation. She told me that Edward Norton had passed on the project and she needed a quick read. Since Joaquin was still not at CAA I figured I might as well try to get one more commission for Iris. I received the script the next day and read it right away. This was the script I'd been waiting for. It was a great black comedy called *Buffalo Soldiers*. It was what Joaquin needed after all these period pieces. I had them messenger the script to him.

Joaquin loved the script. He agreed to meet the director. Then after weeks of waiting, Joaquin lowered the boom that he was going to CAA. Iris's lawyer negotiated a sliding scale commission where Iris would go from 5 per cent to 1 per cent over several-years. This would not include projects that we were already in discussions with. The merger with Endeavor was again cancelled even though she had talked about nothing except the merger to Josh Hartnett's manager. Josh's manager complained to me that Joaquin now had more opportunities because he was with CAA. There was treachery at every turn now. All the clients were restless. They slowly started to leave when their contracts were up. They were heading to the same agencies that Iris should have been merging with. We were also being threatened with a huge commercial strike. The pressure was really on me to keep Josh and his manager happy.

Joaquin loved *Buffalo Soldiers* but CAA did not. They told him not to do the movie. Iris and I argued with them that there was nothing else out there. They kept insisting that they wanted him to do a studio film, but there were none being offered up. He had been out of work for a year by then – this was a good project for him. CAA argued that the financing wasn't in place. Joaquin had worked with the producer of the project, Paul Webster, on *The Yards*. Paul swore that he'd have the money for the movie in a month. He was so sure of it that he offered Joaquin $50,000 with no strings attached if he would wait thirty days. At the end of the thirty days whether they had the money or not, he would walk away with $50,000. Joaquin still refused. I called his mother and explained the situation to her. It was amazing how quickly Joaquin called back and agreed to do the film. CAA was not happy that we had trumped them. They were more than aware of the project but it wasn't in their interests for Joaquin to pursue it.

Iris was still holding on to the dream that Joaquin would stay with the agency and dump CAA. She now had a mission. She was going to make everything as difficult as possible for CAA. Once the agreements were made between CAA and Iris they begrudgingly invited us to lunch. I had no interest in going because I knew it would be wrought with tension. We ate at an Italian restaurant in West Hollywood called AGO. It was a very industry restaurant – a calculated move by CAA so that the town could see that Iris had turned over her star client to another agency and that there were no hard feelings. Everyone knew what Iris had been through with the Phoenix family, so it would have been bad for their image to appear to have 'poached' Joaquin.

It was the most tension-filled lunch I had ever had. Every time one of the agents spoke to me, Iris would shoot steely glances in my direction. It was a large table and difficult to include everyone in the conversation. I don't know why Iris wanted me at the lunch. She was acting as if I had defected to the enemy camp but wasn't about to make this unpleasant. Joaquin was the one who had decided that he wanted to be at CAA. He could have said no. Iris wouldn't have been happy no matter who Joaquin had gone to. All the facelifts, tummy tucks, and fat injections into her wrinkles could not change the fact that she was two months shy of seventy in a business where the average age of agents is thirty.

A producer approached the table about a script. Iris glanced in my direction. Her look was accusatory, like I had forgotten to tell her about something. Joaquin had passed on the project three times. Robert Evans, the super producer and former head of Paramount, sat at a prominent table where he could see everyone and they could see him. He waved over to Iris. She had once handled his son. Iris nodded and then waved. She took great delight in the fact that these power brokers were acknowledging her in front of her rivals.

One of the agents ordered a huge bowl of cherries. I almost busted out laughing when we all started spitting the pits into a bowl. It reminded me of the scene in *The Witches of Eastwick* when the women try to conjure the devil and ate a big bowl of cherries. I don't think we needed to conjure the devil – in Iris' eyes we were already having lunch with him. They seemed to be trying to figure out what made Iris tick. I'd known her a long time and, sadly, I felt the only thing that kept Iris going was anger. Iris lived in the past. She mourned daily what could have been.

When they realized that they couldn't break Iris' shell they turned their attentions on me. It was rumored that CAA agents were required to read and know Sun Tzu's *The Art of War*. They were trying to figure out how important I was to the agency. By Iris including me in the lunch she had elevated my position without having to say anything. I made pleasant conversation with the agents and, like Iris, revealed as little as possible about myself. Even though Iris and I had not studied *The Art of War*, we both knew the art of street fighting. One of the many things Iris taught me was to listen. If you let people talk enough they will reveal everything. Iris kept shooting me looks and I was more than relieved when the lunch was over.

I stepped into Iris' black Mercedes and she waved and smiled at the CAA agents. She put on her big black Jackie O sunglasses and put the key in the ignition. The smile suddenly dropped as we drove out of the restaurant and on to Melrose Avenue.

'Fucking pricks!' She lit a cigarette.

There was no response to that. We drove back to the office in silence.

CHAPTER 22

'A military operation involves deception. Even though you are competent, appear to be incompetent. Though effective appear to be ineffective.'

Sun Tzu, *The Art of War*

I didn't think things could get much worse but then Josh Hartnett's manager told me that she had been having lunch with an agent at CAA. Things then went from bad to worse. Josh had worked in great projects non-stop since we had taken him. I was so frustrated by the stupidity of his manager that I wanted to throw in the towel. I didn't really have the heart to tell Iris because she was already in a tailspin and headed for a crash landing, but she needed to unload Josh to another agency before she ended up with another crappy deal. Once Josh started taking meetings with prospective agents, without Iris in attendance, she would lose any bargaining position that she might have had when it came to negotiating the split of the agency fee.

CAA was careful that no one from Joaquin's team was involved. They set up some new flunky out of the mailroom to approach Josh and make the calls to his manager. That way it would take the blame off Joaquin's team at CAA. It was easier to explain that the newly made agent who wanted to earn his stripes had tried to poach Josh. The agent that they used for the trap reported to the co-head of the Motion Picture Department.

It would be all out war the minute that I told Iris. I waited as long as I could before I told her. Iris sat in front of me and the rage registered in her eyes. She was quieter than I had ever seen her. She had the look of a demonic killer.

'Those motherfuckers.' Iris' spit hit me on the cheek. 'I told you that CAA couldn't be trusted.' She waved her cigarette in my face like I was the one stalking Josh and his manager.

'Calm down, Iris,' I said.

'Don't tell me to calm down. I'll fucking kill them.'

'Iris, it's not good for your health to get upset.'

'You know what would be good for my health? A bunch of dead CAA agents.'

She grabbed her cigarettes and her purse without another word. A few minutes later I heard her car as it left the driveway. The screech that her car made as it sped down the street probably wasn't as loud as the screams that she would make. I didn't hear from her all day. I called all her phones and she didn't respond. Iris didn't know it yet, but her days were numbered.

The whole town watched as Iris was picked apart by the vultures. The bigger defections caused a ripple-down effect. We hemorrhaged clients. They didn't care what happened – they knew that Iris was losing her clout. I was offered several positions at other agencies. I was warned to get out, but the pension money and the dream of eventual freedom kept me sitting at the desk and working for Iris. I just really didn't have the strength to go through all this again. It seemed like the small boutique agencies were a dying breed and our only purpose was to till the garden, plant the seed and carefully nurture the client until they were ripe enough for the big agencies to pluck the fruit and take them to the market. I didn't want to put all my energy into a client and have someone come along, steal them and reap all the rewards.

Actors want to be famous, which is the weakness that the big agencies count on. They tantalize perspective clients with expensive gifts, tickets to baseball games, meetings with studio executives and stacks of scripts. They wine them and dine them just to be able to stuff them and mount their heads on their walls. It is all about the kill. These big agencies just want to prove that they can outmaneuver their rival agents. That way when they see each other at lunch at The Grill in Beverly Hills, they can give each other a smug winning smile. It is all a big game for these big agents. It is literally about who has the bigger dick. Vying for booth space at The Grill is a complicated power game. The stealing of actors, as well as the procuring of a booth, is about ego.

I have to say one thing about Iris: she had plenty of opportunities to steal clients and she didn't do it. If someone had a contract with another agent and she knew that they were the bread and butter of that agency, she left the clients alone. If a prospective client had already left another agency and was making the rounds, then she would take a meeting. Iris was never one to lurk around sets or wine and dine people. She never felt she had to prove anything. She just went about her life.

I was having a really hard time staying balanced. My blood pressure spiked again despite all my hard work to control it. The doctor wanted me to quit my job. I was determined to stick it out until the bitter end. I did increase my acupuncture treatments, which seemed to help. The closing down of the pension proved more taxing than anyone initially thought. If Iris could have found a way to not pay me the money then she certainly would have. With regard to the agency I felt there was nothing left to believe in. I had been brought up to believe that a hard day's work would garner rewards and advancement. That was far from the case in Hollywood. Armani-clad men and women with gleaming smiles and the ability to lie well came in much more useful than hard work. Iris was different than CAA – she didn't make me waste half the day in a staff meeting. I just did my work.

Iris said great things about me to other people. She just didn't know how to express gratitude to me. Maybe she was afraid it would go to my head. A little pat on the back now and then would have helped the horrible situation that we were both in. Iris and I were really caught up in surviving towards the end, so I think everything that should have been said was pushed under the carpet. I knew it was coming but I just didn't realize how hard it would be to watch somebody fall. I wanted to escape to a new life. What that was I had no idea, but $72,000 would go a long way towards helping me find out. I stopped taking on any new clients. When people called seeking representation I told them we weren't taking anyone new. It was, after all, the Iris Burton Agency. If Iris wanted new clients, let her sign them and deal with the crap. I was waiting for parole.

The CAA agents were being incredibly friendly to me. One of them asked me to coffee. I didn't know what he wanted from me but if Iris found out there would be more hell to pay than it was worth. I turned him down. He kept asking about my relationship with Josh Hartnett's manager. My relationship with her had changed dramatically. We went from being great friends to barely communicating. She had put me in a horrible position by taking all the secret meetings.

The bathhouse was becoming my haven. I would stop there on the way home from work and use the steam room and the sauna. Sometimes I would just sit on the deck naked and stare up at the stars. The deck was quiet and peaceful. I felt like I was in another universe, only the occasional slamming of the door from the bathhouse to the patio, as the men cruised each other and looked for action, interrupted my solitude. People rarely spoke at the bathhouse. For some reason they seemed drawn to me and would blurt out their most private secrets. Maybe it was because I had a friendly face and managed to drop my defenses in the bathhouse. Maybe it was because I was a member of a secret club of damaged people, the ones you read about in books like *Less Than Zero* and *Bright Lights, Big City*. I could feel the confusion and unhappiness that the other guests carried around with them. I never understood what it meant to be less than zero until that last year with Iris.

I wouldn't let anyone in too close and I wouldn't allow myself to get attached. It was dangerous to care too much. I re-ran all the stories Iris told me about former clients. They had become her family. They had become her children. One by one they had been snatched away by bigger agencies that had promised bigger things. Iris was still bestowing Hollywood lessons to me even in her miserable downfall. Attachment led to disappointment in Hollywood. Iris had handled Henry Thomas. He was one of her first really big child actors. She had done a tremendous job with Henry after *E.T.* He was one of the hottest kid actors out there. They fired her by telegram from Australia when they went off to do a movie about frogs that she had opposed. They had just stayed at her house in Los Angeles instead of a hotel. Roxanna Zal was another client that was stolen from Iris. She had just thrown Roxanna a sweet sixteen party at Gladstone's in Malibu. Iris returned home from the party to find a telegram from Roxanna's mother that her services were no longer needed. Fred Savage had left and gone to CAA because he was getting older and nobody was buying him as a little boy. It wasn't Iris' fault. Iris was as close to the Savages as she had been to anyone. She used to spend the Jewish holidays at their house. The minute his career started to slow down, they were gone. There had to be some way to find balance so that I could continue to work in the business and not end up like Iris. There was an incredible joy about helping people attain their dreams.

I thought about what would become of me if I accepted any of the offers that kept coming my way. This was not the Hollywood of my childhood dreams. This was certainly not giving me any sense of inner strength. I had long ago abandoned religion in favor of Hollywood and now I was looking at Iris and seeing what would happen to me if I allowed my whole life to become about this business. There was something stirring deep inside me, telling me that there was definitely another life. I just had to find it. When I was young I believed that if I made money and became incredibly wealthy, that happiness would also be included in the package. After watching River and now Iris I knew that all the success and money in the world didn't attract happiness. Happiness was a full-time job. I was far from happy myself. I knew that living through other people's success wasn't enough for me. Iris somehow managed to stay alive by absorbing the glow of her clients' success. I pursued my creative writing and took private lessons with my writing teacher. I derived a new sense of happiness just being a writer. The daily problems of the clients and Iris didn't seem so important any more. I didn't want my life and ego to be linked to a client's success. It certainly wasn't doing Iris any good.

I spent the Thanksgiving holiday in Santa Fe, New Mexico. I had booked myself into a yoga retreat and then my back went out the week before I was supposed to leave. I was told by my doctors I could do yoga, I just couldn't bend over. I arrived at the yoga class early and had a conversation with the owner of the studio to explain my back problem. He assured me that I'd be all right and to just work through the pain. The coatroom to the yoga studio quickly filled up because there was another class in progress. That was when I noticed this woman with poker-straight brown hair, wearing a navy blue pea coat. She seemed familiar to me but I didn't know anyone in Santa Fe. She must be someone famous, but I couldn't think of her name. She smiled at another woman and then it hit me. It was Ali MacGraw from *Love Story!* I loved that movie. I had been in love with her when I was younger. She was also in *The Getaway* and *The Winds of War* and had been married to Steve McQueen. She was a superstar and had a yoga tape out. I remembered that she had a home in Santa Fe.

I needed to make sure not to be anywhere near her in the yoga studio. I'd look like an idiot practicing yoga with an expert like her. The class in the studio finally came out. I followed the woman into the studio. There was not one man in sight. The room was packed. I didn't know where the mats were and by the time I found them there was only one spot left. It happened to be dead in the center of the room. Maybe I should have just left. I didn't want all those people staring at me as I struggled to bend over. I lay my mat out on the floor. Someone tapped me on the shoulder.

'Could you move your mat over a little?' a woman's voice asked.

I turned around to find Ali MacGraw right next to me.

'Sure.' Holy shit! She was right next to me. This was so strange. I only really ever had two movie star crushes and they were Ali MacGraw and Elizabeth Taylor. I admire these women because they live their lives on their own terms and are constantly reinventing themselves. Ali MacGraw represented the fearless person that I wanted to be. She was so full of life.

I tried to concentrate as the teacher guided us through a series of poses. It was hard for me to even bend over and I had to stifle heavy sighs that I wanted to let out. I could bend sideways and stand in place, but I couldn't bend forwards. Was this some strange metaphor for my life? I thought about my third and fourth chakras. For the first time I pondered what blocked chakras actually meant. Could there be some truth to chakras?

I watched as Ali MacGraw somehow managed to drag her head under her buttocks. The teacher was stacking ten blocks in front of me just to help me move my head slightly forwards. No one else had blocks. I was the only one that needed props to do the poses. Just bending over caused sweat to pour from my forehead.

'You're doing fine.' The voice had come from the smiling face of Ali MacGraw. My sweat almost hit her in the face. It was embarrassing.

The teacher rubbed my back reassuringly. 'You're doing fine,' she repeated.

Faces started to pop into my head. Faces and names I hadn't thought of for years. The first man I ever fell in love with. He was tall, had jet-black hair and blue eyes. I met him through the personal ads. When I first met him he put me immediately at ease. I can still remember the feel of his stiff Oxford shirts and the shiny copper pennies in his burgundy loafers. He was a wealthy lawyer. He had a magnificent house in the Hollywood Hills. He romanced me for several months. He was the first man I had sex with. The night we had sex was the last time I ever saw him. It was a wonderful experience except at the end. He left the bed and put on his clothes.

'Will I see you next weekend?' I called out.

He didn't turn around. He just pulled up his jeans and tucked in his starched white shirt.

'I won't be seeing you again,' he said. He didn't even look at me.

I jumped out of bed and pulled him around so he faced me.

'I can't see you any more. I'm getting married.' He moved towards the door.

'To a man?' I asked.

'To a woman,' he replied. Then he closed the door and left my apartment.

I felt the warm stream of tears as they rolled down my cold face.

It took me a year before I wanted to date again. It happened by accident. A friend took me to a play and I met the director. He was older. We dated for four months until I put on ten pounds recovering from bronchial pneumonia. He dumped me on my birthday after we finished having sex.

'You need to lose weight, Chris,' he said as he left the bed. 'My friends in Palm Springs will wonder why I'm with you.'

After that, the dating stopped until I met Richard. I had wanted to cry then but I wouldn't give him the satisfaction. Six years of one-night stands later, sex with strangers in bars and strangers in a bathhouse.

The the yoga and massage were dislodging something – the bottled-up feelings that I'd suppressed since before River's death. I realized suddenly why I was so blocked. I was violated. I had allowed myself to be violated by all those men. They raped my heart and trust. Iris continued to chip away at my ego and kept me unbalanced just so I wouldn't leave. I needed to leave Iris. I needed to regain my self-esteem.

CHAPTER 23

'It is not death that a man should fear
But he should fear never beginning to live.'

Marcus Aurelius

They were having a screening of *Quills*. I hadn't
seen the movie. CAA had seen it and Iris was pissed
that we hadn't. She was furious when CAA took out
congratulatory advertisements in the industry trade
magazines and didn't mention her.

'How dare those bastards ride on my coat tails? What
the fuck did they have to do with any of the movies that
he has out this year? They're making it seem like they
put him in those movies. I want something done to stop
this *now*!' Iris was ranting and raving on a daily basis.
She always found something to gripe about, especially if
it concerned Joaquin and CAA.

'Iris, what would you like me to do about it?' I wanted
to disappear into the ground. My trip to Santa Fe was
long forgotten and I'd been told that the pension money
would not be available until after the New Year.

'Call those sons of bitches up and tell them to stop
taking credit for my work!'

'Are you going to take out congratulatory ads and
spend $3,000?'

'After he left me, you want me to congratulate him? I
just don't want someone taking credit for my work. Let

CAA pay. I just want acknowledgment. I made Joaquin Phoenix not them!'

I called CAA and talked to their publicity department. They told me that it wasn't CAA policy to share congratulatory advertisements but after many days of discussion they decided to put an asterisk after Joaquin's name and at the bottom of the page they added 'Shared client with the Iris Burton Agency'. They were bending over backwards to try to keep Iris calm. They had learned quickly that it was hours of wasted phone conversations if she was stirred up.

We heard that the movie *Black Hawk Down* was going to be made and that Ridley Scott was going to direct it. Jerry Bruckheimer, who had just finished working with Josh Hartnett, was also producing it. This would be a great follow-up movie for Josh. I went after the movie for him and Joaquin. CAA seemed to have little or no interest in the movie for Joaquin. I couldn't understand why as Ridley Scott was also represented by CAA. Jerry Bruckheimer showed Ridley some of Josh's scenes from *Pearl Harbor* because he was unfamiliar with Josh's work. We had Ridley really interested in Josh until his manager decided that she didn't want Josh doing another war movie. We had a huge argument over *Black Hawk Down*. She said that she didn't understand the script. I told her that it was really tough to read an action movie and that she should read the book and trust that Ridley Scott would deliver an amazing movie. She still resisted so I called Josh and he agreed to read the project.

A week later Josh had a tremendous offer to do the movie. He was to be paid the highest payday of his career. It was even negotiated in his contract that they would let him out to do the two-week press junket in Hawaii to promote *Pearl Harbor*. Josh was headed to Leonardo DiCaprio mega-watt fame.

Josh's manager was still taking secret meetings with CAA. She told me that she had lunch with the same CAA agent that had been pursuing Josh for years. Josh was no longer an unfaceted diamond; he was the Hope Diamond. He was headed to at least $10,000,000 a picture if his movies did even half of what was expected. The stakes were higher with Josh than they were with Joaquin. They were going to find a way to steal Josh and then Iris was all but finished. Sure we still had clients, but it would take three to five years to get them to the level that Joaquin and Josh were at.

CAA finally came up with a project for Joaquin. It was right before the two-week Christmas break. The project was called *It's All About Love*. I really liked the script. The studios were not at all interested in Joaquin. Even Ridley Scott was reluctant to use him and he had just worked with him in a worldwide box-office smash. There was something wrong when studios didn't want to capitalize on box-office receipts.

Iris had taken a trip to New York for a week before the holidays. She hadn't done that in years. She loved to look at the Christmas lights, see the Rockettes and go to a few plays. It also gave her an opportunity to wear her furs. She was acting very oddly and I worried that she was eating all the wrong foods in New York. She would fall asleep while talking to me in the middle of the day. She was disoriented and very argumentative. Iris always argued but she was especially bad during the New York trip. I was glad that she wouldn't return to Los Angeles before I left for Florida. I was spending Christmas in Delray Beach.

I waited patiently for the pension money that would enable me to start over. I was diligently working on a book about my experiences in Greece. I had found a new avenue to deal with my high blood pressure. I met another acupuncturist who was also very metaphysical in his treatments. I met him solely by accident in a New Age tea garden near the office. I had been under incredible stress and was looking for something to calm me down. The man behind the counter took pity on me and suggested that I call him for a treatment. I was so desperate at that point that I started regular treatments with him. I felt relaxed and centered after our treatments and my blood pressure was significantly lower.

Things really unraveled during the Christmas holidays. I received a phone call from Iris. She was furious. It was Christmas Eve. Again.

'Chris. Iris,' she said coldly.

'Merry Christmas,' I replied. 'I was going to call you after I put the Christmas Eve dinner in the oven.'

'I don't give a fuck what you're cooking. And I really don't give a fuck about Christmas. What the fuck are you up to?'

'What are you talking about, Iris?' I put the eggplant parmesana in the oven.

'The last I knew I pay your salary not CAA'

'Iris, let's stop playing guessing games. Just tell me what your problem is.'

'Do you know about a film that shoots in Denmark that Joaquin has committed to doing?'

'I didn't know that he committed. But he has read it.'

'Then you do know about it? You fucking son of a bitch – you've joined them,' Iris said.

'Iris, you know about the project too. I told you about it when you were in New York and I left it on your desk with a note explaining all the details.'

'I'm not senile. You never told me about this project!' she screamed.

'I most certainly did, Iris, and if you paid any attention

to the notes that I left, you would know what was going on!' I yelled back

'Who is behind this? Have you joined CAA's side? They offered you a job, didn't they? Then you can be called "agent" instead of "secretary" or "assistant". That *bothers* you, doesn't it?' she said mockingly.

'Why does everything with you have to be some big fucking plot to screw you over, Iris?'

'I know what's going on!' she screamed.

'Really, Iris. Well then you didn't need to call me! Merry fucking Christmas!' I slammed the phone down.

I was shaking. I was so sick and tired of Iris. I wanted to quit that very minute. But if I didn't play this out right she'd tie up the pension money. I just had to hold on a little longer. I didn't know what to do. I turned off the oven and flew out of the house and headed to the beach. I would walk off the anger. I had no other choice. I walked up the beach for about three miles. The wind was blowing and the surf was crashing down. I'd been asked to lunch and coffee by CAA and had repeatedly turned them down. I knew what they wanted: Josh Hartnett. I couldn't do that to Iris. But the fact that she didn't trust me was making it harder to go back to Los Angeles. Any other agent in the city would have taken the meetings with CAA and walked out with the important clients. I couldn't do it any more than Joaquin could make a clean break. Joaquin had actually put himself at a disadvantage by going to CAA. Who did Joaquin think they were going to work harder for – the client that paid 5 per cent or the one that paid them 10 per cent? If a producer called for Joaquin there would be no one to monitor if they didn't try to swing the job to another client. The agency business was about commissions.

There was something really tragic about Iris Burton. It was hard not to feel sorry for her. The waves pounded down on the sand in front of me. The wind blew sand in my face. I made my decision; I would give Iris my notice a week after I had received the pension money. These agencies had finished the erosion that had long been destroying our relationship. Everything was about to crumble. The laughter had left the Iris Burton Agency. In the beginning Iris and I did have incredible laughs, but this last year it was impossible to get even a smile out of her. When I had started working with young adults I hadn't taken into account that the big agencies would chase after the clients. I felt partly to blame for Iris' bad mood because I had been the one to venture into an arena that she didn't want to be in.

When I returned to Los Angeles the situation between Iris and I deteriorated even further. Several clients and one studio executive asked me if I liked my Christmas present. I told them that I hadn't received them. They said that they were sent by messenger to the agency and they had a confirmation that Iris Burton had signed for them. Iris had done stuff like this before, but it was usually when a gift basket came addressed to the two of us. It really bothered her when people lumped the two of us together as a team. She really didn't see it that way. There was no Iris and Chris if the gift cards read only Iris. She could pretend that I didn't exist if my name wasn't in print.

I couldn't have cared less about baskets of candy, muffins and pasta – I didn't need the calories. The baskets were usually recycled to other people that Iris had to give gifts to anyway. Her business manager, lawyer, bankers, other clients, her son and hairdresser would all be the recipients of our shared gifts. But her audacity in rifling through gifts addressed to me and taking them for herself just astounded me. She had a nerve. I decided to confront her when I noticed that she was wearing the ski hat that a network had sent me.

'Iris.' I walked into the house.

She was in her office. 'What?' she screamed.

'I want to talk to you.' I walked into her office, which was in total disarray. Christmas bags and paper were strewn about the floor along with Christmas decorations that had not been put away. I noticed a huge basket from Twentieth Century Fox. It was filled with Neal's Yard products. I saw the tag dangling that read 'Joaquin Phoenix'. The cellophane was torn open and some of the spaces were empty.

Iris saw that I was staring at the basket. 'I gave my son most of the stuff in the basket. Fuck Joaquin if he thinks I'm going to give him that basket. He doesn't need the stuff anyway.' She was beyond bitter.

I decided to let my ski hat and the missing gifts go. I knew she had rifled through my stuff. She knew that she had rifled through my stuff. It just wasn't worth fighting about it any more. I just had a few weeks left until the money was transferred and I could leave.

'What do you want? Don't just stare at me!'

I noticed the remains of what looked like cake crumbs on a plate. She had been at the sweets again. She was out of control. 'I just wanted to make sure that you received my note about the client who called saying that they paid you on residuals that were not commissionable. It's been all over the trades about the big fight between the agents and the Screen Actors Guild.'

'What the fuck do they want?' she screamed. 'I deserve that money. It's my fucking money!'

'Not according to the union, Iris.'

'Fuck the union and fuck the client. Tell them to send me the cancelled checks and I'll give them the money back.'

'Iris, they've been paying you for six years. I told you to send it back.'

'Who the fuck's side are you on?'

'Iris, let's not start this.' I walked out of the office.

'You come back here!'

I went back to my office.

Two weeks later the client fired us. She was on a new CBS series and had been with us for nine years. Another mess that Iris had created.

Iris had come up with the ultimate weapon against CAA. She had accumulated faxes and had spoken to the producers of *It's All About Love*. She believed she could accuse CAA of wrongdoing by saying that they had negotiated behind her back and not consulted with her, causing Joaquin to have a lousy deal. It's true it was a horrible deal, but nobody else was offering him anything. They were not only getting Joaquin for no money, they had him tied up the following winter for a period of time. He was being bought for two years according to Iris, which was not really true. She demanded a conference call with CAA, Joaquin's lawyer, Mrs Phoenix, Joaquin and, of course, me. CAA had called me and asked what the hell the meeting was about. I told them what I knew. They gratefully went off and planned a counter attack against Iris. Now they knew what Iris was up to.

To my great relief the transfer of the pension money finally went through. I wanted to scream for joy when the bank called. I could finally give my notice. At last I had the safety net that I needed to take some time off. I really had no idea what I was planning on doing with my life. I wasn't sure whether to move. Ironically, I had been offered the job running the bed and breakfast in Greece again. It was seven years since I had ran it before. My great-uncle had asked me to move to Florida to take care of him. I had been offered other agency jobs. I wasn't sure what to do but I knew I was taking some time off.

Iris aired her grievances to everybody on the conference call. When she was finished there was total silence. She didn't sound rational and nothing she said had any merit. Nobody knew what to say. It was a desperate plea for attention and control. Joaquin was at CAA and Iris couldn't get him back. His departure essentially forced Iris into retirement. There was no merit to the call. Iris was furious when she hung up the phone. She marched out of the house to the back patio. She slammed her fists on the railing right in front of my open office door.

'Somebody told them! Somebody warned them! SOMEBODY FUCKED ME!' she shrieked and pounded her fists on the railing.

'What the hell are you carrying on about, Iris?' I stood up and walked to the doorway. My face was inches from hers.

'I was fucked. I was fucked.' She just kept hitting the railing.

I reached out and grabbed her hands to stop her from hurting herself. 'Iris, stop this.' I walked up the steps, opened the door to the house and guided her in. I brought her to her office. Everything was in disarray. I sat her at the desk.

'Iris, we need to talk.'

She was huffing and puffing. Her face was all red. Tears were welling up in her eyes. 'What?'

'I need to give you my notice. I can't do this any more. I can't live like this any more. There is no trust left between us. I can't work in a place were there is no trust. Or laughter.'

Iris stared at me. She didn't utter a sound. I didn't know

whether to run or sit because her stare was so vacant. I wasn't even sure that she heard what I was saying.

'So you're leaving me too? I suppose that you took a job at CAA with Joaquin. You probably maneuvered the whole thing!'

'Stop it, Iris! Stop it right now! Joaquin did what he did of his own accord. I didn't take a job with anyone. I've been offered plenty over the years, Iris. I've been more than loyal and that loyalty has only netted me constant accusations of betrayal. If I wanted to fuck you, Iris, I could have done it years ago!'

'Those fucking bastards at CAA, they did this to me! They took you!'

'This is what I mean, Iris. You don't listen to me and you don't trust me. I have tried to make you understand for years that I don't want this business. I never have. I was never the one that you had to worry about trusting. My body just can't take it. I'm sick, Iris. I don't think you understand. The pressure is killing me. I spend most of the little spare money I have trying to lower my blood pressure.'

'I'll pay you more money. I'll make you a partner,' she pleaded.

'Iris, it's too late. I can't do this any more. It's not about money any more. It's about my health.'

'When are you leaving?'

'Whenever you would like.'

'Get my lawyer on the phone. We'll talk about this tomorrow.'

I left her office happier than I had been in years. I didn't shed a tear. I stood firm and never once let Iris intimidate me. It had taken me years to stand up to her. I didn't know where I was headed but I knew that it wouldn't be with her and that I wouldn't take any clients and head to another agency. I didn't want to be like everyone else. The yoga had strengthened me so much that I didn't even cry. I was able to just tell her how I felt for the first time. It felt good.

Surprisingly, Iris wanted me to work a two-month notice period, after it was announced a week later that Joaquin was nominated for the Academy Award for Best Supporting Actor for his performance in *Gladiator*. Iris needed me to run things while she ran around to fittings for gowns to wear to award shows. Joaquin called me at home and thanked me for all my hard work and asked if there wasn't some way that I would stay on with Iris. I told him that nothing would change my mind. I congratulated him and wished him well.

The tension in the office subsided until Josh Hartnett's manager dropped the bomb that they wanted to leave and go to CAA. The agent that had been pursuing Josh and his manager finally won. Josh's manager knew that I was leaving and that Iris didn't hustle appointments. She didn't want Josh or her other clients to be handled by just Iris. In a strange turn of events the agent that had been romancing Josh since *The Faculty* left CAA. In the middle of the night he went to Endeavor to be the head of the Motion Picture Department. The roster of clients that followed from CAA was quite impressive: Ben Affleck, Matt Damon, Christian Bale, Drew Barrymore, Jerry O'Connell, and now he had all but guaranteed Josh Hartnett.

Iris struck a deal with Endeavor immediately. Endeavor gave Iris the deal CAA had not given her. They gave her $100,000 up front and a sliding commission for the rest of her life as long as Josh Hartnett stayed with the agency. They also told Josh's manager that her other clients would also be with Endeavor. They really couldn't have cared less about the rest of her clients. But none of this was my problem.

CHAPTER 24

'May you live all the days of your life.'

Jonathan Swift

When news of my resignation spread around town I received dozens of phone calls from my peers asking me how I had put up with Iris for as long as I had. My answer was that no one else would have ever given me a chance. Hollywood was nepotism of the highest order so what chance would I – a young guy from a small little town in upstate New York – have had? They really didn't know Iris and how much fun she used to be. In the beginning, every day had been an adventure and I sat wide-eyed at the feet of a legend. Iris had more experience in the entertainment business than anyone who currently ran agencies or studios. Her son wasn't interested in becoming an agent, so she decided to pass the knowledge on to someone else. Iris was difficult, opinionated, quirky and a recluse. But she had a great sense of humor. I always said someone needed to just put Iris up on a stage and let her go. Once she started she could have you on the floor laughing. She was outlandish and she had so much money (she called it her fuck-you-money) that she didn't care what people thought.

The biggest lesson in my life I learned from my grandmother when I was six years old. She used to take me to the racetrack and when she was successful she would give me the fifty-cent pieces and dimes that she won.

'Sitto, can I put my money on a horse and win more money?' I handed her four shiny silver dollar pieces. She smiled at me and took me by the hand down to the three-foot-high chain-link fence. The bugles went off and the horses paraded before me one by one.

'Look at the horses, Chrissy, and when you see the one that you like tell me the number and I'll bet on that horse for you.'

'I don't understand, Sitto.'

'Just look at them and the first one you are attracted to is the one you bet on.' She smiled at me. 'It's called a "hunch".'

Iris told me the same thing the first week I worked with her, albeit in a different way. The other agencies that I temped at had a whole room full of videotapes and pictures of the actors. They used to type elaborate letters to the casting directors and messenger the tapes and pictures to producers, casting directors and directors.

'Iris, where are the pictures and tapes for the submissions?' I said.

Iris stood up from her desk, grabbed a cigarette and picked up her lighter. She came around to the front of the desk and just stared at me. 'How long have you been in the business, kid?'

'I went to graduate school for a year. Then I interned for a producer at Warner Bros. Then I did temp work.'

'Hold it. Hold it, kid. I don't need a run-through of the last twenty fucking years of your life.'

'I've worked in agencies for a year. The other agency I was with made me an agent after three months.'

Iris sat on the edge of her desk. She took a long drag on her cigarette and she stared at me. 'I don't send pictures. I don't send tapes. You know why?'

'No.'

'Because I'm Iris Burton. A picture can't tell you if

someone can act. A tape can't tell you someone can be a star. You know how I know who can make it?'

'No.'

Iris walked across the room and stood right in front of me. She punched her stomach. 'It comes from here. From your gut. It's called a "hunch". I get hunches. I don't know fuck about the stock market. I have advisors and I do better than them. Stock market, horse races, actors. Honey, I can smell a winner. Stick with me, kid, and I'll show you a world you only dreamed about. Pictures. I'll teach you how to sell dog shit and people will think it's fucking filet mignon. Are you up to it? Because I don't like weaklings.'

'Yeah,' I said.

Iris just stared at me for a minute as she smoked her cigarette. I felt like she had gained access to my mind and was looking for any sign of weakness. I was committed from that moment on. Just like my yoga classes, people could ask me what they did for me and I couldn't really tell them exactly the feeling they gave me. The same held true for Iris. After all these years through tragedy and triumph, Iris had somehow unknowingly transferred her ability to follow hunches, negotiate and sell to me. I had learned at the feet of the master and it was way past the point when it was time to leave. The master is supposed to tell the student that he has learned all there is to learn and send them off into the world. That was the part that Iris had a problem with. She was a great teacher but a horrible parent. Iris wouldn't let me go because she had no life of her own. She had closed herself up in her own tomb. I needed to get out before the doors sealed.

I was invited to all the pre-awards parties. CAA was throwing Joaquin a party. I was invited to the DreamWorks and Universal parties as well. It was ironic that during my last week with her, Iris fulfilled her promise to me and allowed me to attend all the parties I dreamed about when I was a child.

I made the mistake of agreeing to let Iris drive to the CAA party. I felt embarrassed to valet a 1993 Ford Escort when everyone else would be driving Mercedes, Porsches and BMWs, so for once I agreed to travel in slightly more style, with Iris. I usually made it a point to avoid going anywhere with Iris because she never let you go once she had you trapped in the house or the car. But she had been pleasant so far so I figured I was safe.

I had fun at the party and used it as an opportunity to say goodbye to people I'd never see again. In one week I'd be gone. It seemed hard to believe. I made a point to talk to lawyers, agents, publicists and casting directors who I wouldn't be talking to any more. I'd lose touch with all these people. I looked around and realized that I wasn't a part of anything real. These people were about as fake as they could be. The CAA agents all smiled at Iris from across the room and she smiled back. They all hated each other. They hated that they couldn't get Joaquin without Iris and she hated that Joaquin had left her for younger representation. Everyone politely smiled at each other all night. There wasn't one bit of genuine affection in the room. I will say that they all had great masks.

I noticed that Iris was drinking which was unusual for her. I tried to avoid her. She seemed uneasy in this room full of people. The fact that she had to be there acknowledged that Joaquin wasn't hers and hers alone. She'd lived a personal life with Pete that now mirrored her professional life. Pete had needed more than one woman to satisfy him. Joaquin needed other agents. I felt sorry for her as I watched her from across the room. Once in a while she would let her shield down and I could see the pain. She wasn't going down on top. Rather than just retire Iris had chosen to be dragged around town by a rope attached to a limo until the pavement had torn every piece of flesh, muscle and bone off her body. Iris had stood her ground. The silence of retirement was too much for her. Better to go down fighting. She could pretend she was still in business and let everyone else do the work. At least the phone would ring on occasion.

'Iris, why don't you just retire?' I asked her once, before things became ugly.

'Because no one would call. My phones would go silent.'

I went to the bathroom and bumped into a publicist I knew. We stood outside the one bathroom designated for guests for twenty minutes until I heard Iris calling out my name. This was the reason that I hated going to parties with her – I couldn't be out of her sight for more than a few minutes or she'd assume I'd been kidnapped.

She came around the corner. 'What are you doing?'

'Waiting to go to the bathroom, Iris,' I said.

'Why is it taking so long? You've been gone twenty minutes.'

When it was time to leave, one of the agents grabbed me by the arm and whispered in my ear, 'You better take the keys from Iris. She's having trouble walking and she's slurring her words.'

I went to the valet to retrieve Iris' keys but it was too late – she'd taken them already. Iris was standing by her car with her arms crossed, annoyed because I'd made her wait.

I approached her as she leaned against the car. 'Iris, why don't I drive?' I said calmly and touched her arm.

'I can drive!' She pulled her arm away from me. 'I'm just fine. I can take care of myself.'

People waiting for their cars stared in our direction. Iris was very loud.

'Come on, Iris, give me the keys. Please,' I said.

'No! I can drive just fine and if you don't like it take a fucking taxi!'

I wanted to take a taxi but she couldn't drive like this. She'd never make it. She couldn't see that well at night, let alone drunk. I went to the passenger door resigned to my fate. It was no use fighting with her any more.

'Are you sure you'll be all right?' one of the CAA agents said.

'I'll be fine.'

I didn't really believe it as I stepped into the black Mercedes. Iris gave me a dirty look as I closed the door. Sunset Boulevard had treacherous curves from the Palisades to Beverly Hills. I had my eyes glued to the road as Iris started the descent down to Beverly Hills. She had trouble with the steering wheel and I kept my arms ready to go over and pull it if she veered too far into oncoming traffic. We rounded a corner and she headed right into the oncoming traffic I yanked the steering wheel quickly to the right. The car horns blared.

'I can drive!' she screamed and pushed my hand off the steering wheel. Her foot pushed on the accelerator as I heard the engine rev up.

'Iris, slow down for God's sake,' I pleaded.

'I'll show you. I'll show everyone. I'm still in control.'

The car veered once again towards the oncoming traffic. I pulled the wheel over just in time.

'Stop touching the wheel. God damn it!' she screamed.

'I will when you slow down, Iris.'

'Those motherfuckers taking credit for my hard work. Throwing a party to celebrate work that I did. It made me sick to sit there and smile for those motherfuckers. I wasn't going to show them it bothered me,' she yelled.

'Iris, slow down.'

'I've lost. They've taken everything from me including you,' she sobbed.

I grabbed the wheel again. Mercifully we were headed into Beverly Hills. It was a straight road to Doheny where we would turn to head back to Iris' house.

'It's all right, Iris. It will be all right,' I tried to comfort her.

'It's all over for me. Don't you see?'

The only thing that I wanted to see was Iris' driveway. I could finally see my car sitting out in front of Iris' house. I couldn't wait to get away. I helped her out of her car and opened the door to the house. I walked her in and sat her down on the couch. I gave her a quick hug.

'I'll see you tomorrow.' I closed the door not wanting to end up sitting with her all night. One thing I knew for sure: tomorrow night she wasn't driving.

I told Iris that I would meet her and the Phoenixes at Il Cielo, where Universal's Oscar party was being thrown. I would walk over from the office and then take Joaquin's limo with them to the rest of the parties. When I arrived at Il Cielo it was like prom night. I watched as lines of limos let off one celebrity after another. Julia Roberts and her boyfriend Benjamin Bratt, Russell Crowe, and Jamie Bell from *Billy Elliot* were just a few of the stars that headed into the Universal party. In all the years I had been in Hollywood I had never seen anything like this. The security was unbelievable and the President could have just as easily been attending rather than Hollywood stars. I walked through the security line and was asked my name at a table that was set up. I was allowed into the secret world of celebrity.

Flashbulbs went off constantly; the photographers would snap first and ask questions later. Once inside the small courtyard the wine flowed. I was early so I was able to just stand back and watch the celebrity scene. Agents dressed in black leather jackets, black pants and expensive dress shirts hovered around their clients. They looked like a sea of Terminators protecting their clients from rival agencies. There was no room for people like Iris. There was certainly no room for me. I didn't want to be one of those agents in black uniforms hovering and waiting to pounce on some other agent's client when their guard was down. The limos kept arriving and at last Iris arrived with the Phoenixes. It was hard for Iris to find me and even harder to navigate the small courtyard. The party was so overcrowded that people started to leave the minute Julia Roberts and Russell Crowe left.

We left to go to Spago where DreamWorks was throwing a party. Joaquin's limo dropped us off and the doors to Spago were opened and the ten of us were whisked into the building. There were no questions and no lists to check as we were with an Oscar nominee. Again I was allowed into the inner sanctum.

Steven Spielberg, studio heads and a who's who of Hollywood were at the party. Iris tried to flag down Spielberg but he just walked right by. I slipped off to enjoy the huge tables of food that were placed intermittently around the room. There was a huge twelve-foot long table that was filled with desserts and looked like something out of *Willy Wonka and the Chocolate Factory*. The food and the evening seemed like a dream. Waiters passed out finger foods and champagne flowed. Iris sent out a search party for me in the form of Casey Affleck and Summer Phoenix. I told them to pretend that they hadn't found me. This was my farewell to Hollywood. In five days I would be leaving Iris and all this for good.

'Where the hell have you been?' Iris snapped.

'Eating.' I held up a huge chocolate-covered strawberry then bit into it. 'I plan on eating one of everything.'

'My shoes are killing me. I want you to come and sit with me. I can't even get Joaquin's attention.'

'Iris, he's enjoying himself. Leave him alone.' I picked up a chocolate mousse.

'I want someone to sit with me,' Iris whined.

'Go find a table.' I was eyeing the next dessert I planned to attack. Funny, I never really ate dessert, but this was a celebration.

'I want you to come with me now!' Iris commanded.

'Fine, Iris.' I grabbed two more desserts to take with me.

'How many of those are you going to eat for Christ's sake?'

'As many as I want!'

Iris was just pissed that too many people were watching her and she couldn't sneak anything. We would all give her hell about her diabetes. As it was she had a drink in her hand. We found a table and were soon joined by Mrs Phoenix, Summer and Casey. I watched the people parade by.

The week after the Oscars was my last. Iris was miserable the entire time. As we approached the end the tension mounted. I took my things home a little at a time so she wouldn't notice. I made up lists of numbers she would need. I pulled the files of the projects that were currently active and made detailed notes regarding the key people that I'd been dealing with.

'Iris, we need to go over some things,' I said and handed her the files and a folder with all the information I'd compiled.

She glanced down at the papers like they were written in Greek. 'I always knew this would happen. You have everything up in your head. That memory of yours. I knew that I'd be left holding the bag.' She swiped the files from the table onto the floor. The anger poured out of her eyes. This was not going to be easy.

I bent over and started to retrieve the papers. 'Iris, let's not do this. Let's not make it ugly.'

'I can't do this right now. We'll do it later.' She walked into her bedroom and closed the door.

A few hours later she came out into the office and handed me an envelope.

'What's this?' I said.

'Happy birthday,' she said.

My birthday wasn't until next week. This was peculiar but I opened the card. The card read 'Happy Secretaries Day'. It wasn't anywhere near Secretaries Day and she hadn't ever given me a card on Secretaries Day. There were fifty dollars inside and she had handwritten on the card: 'That's all you'll ever be – a secretary'.

I smiled at Iris. She wanted a fight. I wasn't going to give it to her. 'Thank you. That's so thoughtful.' I gave her a big hug. I wasn't about to let her get to me on my last day.

She left the office with a perplexed look on her face.

She came back an hour later right before my lunch break. 'I need to know how to get ahold of you if I need something.'

'Iris, I'm gone as of today. I am not on a retainer so please don't call me to ask me questions. I'm just a lowly secretary.'

'How dare you? How dare you after all I've done for you! You would refuse my calls? You're an ingrate!'

I didn't say another word. I picked up my briefcase and my keys and headed out of the door. She wanted World War III. I'd already slipped in the comment about the secretary, which I shouldn't have.

'DON'T YOU DARE WALK OUT ON ME! I WON'T HAVE IT. YOU COME BACK HERE!' SHE SCREAMED.

I kept walking. I continued the long walk down the driveway blocking out the obscenities that came out of her mouth. I never looked back. I decided after lunch I would leave. I returned from lunch and tossed my key on the desk and never saw Iris Burton again. There was nothing left to say.

The first week was weird. I didn't know who I was. I remember talking to my father the first morning after I left Iris. He told me to have a daily routine and stick to it or I'd never accomplish anything. He was right; it was the best advice he ever gave me.

CHAPTER 25

'What lies behind us and what lies before us are small matters compared to what lies within us.'

Ralph Waldo Emerson

The casket was being pulled out of the hearse when I arrived at the gravesite. The mound of dirt high up on the hill marked the location of Iris' final resting place. It was a steep hill and Iris was pretty near the top. She now had an unobstructed view of the studios she had done most of her business with.

I was informed that being an honorary pall-bearer meant that I was supposed to follow behind the casket and not have to bear the burden of actually carrying it. I moved in the direction of Mrs Phoenix since I would join her behind the casket. But the funeral director approached me before I could reach her.

'You're a big guy. Would you mind carrying the head of the casket?'

'No. Not at all.' I moved to the head of the casket and joined the rest of the pall-bearers. I was surprised at how heavy it was. Even though Iris and I had spoken in the past seven years I hadn't seen her face since I'd left. Now she was inches away from me, separated only by the wooden lid of the casket. I kept expecting her to yell: 'Hurry up. Let's get this over with,' or 'What was that bitch doing at my funeral? I hated her,' Or 'Why the hell was the rabbi calling me Irene? My name is Iris.' I would miss Iris' banter and tell-it-like-it-is comments.

The sun seemed to get hotter and I broke a sweat in my blue suit. Someone approached me from the side. Out of the corner of my eye I could see it was Iris' son. The heat seemed to intensify as the casket grew heavier. Finally we reached the lift that would lower the casket into the ground. It was a relief to finally rest the casket down.

The mourners had filtered down to about twenty. There were two rows of chairs but only three people sat down. The rest of us stood awkwardly behind the chairs, not wanting to sit. The rabbi pronounced the last rights over the casket in Hebrew. I listened, not knowing what he was saying and then he spoke in English. 'Could you each lovingly place the first layer of dirt on the casket with either the shovel or your hand. We think it's important that the first layer be from loved ones.'

I watched as the workmen lowered the casket into the hole. Then they placed a cement slab over it. No one spoke and the only sounds were from the occasional breeze that stirred. Once the workmen left everyone just stood stiffly. No one wanted to be the first to approach the grave.

My palm started to itch and I wanted to laugh because Iris used to say if her palm itched it meant money was coming. Iris was a very superstitious woman. I don't know how many times when we were driving she would screech to a halt because a black cat was walking across the road. She went crazy if the maid put one of her hats on the table or the bed because it meant bad luck. She yelled at me whenever it rained because I'd open the umbrella before I left the office and she said it brought bad luck to the people living in the house. She always saved the wishbone from the Thanksgiving turkey and the Monday after Thanksgiving she used to make me pull one end to see who'd get the bigger piece of wishbone. Iris always seemed to win. She lit candles for her dead mother on special holidays and when someone close to her died she lit a religious candle that burned for seven days. She said it gave the dead a light to follow to heaven. I'd had a candle burning since I'd learned of her death.

I wondered if someone had remembered to attach the safety pin with her charms to the inside of her bra.

I was the one that started our sage ritual. I was walking on Venice Beach one day and I saw people selling these sage sticks. I stopped to ask what they were and was told by one of the vendors that if I smudged the house with sage it would clear away the bad energy. I bought a bunch of the sage and brought it to the office. When I told Iris what it was for she just looked at me deadpan and said, 'Honey, you better buy that shit by the bushful with all the bad energy in this town.' Iris then lit the sage stick and went around the office and her house smudging the whole place. It became a ritual. Every time we got off an unpleasant call with a lawyer or a studio Iris would call out, 'Honey, fire up the sage!' We would laugh uproariously as she danced around the office with the sage stick.

Iris never let anyone get the better of her and she knew exactly the right moment to move against her enemies. She had uncanny instincts and sold stocks on impulse and was always right. I looked around at the mourners and I wondered if anyone knew Iris as well as I did. She had exposed sides of herself to me that I don't think anyone else ever saw.

Not wanting to be first, I waited until her son had placed a shovel full of dirt in the grave. I grabbed the shovel after him and went to the head of the grave and shook some dirt onto the slab of cement. Then I put down the shovel and made the sign of the cross to bless Iris. I inhaled deeply as I turned to head towards my car. As I walked away from the grave I swear I smelled wild sage from the hills that surrounded us. I broke into a smile as I walked away from the grave and knew exactly what I had to do. I needed to go home and sage the house and clear away all the old energy and start a new life without Iris.